JUDAS

JUDAS

Images of the Lost Disciple

KIM PAFFENROTH

Westminster John Knox Press
LOUISVILLE • LONDON

© 2001 Kim Paffenroth

Scripture quotations from the Revised Standard Version of the Bible are copyright © 1946, 1952, 1971, and 1973 by the Division of Christian Education of the National Council of the Churches of Christ in the U.S.A. and are used by permission.

Lyrics from "Steeler" reproduced by kind permission of JUDAS PRIEST

"Judas' Kiss" © 1982 Dawn Treader Music. All rights administered by EMI Christian Music Publishing.

Book design by Sharon Adams

First edition
Published by Westminster John Knox Press
Louisville, Kentucky

This book is printed on acid-free paper that meets the American National Standards Institute Z39.48 standard. ∞

PRINTED IN THE UNITED STATES OF AMERICA

Library of Congress Cataloging-in-Publication Data

Paffenroth, Kim, 1966–
    Judas : images of the lost disciple / Kim Paffenroth.
       p. cm.
    Includes bibliographical references and index.
    ISBN 0-664-22424-5 (alk. paper)
    1. Judas Iscariot. I. Title.

BS2460.J8 P34 2001
226'.092—dc21   2001045552

For Leslie and Jack:
mentors, colleagues, and friends

Catch the play now, eye to eye
Don't let chances pass you by
Always someone at your back
Biding their time for attack

Check for decoys, stay sharp edged
Double-crossers get your head
Carpet-baggers bluff and strike
Kiss of Judas, spider like

"Steeler," by G. Tipton,
R. Halford, and K. K. Downing,
Judas Priest, *British Steel*
(New York: CBS Records, 1980)

Contents

Preface

It is perhaps not an accident that my favorite band has been Judas Priest since the day in 1980 when I bought their album *British Steel* (on vinyl, of course).[1] Besides the partial coincidence of their name with the subject of the present work, I believe that the power and anger of their music can be seen as capturing the essence of Judas's character as well as our frustration with understanding him. Bach had done this explicitly (as well as much more artfully and subtly) in aria 51 of his *St. Matthew Passion.*[2] Angry at Jesus, angry at the evil men who encouraged and then abandoned him, angry at his own mistake, angry at God, angry at fate: all of these are implied as Bach has the bass echo Judas in his aria, singing, indeed demanding, "Give me back my Jesus!" The response is futile and self-destructive, but it is completely understandable as well as undeniably moving.

Judas fascinated the authors of the Gospels and their predecessors, and he has continued to captivate authors, artists, composers, and filmmakers throughout twenty centuries of Christianity. My own initial encounter with him was shortly before I was introduced to Judas Priest and long before I read the Bible, when I first watched *Jesus Christ Superstar* on a late show on television. In this production and throughout the centuries, Jesus awes us with his otherworldliness, Mary Magdalene lures us with her sensuality, Peter amuses and perhaps endears us with his simplicity and bluntness, but Judas fascinates us with his humanity—his dirty, noble, inscrutable humanity that demands and defies our understanding.

I fear the present work will disappoint if the reader is looking for the answer to the question "Who was Judas, *really?*" Although the question of the historical Judas will be addressed briefly in chapter 1, I do not intend to find *the* unique Judas who walked through Palestine two thousand years ago. Indeed, I find the present mania about such a question in relation to Jesus terribly misguided, both because of the utter poverty of the reconstructions themselves and the naive simplicity they assume in both human nature and human knowledge. What person is so shallow and uniform that he or she can be captured in merely one depiction, known in his or her entirety and experienced as a real presence from a handful of incidents and utterances? Certainly no one would claim such a facile reduction for Oedipus or Lear, nor for Hitler or Gandhi, and I do not think we should try to do it for Jesus or Judas either. Since we usually believe that truth as well as fiction is strange indeed, then surely the depth and complexity of character that we acknowledge in other historical figures and in the figures of great literature should also be expected from the historical figures in our religious literature. If there was a Judas walking in Judea two thousand years ago, then I am sure he was as complex and ambiguous as any other person, and to reduce him to just a thief, or a traitor, or a friend, or a hero is simplistic and misleading.

As soon as Judas (or Jesus, or any other person) did anything, there were several different versions of that event in the minds of the audience, and subsequently in the minds of the hearers or readers of the stories that were told. Nor is the necessary subjectivity of such records to be regretted. It is simply a fact of all knowledge that it must have a subject, and that subject must impute meaning to the knowledge as it is known and expressed: "Every person we know is a person with some significance or other for us, either positive, negative, or both. A person devoid of any significance to anyone would be an abstraction. No one knows any such person."[3] Brendan Kennelly also tries to capture this paradoxical subjectivity in his work *The Book of Judas*,[4] a long meditation on the many types and instances of betrayal that surround us. One of the poems in it is entitled "No Image Fits," and it begins with just this paradox: "I have never seen him and I have never seen/Anyone but him." We will never see Judas, and we will never not see him because, like every historical or literary character, he is found everywhere and in everyone, and he is also not just in one place or identified with one person. From the earliest sources on, there were a number of depictions of Judas (as there were also of Jesus), each with its own emphases, its own meaning, and ultimately, its own importance for our understanding of Judas, Jesus, God, good and evil, human nature, and ourselves.

From the earliest sources, Mark and an aetiological legend about a "Field of Blood," we know almost nothing about Judas: he was one of Jesus' disciples; he helped the authorities arrest Jesus; and a place in Jerusalem was somehow associated with him. It is this ambiguity that left the story open for subsequent traditions to develop their versions of Judas.

Many of the traditions have filled in the original silence about Judas with negative portrayals of him. Luke does this by developing Judas into a typical villain, evil and under the power of Satan. Luke's particular addition is to add an account of the ghastly and deserved death of the arch-sinner, a standard part of such stories in antiquity. Developments of Luke's account can be seen in later versions, such as Dante's elaboration and extension of Judas's grotesque suffering into all eternity for the sin of betrayal. John also develops Judas as a villain, his addition being the added accusation of thievery and greed against Judas. John's version has been particularly influential as anti-Semitic propaganda, such as that found in the medieval passion plays.

But there have also been positive portrayals of Judas. These may have been a minority, but they have been a curious and constant part of the tradition. These versions also rely on the silence and ambiguity of the Gospels about Judas and fill in the story in very different ways. The Gnostics may have revered Judas as the disciple who saw Jesus as he truly was and who acted to help Jesus by hurrying him on his way back to God; this act of Gnostic insight was of course only "misunderstood" by the other unenlightened disciples. The Middle Ages and beyond saw versions of Judas that combined his story with that of Oedipus. These versions sometimes saw Judas as deserving or contributing to his fate. On the other hand, some of these depicted him as doomed (by God?), even to the point of having him try (unsuccessfully) to avoid his fate; such versions almost seem to delight in the theological difficulties that this would pose in a Christian context. In the nineteenth and twentieth centuries the depiction of Judas as a revolutionary and patriot who became disillusioned with Jesus' refusal to establish an earthly kingdom has been perhaps the most popular, offering to the modern mind a psychologically plausible as well as refreshingly secular version of a religious tale. Finally, Matthew's account of Judas's ambiguous "repentance" and suicide has been developed into versions that either depict him as damned because of the sin of despair—not treachery or betrayal—or as saved through repentance, the ultimate sinner become the ultimate penitent and therefore a powerful and humbling object of emulation and admiration for the audience. Such a portrayal is seen in versions as diverse as Theophylactus (eleventh century), J. S. Bach (eighteenth century), and R. S. Anderson (twentieth century). It can also be made into a meditation on the necessity of Judas's role in our salvation, in which our attitude towards him is one of gratitude, not revulsion, seen quite powerfully in Scorsese's *Last Temptation of Christ*.

A final note on the comprehensiveness I am attempting in this book: I have tried with my examples and my analyses of them to be suggestive and representative of all the strands, streams, or branches of the tradition, but I myself have not read nor do I offer here analyses of every depiction of

Judas. As I have read more and more, I have found two different ways to look at the quantity of material. On the one hand, as one reads through a large number of these depictions, one is struck by how typical they all are, how often the same constellations of themes or images recur. So I think that a representative sample as is offered here does provide an accurate view of the overall picture. But at the same time, I have been struck by how each version, no matter how typical (or artless), has something unique to add, something no author had ever thought of before. Thus no survey can ever fully complete the picture, because the depiction of Judas hidden away in a library somewhere or the one that will be published next year will add something new. What is offered here is a guide or map, or, better yet, a family tree that traces the genetic resemblances between generations of Judas's story: as new ancestors are discovered or new descendants are created, they can be added to the tree, making it different but without altering the basic structures and insights I have tried to show here.

The present work has been through many reworkings, versions, and stages itself. I first made an attempt to say something interesting about Judas in a paper I wrote as an undergraduate at St. John's College for Dr. John Verdi's music class; it was eventually reworked and published.[5] As I began my graduate work in biblical studies, one of my first papers was an examination of the accounts of Judas's death in the Gospels and Acts; it was written with the help of Dr. Adela Yarbro Collins for the Christianity and Judaism in Antiquity Seminar at the University of Notre Dame and later presented at a regional conference of the Society of Biblical Literature.[6] Parts of this work have also been presented as papers at meetings of the Mid-Atlantic Region of the Society of Biblical Literature and at the International Conference on Patristic, Medieval, and Renaissance Studies. Work on this project has been supported in part by a Research Grant from the Society of Biblical Literature. The research has also been assisted by my participation in three summer seminars: in 2000, a Summer Seminar in Christian Scholarship at Calvin College led by Dr. Lamin Sanneh of Yale Divinity School and sponsored by the Pew Charitable Trusts; and two National Endowment for the Humanities Summer Seminars, one in 1996 with Dr. Leslie Brisman at Yale University and one in 1999 with Dr. Roger Bagnall at Columbia University. I began the initial research on the present work with Leslie, and I have continued it while at Villanova University working with Dr. Jack Doody of the Core Humanities Program. Their encouragement and assistance far surpass any acknowledgment I can offer here: in an academic world that often associates effectiveness with ruthlessness and detachment, these two gentlemen are passionate teachers as well as kind and generous colleagues who treat everyone around them with the utmost of respect and consideration. I am richer for having known them, and I dedicate this work to them. It is, indeed, the least that I can do.

In doing the research on this project, the interlibrary loan staffs of Falvey Library at Villanova University and of the Hekman Library at Calvin College have been wonderfully prompt and helpful in procuring books and articles from other libraries. In particular I would like to thank Catherine McGowan, Phylis Wright, Sue Facciolli, Bente Polites, and Kathleen Struck for their assistance in obtaining difficult-to-find items. Dr. William Klassen, whose work on Judas is so different from my own, has nonetheless been very helpful in offering his comments and helping with bibliographic references. Special thanks are also due Jon Levenson, Thomas Bertonneau, Daniel Morehead, and Rick Bolles for their suggestions on the manuscript, as well as my editor at Westminster John Knox, Carey C. Newman, whose enthusiastic support of my idea has made this book possible. Again, in a world where great minds are not always possessed by good people, all of their help has been most gracious and appreciated.

Finally, no introduction would be complete without some acknowledgment of the most beloved and supportive people around me, my students and my family. Everything I have ever written has in some way come out of the honest and insightful things said by my bright and wonderful students at Notre Dame and Villanova. As for my family—my wife, Marlis, and our children, Charles and Sophia—they have patiently endured the difficulties of an academic life and have always remained loving and supportive. Both my students and family have always generously put up with my idiosyncratic interests and especially my ongoing fascination with the darker side of the human story. At home and at work I am constantly surrounded by people who are the bright side of my life, a fact of which I am ever mindful and always grateful.

Kim Paffenroth
Villanova University
Christmas 2000

Chapter One

Judas the Obscure:
Object of Curiosity

Introduction

This chapter will examine the portrayals of Judas in the earliest traditions: Paul, the Gospel of Mark, and legends about a "Field of Blood" somewhere in Jerusalem. We will use the redactional and tradition-historical methods of analysis to get at what lies behind the final versions preserved in the canonical Gospels. For the purposes of redaction criticism, I will assume the two-source hypothesis; since the present subject does not include any Q material,[1] however, this will really only be an assumption of Markan priority (i.e., that Mark did not use Matthew in his composition). Although Paul does not mention Judas by name, the other two early traditions do, thereby showing that speculations about Judas's life and death arose early indeed: people's literary and moral imaginations long for villains, heroes, scapegoats, or victims, and their ability to create these almost always equals their need.[2] On the other hand, Paul's silence and the simplicity and ambiguity of the other early portrayals show that this early stage of development lacked the details and embellishments of later versions. Indeed, their very silence or ambiguity invited or even demanded such later elaborations.

Paul: Judas the Absent

Paul, the earliest of the New Testament writers (ca. 50–60 C.E.), never mentions Judas by name. In fact, it is not clear that he even knows that there was a betrayer. Paul mentions several times that Jesus was "handed over" (παραδίδωμι) to death, but this is usually presented as a theological statement of the meaning and purpose of Jesus' mission, not a description of the historical facts of Jesus' life.[3] Paul once describes this "handing over" without specifying who did it: "Jesus, who was handed over to death

1

for our trespasses" (Rom. 4:25). In another place he describes God as the one who "did not spare his own Son, but handed him over for us all" (Rom. 8:32). Also in Paul, Jesus hands himself over to death, "[Christ] loved me and handed himself over for me" (Gal. 2:20), and this is repeated in the subsequent Pauline tradition: "And walk in love, as Christ loved us and handed himself over for us. . . . as Christ loved the church and handed himself over for her" (Eph. 5:2, 25). There is only one Pauline reference to Jesus being "handed over" in the specific context of his arrest. In his description of the institution of the Lord's Supper, Paul refers to "the night when he was handed over" (1 Cor. 11:23). Given Paul's usage elsewhere, it would seem unlikely that this refers to the actions of someone other than Jesus or God: at the very least, the existence of such a person is not demanded by the text. As we shall see, this raises serious questions about the historicity of Judas.[4]

Just as interestingly, it shows that it is quite possible to proclaim an idea of Jesus, his mission, and his passion without any idea of his betrayer. I would say that it is possible to have an *idea* of Jesus like this but practically impossible to have a *story* of him that lacks the crucial poignancy of the betrayer: at the very least, it would be a story of much less power and vitality. To see what such a story might look like, consider the film *Jesus of Montreal* (1989), by French-Canadian director Denys Arcand.[5] Although the movie starts with actors putting on a scene from Dostoyevsky's *Brothers Karamazov* that is highly reminiscent of Judas's suicide,[6] the rest of the movie does not contain a Judas character.[7] The main character, Daniel, and four of his friends are asked by Father Leclerc to put on a play of Jesus' life. The friends come up with a version that is based on current historical research: they dismiss the virgin birth and make Jesus the illegitimate son of a Roman soldier; they reduce his miracles to the magical antics carried on by many other men of his time; they remove from his teaching anything that is apocalyptic, judgmental, or threatening; and they spiritualize the resurrection to be his living on in the hearts of his followers. The crowds enjoy the play as a novel spectacle, but Father Leclerc and his superiors are outraged and demand that the play be stopped. (Indeed, for me the movie succeeded remarkably in showing how meager and rather uninteresting are the results of historical criticism, and yet how threatening those results are perceived to be.) Meanwhile, Daniel's own life starts to resemble many of the parts of the gospel story that he and his friends have excised from it: he uncharacteristically flies into a rage and destroys a television studio, wielding a scourge of video cables to drive out the wicked, exploitive directors; with a panoramic view from the top of a skyscraper, he is tempted by the devil in the form of an evil lawyer to sell out to the culture and the market; in his final moments, while his brain is hemorrhaging after someone accidentally knocks over the cross he is on during the play and crushes his skull, he goes into apocalyptic rantings that are a long way from the "feel-good" message he had been preaching in the play; and finally, in a rather gruesome and heavy-handed scene, he is strapped to a hospital bed with his arms sticking out to his sides, crucifixion style, and he is torn open, his organs being harvested and flown all over the world, where they are physically "resurrected," giving new life to others.

The film has been rightly praised, winning at the Cannes Film Festival and being nominated for an Academy Award. But without a Judas character (and, indeed, in the metanarrative without a Pilate character either), the dramatic "hole" left by having no villain is noticeable. As social commentary, the film succeeds admirably by having the actor killed accidentally (but inevitably) by a combination of forces in which no one is really to blame: the narrow-minded church hierarchy, the ignorant crowds, the arrogant and venal media, the callous and inefficient bureaucracy of the health care system. As a biting, cynical critique of these groups (the film's black humor is irresistible), it is extremely effective; as the story of a man's life and its meaning, it is disappointing. Daniel's death makes us sad; it may even make us angry at the people and forces that have brought it about. But it is hardly heroic or tragic: he might as well have been hit by a bus.[8]

An interesting analog to this phenomenon may be found in early Christian art, where images of Judas are not essential parts of the passion cycle until the sixth century,[9] even though stories of him were already rich, varied, and widespread: it is quite possible to have a pictorial *image* of Jesus and even of the events leading up to his passion without including the betrayer. Both theological ideas and visual images are gleaned from the narrative, like frames taken out of a reel of film, but they then have a static existence separate from the demands of narrative. (It is another weakness of *Jesus of Montreal* that it often has the annoying look of a "set-piece," a bold visual image that the director wanted to put on the screen rather than an integral part of the narrative: I knew at the death scene that some excuse would have to be made to get rid of one of the women characters so that there could be just one woman cradling the dead Daniel, thus making it look like a *pietà*, the highly stylized representations of the virgin Mary holding the dead Jesus.)[10] Paul, for all his gifts as a preacher and theologian, was not much of a storyteller. Indeed, his rather heavy-handed and univalent use of Old Testament stories shows a mind of limited literary sensibilities. Visual artists were similarly not engaged in creating a narrative, nor obeying the rules of the very different craft of storytelling. Paul created powerful exhortations and theologies based on Jesus' life and message while artists created beautiful and moving images of the last days of Christ, but neither were capable nor interested in telling Jesus' (or Judas's) story. Such stories were probably already widely circulated in Paul's time by oral performers, but it would be another generation before they would be set in writing by men with much less elaborate theologies than Paul but much richer literary imaginations and skills.

Mark: Judas's Name, His Role, and the Historical Judas

Mark, most likely the earliest of the canonical Gospels (ca. 70 C.E.), and one that preserves traditions that go back even further, first mentions Judas by name in the list of the twelve (Mark 3:13–19). The special status of the twelve in Mark seems to be spelled out in verses 14–15: they are "to be with him" and to "have authority." Unlike other characters in Mark who are favorably disposed towards Jesus and his message and may even be termed followers in some loose sense, Mark portrays Jesus as appointing this special group who will accompany him and will share in his work of preaching and casting out demons. This latter ability is portrayed as a "power" or "authority" (ἐξουσία) given to them by Jesus. As a part of this special group, Judas receives the same "authority" and "power" as the others. Mark uses his typical device of bracketing one episode between two others to highlight the importance of exorcism here,[11] as the disciples are given "authority" over the demons immediately following a summary of Jesus' exorcistic activities (Mark 3:7–12), and right before Jesus is accused of being himself possessed by Beelzebul (Mark 3:20–27). As with Jesus' own power and authority, that granted to the disciples will cause them conflict and persecution; also, their own misunderstanding of the implications of Jesus' authority will cause them conflict with him. Judas clearly shares in the general incomprehension and misunderstanding of the disciples.

What was the significance of the name "Judas Iscariot"? That of the first name—Judas or Judah—is easier to answer, since it is well known. It may indeed have been the real name of one of Jesus' disciples as the name was very common among Jewish males in the first century.[12] The popularity of the name is partly confirmed by the fact that no fewer than eight different characters in the New Testament are named Judas or Judah. Besides Judas Iscariot are Judah, son of Jacob, patriarch and ancestor of

Jesus (Matt. 2:6); Judah, another ancestor of Jesus (Luke 3:30); Judas, the brother of Jesus (Matt. 13:55; Mark 6:3); Judas, the son of James (Luke 6:16; John 14:22; Acts 1:13); Judas the Galilean (Acts 5:37); Judas of Damascus (Acts 9:11); and Judas Barsabbas (Acts 15:22, 27, 32). To this evidence may be added the frequent appearance of the name in Josephus (ca. 37–100 C.E.).[13] However, the name would also have proved particularly apt for the Gospel tradition: the patriarch Judah, who sold his brother Joseph into slavery, provides a fitting analogue to Judas handing over Jesus for money in the gospel story.[14] Even in the particulars of the betrayal, a parallel may have been sensed: "Just as Judah and his brothers were eating when they decided to sell their brother Joseph, so Jesus during a meal expressed his premonition that there was enough unhappiness among the disciples about his mission that one of them would certainly communicate his concerns to the people in charge."[15] However, since Jesus himself was also thought to have descended from Judah, Judas's name gives him a special connection and even identity with Jesus.[16] The patriarchal name thus carries the implications both of greatness and valor, accentuated by its association with the great warrior and revolutionary Judas Maccabeus (second century B.C.E.) as well as its echo of a shameful story of jealousy and betrayal of a family member.

As for Iscariot, there has never been a satisfactory answer.[17] The most popular still seems to be that it represents *ish kerioth*, "man from Kerioth,"[18] although the location of a village with such a name has never been determined. (The phrase "from Kerioth" in some manuscripts of John 6:71 has been taken as confirmation of this identification, but it could just as easily be a later scribe engaged in the same sort of speculation as we are.)[19] It could be related to the tribe of Issachar,[20] or from Aramaic *saqor*, "of red color," either in the sense of "a ruddy complexion"[21] or "a worker in red dye."[22] It could be pejorative, either related to Latin *sicarius*, "assassin,"[23] or from some Semitic root (*sakar*, "to hand over";[24] *shaqar*, "fraud, deception"[25]), or an amalgamation that would come out to "he who makes a business out of friendship."[26] If it is pejorative in this way, and especially if it is a label that indicates Judas's narrative role, then this would almost certainly make it part of later tradition and not the name of a historical character.[27] None of these explanations has ever commanded general agreement.[28] Regardless, for this study what is important is that the name seems meaningless to the evangelist:[29] he does not explain it as he does another name in the list, "Boanerges," or as he explains the Aramaic at Mark 5:41. It is part of the tradition whose meaning was already lost by the time of the composition of the Gospels. And like other parts of the tradition, it was an ambiguous piece of the puzzle that was subsequently provided with a myriad of different meanings.

Judas's placement in the list should also be noted. It has been speculated that his name once stood much higher on the list, perhaps even first, and was only later moved to the end in order to cast him in a negative light.[30] While this may certainly be so, it would not really affect our reading of Mark, who clearly does place Judas last. I do not think, however, that this placement necessarily functions to denigrate Judas or lessen his status but rather to draw attention to him. Being at the end of a list does not imply inferiority,[31] but it does make the person listed last seem more important and more memorable. Readers would not expect Bartholomew, Matthew, or Thomas to figure prominently in the rest of the narrative, and they would be right, as these names are never mentioned again in Mark's Gospel.

But if Judas's placement on the list does not imply anything negative about him, the label placed after his name certainly does. Judas's role in the story is told to the reader as soon as he is introduced: he is the disciple "who handed him [Jesus] over." Although Klassen has argued persuasively for the translation "handed over" instead of the traditional "betrayed,"[32] Judas's act still seems clearly to be intended by Mark as a negative one, part of the plot of Jesus' enemies that has already been mentioned right before the disciples are introduced (Mark 3:6). Judas's label is the first indication of the failure of the disciples as a whole, a consistent theme in Mark,[33] although another foreshadowing of their failure may also be implied by the prominence of exorcistic power in their introduction, as they will later prove incapable of exorcism (Mark 9:14–29) or of understanding its significance (Mark 9:38–41). But none of the other disciples are introduced by labeling them with their future failures: it is not "Peter, who denied him," or "James and John, who foolishly asked for preeminence," or "Andrew, Philip, and Bartholomew, who misunderstood and abandoned him." Only Judas is introduced in this way, focusing and limiting his character to its narrative role.

The next time Judas is mentioned in Mark the bracketing technique is once again used, though this time the story is part of the bracketing material. The anointing at Bethany (Mark 14:3–9) is bracketed by a mention of the plot by the chief priests and scribes to kill Jesus (Mark 14:1–2) and a description of Judas's approaching them to join their plot: "And Judas Iscariot, who was one of the twelve, went to the chief priests in order to hand him over to them. When they heard it they rejoiced and promised to give him money. And he sought an opportunity to hand him over" (Mark

14:10–11). Mark has again used one story to highlight another, though this time for the purpose of contrast. An anonymous woman with whom Jesus has no previous connection shows him kindness and trust while the religious leaders and one of his own disciples show him malice and treachery; she has lovingly prepared him for death while they are hatefully and enviously preparing him to be killed. The scene is one of typical Markan irony,[34] as the people whom one would expect to side with Jesus are against him while the appropriate, even extravagant, response to Jesus comes from someone totally unexpected. Judas's status as a disciple is underlined in this story as we are reminded that he is "one of the twelve" (v. 10), making this another example of the general and ongoing failure of the disciples.

But just as important to note in this story is what is not said. Although it is connected to the anointing at Bethany by way of contrast, it is not suggested in Mark that the woman's "waste" motivated or even upset Judas: he is not the one who objects in the Markan version (Mark 14:4–5). Despite the overall negative portrayal of the disciples in Mark, it is not even they as a group who do so but only an unidentified "some" people, who may have been disciples or other bystanders. Also, the offer of money by the high priests is an afterthought first mentioned by them, not Judas, and about which there is never any further elaboration. Neither concern about money, nor greed for it, is ever attached to Judas in Mark. This leaves us, however, with a character who is disturbingly or disappointingly without motives. Although Mark's descriptions can often be vivid, his characterization is usually minimal. Judas must fulfill the narrative role of handing over Jesus: motives are a speculative extravagance or distraction in which the author does not indulge.

At the Last Supper, Judas is not mentioned by name, but his act is explained and interpreted:

> And when it was evening he came with the twelve. And as they were reclining and eating, Jesus said, "Truly I say to you, one of you will hand me over, one who is eating with me.". . . He said to them, "It is one of the twelve, one who is dipping with me in the bowl. For the Son of Man goes as it is has been written of him, but woe to that man by whom the Son of Man is handed over. Better for him if that man had not been born." (Mark 14:17–18, 20–21)

Again, Judas's act as yet another example of the failure of the disciples is highlighted by the repetition of "the twelve" (vv. 17, 20): Judas does not act as an individual but as a member of "the twelve" and a representative of their continuing and worsening failure.

The theme of Jesus' life and death as fulfillment of scripture is explicit in this section, both from Jesus' reference to what "has been written" (v. 21) and from the description of the unfaithful disciple as sharing bread with Jesus, meant to evoke Ps. 41:9: "Even my bosom friend in whom I trusted, who ate of my bread, has lifted his heel against me." As before, the scriptural allusion and the whole scene are bitterly ironic.

The "woe" (v. 21) is designed to separate and balance two conflicting and therefore problematic parts of Judas's act: Judas's part in the action, which Mark wants to condemn, and Jesus' part in the action, which Mark wants to commend as the fulfillment of God's plan and Jesus' obedience to it. This is why he alters the form of the "woe" by including "the Son of Man" as well as "that man": Jesus acted in submission to God's will; Judas did not, even though his act is part of the divine plan.[35] The ambiguity of the last part of the "woe" should also be noted. The referent of "for him" (v. 21) is grammatically unclear. From proximity it should refer to "the Son of Man," and on the literal level this would make sense: better for the one about to be handed over to execution if the one who handed him over had never been born. But this would be a rather flat and trivial reading of it, for we know that on a deeper level "the Son of Man" will be victorious and "that man" is the one who will be worse off.

The final appearance of Judas in Mark is to fulfill his narrative role of aiding in Jesus' capture in a scene that seems almost anticlimactic:

> And immediately, while he was still speaking, Judas, one of the twelve, came up, and with him a crowd with swords and clubs, from the high priests and scribes and elders. The one who handed him over had given them a sign, saying, "The one whom I will kiss is he; seize him and lead him away under guard." And when he came, he immediately went up to him and said, "Rabbi," and kissed him. . . . And Jesus said to them, "Have you come out as against a robber, with swords and clubs to take me? Daily I was with you in the temple and you did not seize me. But let the scriptures be fulfilled." And they all left him and fled. (Mark 14:43–45, 48–50)

The same Markan themes seen before are once again emphasized. Judas as "one of the twelve" is again repeated, and the painful irony of his collusion with Jesus' enemies is given a final embellishment: a respectful greeting (used elsewhere of Jesus at Mark 9:5; 10:51; 11:21) and a gesture of affection or familiarity are his final acts as he hands Jesus over to a shameful death.[36] The scene is again depicted as the fulfillment of scripture, though the reference is vague: with the reference to "swords" and the scattering of the disciples it may be another reference to Zech. 13:7 (already quoted at Mark 14:27): "'Awake, O sword, against my shepherd, against the man who is my associate,' says the Lord of hosts. Strike the shepherd that the sheep may be scattered." Having fulfilled his narrative role, nothing more is said of Judas in Mark.

Finally, since the other Synoptics are most probably based on Mark's account and therefore do not provide independent witness, the issue of Judas's historicity should be addressed here.[37] Did one of Jesus' disciples help in his capture, and was that disciple named Judas? The answers to both must be in the form of probabilities: biblical scholars who claim more than this are being less than honest. To the first question I would say that the probability is high indeed. The story obviously existed before Mark's Gospel, and its absence in Paul tells us nothing other than that Paul either did not know or was not interested in the tradition:[38] Paul can be used to confirm Gospel traditions, not disconfirm them, as it is clearly an argument from silence. It is difficult to imagine any apologetic purpose that the early church would have had to invent the story of one of the chosen disciples helping in Jesus' capture.[39] The later tradition is indeed at pains to rehabilitate the disciples as much as possible. And although another negative episode for the disciples in Mark might make sense, would it cast Jesus in a more favorable light so that someone in the tradition might be tempted to create such a story? It is hard to imagine this. On the one hand, if Jesus chose the disciple not knowing he would hand him over, it would suggest a rather unflattering lack of foresight and planning. This was apparently the exact objection raised by Celsus (second century C.E.), a pagan critic of Christianity, as we find it now in Origen's (ca. 185–254) rebuttal:

> And the following appear to me to be childish assertions, viz., that "no good general and leader of great multitudes was ever betrayed; nor even a wicked captain of robbers and commander of very wicked men, who seemed to be of any use to his associates; but Jesus, having been betrayed by his subordinates, neither governed like a good general, nor, after deceiving his disciples, produced in the minds of the victims of his deceit that feeling of good-will which, so to speak, would be manifested towards a brigand chief."[40]

On the other hand, if Jesus chose the disciple knowing he would hand him over and bring all the resulting shame and guilt upon himself, then we have a scenario that is so problematically hard-hearted on Jesus' part that it is difficult to imagine why anyone would think to invent such a story.[41]

As to the question about a disciple named Judas, I think that the name Judas was common enough at the time to be believable as that of one of Jesus' disciples. But was it invented as an anti-Jewish attack?[42] Certainly in subsequent polemic it has been tragically effective in just such a way: the disciple named "Jew" turned Jesus over to "the Jews" to be tortured and killed. If the name only appeared in later tradition, I would certainly be inclined to dismiss it for this reason. But to posit in the pre-Markan tradition such a subtle, allegorical, anti-Jewish invention that is simultaneously unflattering to Jesus seems less likely.

To conclude, Judas is an enigmatic figure in Mark whose only role is to hand Jesus over to the authorities. He has no character beyond this, and no details are given about him that do not contribute to this role. His character is effectively confined or limited to its narrative function.[43] Judas's role in Mark is seen as fulfilling scripture and also as epitomizing the ironic and tragic failure of the disciples in general. While all the other disciples also fail, indeed do so more frequently, Judas is the greatest and most consistent failure: the other disciples often fail, but Judas does nothing but fail. He is a figure of simple, unadorned irony and poignancy. We do not feel for him, but because of him we do feel more deeply the pain that he and the others cause Jesus. And while we wonder at his lack of motives and know that he is not absolutely necessary to the plot, we aesthetically or emotionally feel the need for this deeper pain that he brings to the story.

A Modern Version of Mark's Enigmatic Judas

Practically every version of Judas's story since Mark's has sought to fill in Mark's silence about Judas's motives and character, but an interesting exception to this is found in perhaps the best-known Jesus film of all time, *The Greatest Story Ever Told* (1965), directed by George Stevens.[44] Among the film's many shortcomings (its most noticeable being its numerous and absurd miscastings) is its flat, static quality—its attention to visual effect without any equivalent interest in characterization or narrative: "Yet, the viewer may also discover that *Greatest Story* is less a story . . . because it contains less narrative structure, less plot, and less character interaction."[45] Although sensitively played by David McCallum (who went on to huge fame as Robert Vaughn's sidekick in *The Man from U.N.C.L.E.*), Judas is a glaring example of this lack of characterization. He is the first disciple called, and in an early scene (with Martha, Mary, and Lazarus), he is even seated closest to Jesus. But nothing is ever made of this. At the confession at Caesarea Philippi, Judas is given his own confession: "You are a great leader, and the greatest teacher I have ever known." This is again a good start, hinting perhaps at the kind of nationalistic, revolutionary tendencies that we will see in many depictions of Judas in chapter 4, but again there is no sequel. Judas is outraged at the anointing, but we have no idea why, as he has evinced no special interest in the poor, nor does he show any interest in money himself. At the betrayal, Judas seems distraught, but there is no indication why he is betraying Jesus nor why he would be distraught over it. Finally, his death is visually stunning: in an extreme long shot we see him throwing himself into an enormous sacrificial fire in the temple. But again there is no indication whether we should take this as remorse, despair, or just punishment for his evil deed.[46] (Much the same could be said for Jesus' crucifixion, which is shot from way too far away for it to be compelling or even emotional.)[47] In a fast-paced story like the Gospel of Mark, an enigmatic character like Judas is intriguing; in a four-hour biblical epic like *Greatest Story* that lacks any fleshed-out characters, he is annoying.

The Field of Blood

Although discussions of the full versions of Matthew, Luke, and Papias will come later in our analysis, it is possible here to untangle one strand of tradition that they all used: a legend about a "Field of Blood" somewhere in Jerusalem, a site that is still included in tours of the city.[48] This will enable us to consider this part of Judas's story on its own as well as appreciate the different functions it fills in the fuller versions of the story.

Matthew is the earliest extant mention of a Field of Blood associated with Judas (ca. 80 C.E.). Just like Mark, however, it should be remembered that Matthew preserves traditions much older than the final edition of his Gospel. After Judas has returned the silver pieces to the chief priests and has hanged himself, the chief priests are confused as to what to do with this money: "But the chief priests, taking the pieces of silver, said, 'It is not lawful to put them into the treasury, since they are blood money.' So they took counsel, and bought with them the potter's field, to bury strangers in. Therefore that field has been called the Field of Blood to this day" (Matt. 27:6–8). Given how tightly Matthew has woven these sentences into his overall work, we must first consider whether the Field of Blood is his own invention or whether it is more likely that it came to him from some preexistent tradition.

There are two compelling reasons to think that the Field of Blood is from a tradition that predates Matthew's Gospel. First, as we shall see later in our fuller analysis, the main points that Matthew wishes to stress here are scriptural fulfillment and the guilt of the chief priests and elders. The mention of the field advances neither of these points directly.[49] The chief priests and elders are rendered guilty by the return of the "blood money," not by the purchase of the field. And Matthew is at pains to connect the field into his prophetic quotations: it is not simply manufactured from the scriptural quotations, as if Matthew built his story out of them, but the scriptural quotations must be made to fit with the mention of the field. This suggests that the field's name was the nucleus around which Matthew built his passage, though the final product more or less abandons the purposes of the etiological legend (to explain the curious name of a place), subordinating it to Matthew's real interests—to blacken further the chief priests and elders and to show Jesus' life and death as the fulfillment of scripture.[50] Second, the Field of Blood is about the only similarity between the versions of Matthew and Luke, thereby strongly suggesting that it was part of a tradition independently available to both of them.[51] So sometime before 80 C.E., people told of how a Field of Blood was somehow associated with Judas.[52]

Is there any way to tell where this field was? With all due respect to biblical scholars and contemporary tour guides,[53] I would have to say no. Or perhaps, at the very least, we could reconstruct the content of the original legend. Given the complete subordination of the etiological legend to Matthew's own literary purposes,[54] the answer would again have to be negative. For Matthew, the Field of Blood is now primarily a part of scriptural fulfillment. Beyond that, it is an image of anonymous, failed potential: it becomes the resting place of the unmourned dead, for those who are not merely forgotten but were never known. As we shall see, the place takes on very different valences in other versions almost contemporary with Matthew's, so there is no need to believe that this particular meaning was intrinsic to the legend: it was most likely part of Matthew's contribution to the evolving tradition.

Shortly after Matthew wrote his Gospel, Luke wrote his Gospel and the book of Acts (ca. 80–90 C.E.), again preserving much older materials. Although Luke's version of Judas's death is almost completely different from Matthew's—it differs as to the manner of Judas's death, who bought the field, and whose blood lent it its name—they agree as to the detail of a Field of Blood. In a speech supposedly given by Peter to the congregation in Jerusalem, there is a digression to explain the death of Judas: "Now this man bought a field with the reward of his wickedness; and falling headlong he burst open in the middle and all his bowels gushed out. And it became known to all the inhabitants of Jerusalem, so that the field was called in their language Akeldama, that is, Field of Blood" (Acts 1:18–19). As spoken by Peter, the sentences make little sense. Peter is speaking to "the inhabitants of Jerusalem," so why does this need to be explained to them? And the language of Peter and his audience is Aramaic, so how could he call it "their language"? The sentences are intended for Luke's audience, but our question is, Did they come to Luke as part of a tradition about a Field of Blood, or were they created by him?

There are at least four reasons, each of them suggestive on its own, that verses 18–19 are pre-Lukan. First, the idea of scriptural fulfillment is raised in verse 16, but it is not resolved until verse 20: the account of Judas's death and its relation to the Field of Blood appear therefore as a rather awkward aside or parenthetical remark that interrupts the flow of the speech that Luke has created, thereby increasing the likelihood that he is here trying to incorporate preexisting material.[55] Second, the phrasing of these verses shows a much lower incidence of Lukan style and vocabulary than the rest of the speech.[56] Third, the verses stand on their own as "a self-contained whole, an aetiology-story."[57] Finally, the fact that this is one of the few points of connection with Matthew's version again suggests that it was a tradition independently available to both.[58] Luke, like Matthew, has preserved an earlier tradition and subordinated it to his own literary ends. It is in his literary ends, in the meaning that he wishes this etiological legend now to convey, that he differs most from Matthew. For Matthew, the Field of Blood conveys a sense of poignancy, loss, and anonymity, while for Luke the same field is an image of grotesque and deserved punishment at the providential hand of God, and everyone remembers precisely who was so punished there.

Finally, one or two generations after Matthew and Luke, Papias (ca. 130 C.E.) preserved another tradition of Judas's death. In this version, Judas died from neither hanging nor falling but instead from a horrible, disfiguring, and, most of all, shameful disease. But as different as the account may be from the two canonical versions about the cause of death, it is consistent in associating Judas with a field:

> After many such tortures and punishments, they say that he died on his own property, and that on account of the stench the place is desolate and uninhabited even until now, and that even today no one can go through that place without stopping up his nose with his hands, because the stench of his flesh spread out over the land so much.[59]

Again, the fact that the field is about the only point of connection between this and the two canonical versions increases the likelihood that it was part of a tradition that circulated independently.[60] But even if Papias invented it himself, or adapted it directly from one or both of the canonical versions, it still shows the same sorts of developments. The tendency we already saw in Luke's version to make the Field of Blood into a grotesque detail of the traitor's deserved suffering and death has been accentuated in this version, so much so that the actual name of the place has been forgotten in favor of including more details regarding the stench: it is no longer the Field of Blood, a reminder of Jesus' passion, but only a vile, foul-smelling place. No longer is the field even part of a lesson on the terrible results of sin, but only a grotesque fact of geography that people try their best to avoid or mock, showing that literary traditions do not only evolve, they also degenerate.[61]

The obvious similarity of these references, together with the marked differences of these versions, point to the fact that, although a Field of Blood was somehow associated with Judas at quite an early date, the exact connection was not solidified or specified in the tradition but could be elaborated in several ways: many people thought there was a Field of Blood, but no one knew for sure where it was or why it was called this. It is perhaps a perfect encapsulation of all of the Judas traditions that one of the earliest traditions never had one "canonical" version but existed in the amorphous and multiplicitous world of oral traditions for fifty years,[62] and when the written word sought to oust this vibrant but confusing tradition, it did so only by paradoxically canonizing two divergent explanations of the Field of Blood, and allowing a third, noncanonical version to continue its influence for hundreds of years.

Conclusion

By the end of the first generation of Christian storytellers, there was already some speculation about Judas, but it was caused by a continuing ambiguity and vagueness surrounding him. If Paul is any indication, some first-generation Christians probably did not even know that one of Jesus' disciples was supposed to have betrayed him, nor what that person's name might have been. Those who did know of Judas knew only one thing about him: he was the disciple who cooperated with those who arrested Jesus. But why he would do this, or why even the people who arrested Jesus would need his help, seem to have been completely unknown to the first generation of Christians, for there is no surviving record of their beginning to speculate on these questions. Nor is there any record of speculations on what would become the most fertile ground for speculation—Judas's life previous to his following Jesus. Some Christians knew of conflicting legends about Judas's death, but the interpretation of these was still left wide open, and they could be seen as tragedies, warnings, or sick jokes with equal justification. No systematic or satisfying portrayal of Judas had yet been created. Like some evil version of the anointing woman (Mark 14:9), his terrible act was told everywhere in memory of him: everyone knew what Judas did. But also like the anointing woman (whose name even is forgotten), no one knew who Judas was. All the details of his life had been lost, or, more accurately, they had yet to be created: when later storytellers looked at Judas, they saw the perfect cipher on which to practice their art, shaping him into the kind of man or monster that their individual stories needed. Here was the perfect foundation on which to build a character and a story: here was a man who, on the one hand, needed no introduction but, on the other, definitely needed a conclusion. As we shall see, there were many possibilities for what that conclusion could be, and with each new conclusion, a new meaning and purpose for Judas's story was crafted.

Chapter Two

Judas the Arch-Sinner:
Object of Horror

Introduction: Judas as a Lesson against Evil

The ambiguity and enigma of Judas in the earliest traditions proved unsatisfying to many. Enigmas usually have a point, but it is one that is too often missed, and storytellers have sought to make the lesson of Judas more explicit and accessible to their audiences. To this end, some versions of Judas's story show a much greater interest in depicting Judas like other archetypally evil characters. They also try to balance two conflicting tendencies of the story of Jesus' enemy. On the one hand, Jesus' most appropriate adversary would be Satan, another daimonic being possessed of superhuman powers,[1] and versions such as Luke's are careful to accentuate the devil's role.[2] But storytellers also know that there is a special delectation and horror at the enemy who is also an intimate: Cain, Absalom, Brutus, and Iago will always be more powerful and terrifying than Satan, Goliath, Hector, or Shylock because something has gone much more profoundly wrong with them, and the bonds they have broken are more essential to who they are, just as the rupture is more essential to what they have become. Of course, in a polytheistic context, the divine and intimate adversary can be one and the same, as in the story of Osiris, who is tricked and killed by his brother-god Seth/Typhon.[3] But in the gospel story this would not seem possible,[4] and therefore the role of Jesus' adversary is essentially split between Satan and Judas, giving him both a demonic and a human opponent. But at the same time, Luke is careful to tie the two together as closely as possible, making it explicit that Satan is in Judas and is working through him (Luke 22:3), so that Jesus is not defeated by a mere human. And while his demonic opponent might be an object of fear or even awe, his human enemy, Judas, is made into a lesson on the wages of sin. Punishments are heaped on him to drive home the message to the audience that they must avoid sin or face similar consequences. Such depictions were especially popular in antiquity and the Middle Ages, but we will see that their echoes persist until the present day in many popular beliefs and practices all over the world.

Early Versions

Two early versions—those of Luke and Papias—took the ambiguity of Mark and the Field of Blood and developed it into two similar stories focusing on the death of Judas. The point of both of these versions is that the wicked are punished by the just and providential hand of God. But another early version—that of the Arabic infancy gospel—began the tradition of speculating on Judas's life before the betrayal. As the other versions projected the results of his evil forward to his horrible death, this gospel projected the origins of his evil backwards to his childhood. By doing this, it began a long tradition of using Judas's story to meditate on the nature of evil as well as to consider whether the idea of evil is compatible with either fate or free will.

Luke

As in Mark, Luke first mentions Judas as the last member on his list of the Twelve: ". . . and Judas Iscariot, who became a traitor" (Luke 6:16). The term Luke uses here, προδότης, is less specific about the act that will be committed by Judas: it does not designate him as the one who would "hand over" Jesus.[5] But if the term is more vague about what act he will commit, it is also more definite in its evaluation of him as negative. The word clearly designates someone who commits an evil, treacherous, unfaithful act, as Luke uses it elsewhere in Stephen's speech: "Which of the prophets did not your fathers persecute? And they killed those who announced beforehand the coming of the Righteous One, whom you have now betrayed and murdered" (Acts 7:52; cf. 2 Tim. 3:4).[6] With his first reference to Judas, Luke has already sought to remove some of the ambiguity with which Mark had surrounded him. But although Luke seeks to blacken Judas's character more unambiguously right from the beginning, he has more of a problem in doing so than would Mark, because Judas is one of the "Twelve," a designation that is much more theologically loaded in Luke–Acts than it is in Mark.[7] For Luke, the Twelve are not just disciples who are especially close to Jesus; they provide the crucial link between Jesus' ministry and the nascent church (Acts 1:21–22), and it is imperative that their number be kept at twelve, representing the twelve tribes of Israel. The presence of a betrayer among them is not just a terrible irony that also epitomizes the failure of the disciples in general (as it is in Mark), but a much deeper problem that threatens the foundation of the church. As we shall see, Luke's treatment of Judas is to a large extent constructed to answer this challenge.

Luke has omitted the anointing at Bethany, instead including a similar anointing of Jesus much earlier in the Gospel (Luke 7:36–50).[8] There are numerous differences between this anointing and Mark's,[9] but one is worth noting for its different portrayal of Judas and the disciples. Mark had "some" people object to the anointing, but Luke has specified that it was only Simon the Pharisee who objected (and for the totally different reason of the woman's character, not for the wastefulness of her act). This is interesting, as it further distances the disciples (including Judas) from any wrongdoing or misunderstanding (at this point at least). It is part of a general improvement in the depiction of the disciples, as they will have to go on to lead the church in Acts, so they cannot be the unmitigated failures that they are in Mark. It is also part of the more ambiguous depiction of the Pharisees in Luke–Acts, for they are sometimes favorably disposed to Jesus (Luke 5:17; 13:31; Acts 5:34) and sometimes opposed to him (Luke 6:11). This leads Luke to a more ambiguous portrayal of both Judas and the Pharisees. Whereas Mark had the latter as simply villains, Luke must be more careful: insofar as they accept Jesus, they show themselves to be the legitimate interpreters of the Jewish tradition, but insofar as they reject him, they fatally break with their own tradition.[10] Likewise with Judas, who may be an ironic or enigmatic villain in Mark but also clearly evil: for Luke, he has to be good insofar as he is an apostle but evil insofar as he is the betrayer.

Luke solves this in part by accentuating and expanding the role of Satan in the Gospel in general and in the betrayal in particular. Only Luke notes after the temptation by the devil that he departed "until an opportune time" (Luke 4:13; cf. Mark 1:12; Matt. 4:11).[11] And this temporary departure is specifically referred to at the betrayal when Satan returns:

> Then Satan entered into Judas called Iscariot, who was of the number of the twelve; he went away and conferred with the chief priests and officers how he might betray him to them. And they were glad, and engaged to give him money. So he agreed, and sought an opportunity to betray him to them in the absence of the multitude. (Luke 22:3–6)

Luke has a marked interest in Satan and the demonic as Jesus' opponents[12] for the reason already mentioned. Merely human opponents are not sufficient for the battle Luke wishes to portray nor for the higher

Christology he has over Mark's: "This gives what in the Third Gospel had earlier appeared to be a struggle among humans and human institutions an even more profound and cosmic dimension."[13] (One of the few artful touches of the movie *The Greatest Story Ever Told* is to have the rather avuncular Satan, played by Donald Pleasence, reappear at the betrayal, the denial, and the crowds' shouting for Jesus' crucifixion: it really does make these scenes seem much more dramatic and purposeful, as they are driven forward by cosmic forces but are still totally in the hands of willing, human participants.) This Satanic influence over Judas allows Luke partly to resolve his problem of Judas's dual nature: insofar as he was a chosen apostle of Jesus, he partook of all the authority that Jesus granted him, including the ability to perform miracles (Luke 9:1–6); but insofar as he was a chosen instrument of Satan, he partook of Satan's evil and relinquished any claim to be Jesus' follower. Satan provides Luke with an important explanation for the transformation of an apostle into an enemy.

At the Last Supper, Luke reproduces Jesus' prediction of his betrayal and the resulting "woe" fairly closely: "'But behold the hand of him who betrays me is with me on the table. For the Son of man goes as it has been determined; but woe to that man by whom he is betrayed!' And they began to question one another, which of them it was that would do this" (Luke 22:21–23). Luke has omitted reference here to the Twelve, and he has shortened the "woe," omitting reference to it being "better for him if that man had not been born" (Mark 14:21). Again, this seems to be part of Luke's slightly more positive depiction of the disciples and his more elevated depiction of Jesus. The betrayal by an intimate, which was so painful, ironic, and mysterious in Mark's version, becomes in Luke's version another example of Jesus loving his enemies and sharing his table with them, as he has throughout Luke's Gospel.[14] The epitome of this would be Jesus' words on the cross, "Father, forgive them; for they know not what they do" (Luke 23:34),[15] found only in Luke's version. But in Luke's portrayal, all of this is done to highlight and accentuate Jesus' goodness, not to lessen Judas's evil.

Much the same motivations guide Luke's redaction of the arrest scene: "While he was still speaking, there came a crowd, and the man called Judas, one of the twelve, was leading them. He drew near to Jesus to kiss him; but Jesus said to him, 'Judas, would you betray the Son of man with a kiss?'" (Luke 22:47–48). On the one hand, Luke has added a direct address by Jesus to Judas, emphasizing Jesus' disappointment and his willingness even now to forgive his disciple and remind him of the love they share.[16] But Luke omits the actual kiss, probably because of his general aversion to depicting Jesus as physical or emotional.[17] At the end of the scene, Luke also adds Jesus' statement "But this is your hour, and the power of darkness" (Luke 22:53), again emphasizing that what is happening goes way beyond the human actors involved and includes cosmic evil at work in them.[18] In Luke's version of the arrest, Jesus expresses his willingness to forgive and his submission to the present powers, and he does so in a way that is in keeping with his depiction throughout the Gospel, where Jesus is almost always regal, detached, and in control (condescending, one could say, in its original, nonpejorative sense).

So far, all of Luke's depiction of Judas tends to mitigate his responsibility somewhat by shifting the blame onto Jesus' real, demonic opponent, Satan. But at the beginning of Acts, Luke makes it clear that Judas still justly suffered punishment for his deed. In a speech attributed to Peter, Luke describes Judas's fate:

> "Brethren, the scripture had to be fulfilled, which the Holy Spirit spoke beforehand by the mouth of David, concerning Judas who was guide to those who arrested Jesus. For he was numbered among us, and was allotted his share in this ministry. (Now this man bought a field with the reward of his wickedness; and falling headlong he burst open in the middle and all his bowels gushed out. And it became known to all the inhabitants of Jerusalem, so that the field was called in their language Akeldama, that is, Field of Blood.) For it is written in the book of Psalms,
> > 'Let his habitation become desolate,
> > and let there be no one to live in it';
> and
> > 'His office let another take.'" (Acts 1:16–20)

The beginning and the end of this quotation highlight what are Luke's interests in relating Judas's death. What happens in Jesus' life and in the life of the church is not chance, but it is what "had to" happen (v. 16), and this necessity was predicted in scripture. And at the end of the quotation, we see exactly what scripture has been fulfilled by the predicted death of the betrayer (Ps. 69:25) and what scripture warrants what now "has to" happen (vv. 21–26) in the election of a new apostle to replace Judas (Ps. 109:8).[19] Luke's description of Judas's death emphasizes that it was in fulfillment of scripture and that it was the just punishment of God for his terrible act of betrayal.[20] As we shall see, in its overall emphasis on scriptural fulfillment, the motivations behind Luke's description are quite close to Matthew's, though the actual details of the two accounts are irreconcilable.[21]

But this difference in content creates quite a different meaning for Judas's death in Acts. Luke's version of Judas's death does not include the poignancy (or nobility) of suicide (as in Matthew), but rather portrays the death as the kind that should (or must?) happen to wicked people,[22] similar to the deaths of Ananias and Sapphira (Acts 5:1–11), and Herod Agrippa (Acts 12:20–23).[23] Even in some of its details, the account echoes the presumed retribution that would be visited on the godless: "After this they [the unrighteous] will become dishonored corpses, and an outrage among the dead forever; because he will dash them speechless to the ground" (Wis. 4:18–19).[24] Later elaborations of Judas's punishment are all similar to Luke's version, in which he is possessed by Satan, and his death is by a horrific fall that was in fulfillment of scripture. Although Luke's main focus in his description of Judas's death is on the idea of scriptural fulfillment, he does show an interest in relating the death more graphically and grotesquely when he adds the detail that "all his bowels gushed out." It is similar to his description of the death of Herod Agrippa (Acts 12:23), and it also contains the kind of stereotyped details found in the descriptions of the deaths of other notoriously wicked people in nonbiblical literature.[25] Luke, his contemporaries, and generations of storytellers since then did not believe these were chance coincidences but rather saw them as direct and necessary punishments from God, who shows how "those who commit sin and do wrong are their own worst enemies" (Tob. 12:10).[26] Such acts of retribution reestablish justice in the world as well as promote it in the future, for the threat that a dire, ghastly death and eternal judgment were just around the corner might well scare the wicked into repentance and reform as well as chasten the righteous so that they would not stray in the first place. For these versions, there was no better way to use the story of the worst sinner than as a lesson that would diminish the likelihood that their audiences would commit sin in their own lives.

All in all, Luke's portrayal of Judas seeks to resolve many of the ambiguities of Mark's: Judas's act was not simply "handing over"; it was the act of a "traitor." The source and motivation of his evil were clarified by its coming from his master, Satan; and although Satan was ultimately to blame, this did not lessen Judas's guilt, as shown by his fate subsequent to Jesus' arrest. This fate was not left unstated but was vividly described as a stereotypically and deservedly gruesome death—a death providentially from the hand of God, as had been foretold in the scriptures, one that should be taken by the audience as a lesson against sin in their own lives.

Papias

As grotesque as Luke's description is, the punishment was not extended or excruciating enough for many later authors. Soon after Luke's time, a tradition was circulating that sought to remedy this. It is found in a fragment attributed to Papias (ca. 130 C.E.):

> Judas wandered in this world, a great example of impiety. His flesh swelled so much that where a cart went through easily, he was not able to go through, not even the mass of his head; they say that his eyelids swelled so much that he could not see any light at all, and his eyes could not be seen even with a doctor's instruments, because they had sunken so far from the surface of his face. His genitals were more enlarged and unsightly than any other deformity, while blood and worms flowed from all over his body, necessarily doing great harm just by themselves.[27] After many such tortures and punishments, they say that he died on his own property, and that on account of the stench the place is desolate and uninhabited even until now, and that even today no one can go through that place without stopping up his nose with his hands, because the stench of his flesh spread out over the land so much.[28]

Now here is a punishment that fits the crime and satisfies our moral and aesthetic sensibilities as well as provides a much more powerful and memorable lesson on the results of sin.

Although Papias's version is similar to Luke's,[29] it shows slightly different emphases in its development of traditional material.[30] The etiological legend about the name of a place in Jerusalem has been subsumed so much to other concerns that it is not explicitly named as the Field of Blood, and the details of how it got its name are now used to describe more graphically the grotesque and painful death of Judas. Scriptural fulfillment, so crucial to Luke, is also subdued: an implicit fulfillment of Psalm 69:25 might still be seen in the final part of the story, but it hardly seems to be an important point that the author wishes to emphasize. Rather, the author's point seems to be not that these events were in fulfillment of scripture but that Judas's death was just the sort of death that his audience would expect an especially wicked person to suffer at the hands of a just God (or gods, or Providence). In this, Papias's version shows further development towards a common extrabiblical genre of stories that relate the horrible (and deserved) ends of wicked people. Although Luke's version contained the common detail of bursting, Papias's contains more such details that are found in many other stories from the ancient world:[31] grotesque swelling;[32] unnatural effluxes from the body, especially blood, intestines,[33] or worms;[34] focus on the particularly shameful location of these symptoms in or around the genitals;[35] premature putrefaction with accompanying stench;[36] and all of these leading to great and prolonged pain and suffering before death. Such stereotyped material may make the story seem less compelling to us, for we look for diversity and uniqueness in characterization. But, as we shall see, stereotypical elements made this version seem more appropriate and real to many who have tried to imagine Judas's death: what "better" way to have the worst sinner die than to have him die like other sinners, only worse? And while the details of his death were stereotypical, the detail of stench also became useful much later as part of anti-Semitic slurs.[37] Papias's version also resurfaces in the repertoire of the virulent anti-Semite, Abraham a Sancta Clara.[38] Because of its stereotypical treatment of evil and its usefulness for anti-Semitism, Papias's version of Judas's death, although uncanonical, has often been as popular and influential as the canonical versions.

Arabic Infancy Gospel

As early as the fifth or sixth century, Judas's evil and its punishment were not only being projected forward into a miserable life and excruciating death following the betrayal but also backwards into his earlier life, showing that his role as Jesus' implacable and demonic adversary did not begin in adulthood. This is the scenario described in the Arabic infancy gospel.[39] Amidst all the miracles performed by Jesus as a child, he first encounters his future betrayer:

> Another woman was living in the same place, whose son was tormented by Satan. He, Judas by name, as often as Satan seized him, used to bite all who came near him; and if he found no one near him, he used to bite his own hands and other limbs. The mother of this wretched creature, then, hearing the fame of the Lady Mary and her son Jesus, rose up and brought her son Judas with her to the Lady Mary. In the meantime, James and Joses had taken the child the Lord Jesus with them to play with the other children; and they had gone out of the house and sat down, and the Lord Jesus with them. And the demoniac Judas came up, and sat down at Jesus' right hand: then, being attacked by Satan in the same manner as usual, he wished to bite the Lord Jesus, but was not able; nevertheless he struck Jesus on the right side, whereupon He began to weep. And immediately Satan

went forth out of that boy, fleeing like a mad dog. And this boy who struck Jesus, and out of whom Satan went forth in the shape of a dog, was Judas Iscariot, who betrayed him to the Jews; and that same side on which Judas struck Him, the Jews transfixed with a lance.[40]

Here is someone whom Jesus is not able to heal, at least not without cost to himself, and not in any permanent way. There are some people who remain outside of Jesus' control: even though he can defeat them, he cannot save them.

The fact that this occurs when both are children points to an interesting development in the portrayal of evil: evil is especially disturbing and compelling when it is found in children. What we find so horrifying about Columbine and other school shootings is the youthfulness of the perpetrators: children who should be playing cops and robbers, or teenagers who should be getting their first kiss, are instead acting with the kind of brutality and detachment that we would find disturbing even in the most battle-scarred soldier. And in a literary context, consider how prevalent the image of evil children is in the modern horror genre. It is exploited most effectively in movies such as *The Exorcist, Rosemary's Baby, The Omen, Children of the Corn*, and the opening sequence of *Halloween*, and in the classic *Twilight Zone* episode "It's a Good Life," in which a town is held hostage by a maniacal little boy who has paranormal powers.[41] I myself find that the most chilling part of a haunted house attraction at Halloween is not being menaced by a man wearing a hockey mask and wielding a chainsaw (the most common element to these places), but being confronted, amidst all the dismemberment and blood, by a child in ghastly black and white makeup, who either jumps out at you or just stares blankly but menacingly. He obviously poses much less physical threat than the man with a chainsaw, but the terror lies in contemplating that the epitome of innocence may be, in reality, the embodiment of the ultimate evil: this is utterly paralyzing and chilling. The same dynamic can be achieved by having a beloved childhood object take on sinister characteristics, as in *Poltergeist* or *Child's Play*, though this has the tendency to slide into comedy, as in *Ghostbusters* ("I thought of the one thing that could never harm us—the StayPuff marshmallow man!") or *Gremlins*.

This tendency for horror to slip into comedy points to a problem in this kind of depiction of evil: by associating evil with childhood, there is a tendency to trivialize it. (As, indeed, there is a tendency to trivialize goodness that is associated with childhood: it is hard to appreciate the mysterious and tragic joy of Easter if there is a large, talking rabbit prancing around to entertain the kids and give them candy, just as it is hard to appreciate the solemnity and awe of Christmas when Santa and his elves are there to distract you and your children.) If evil has taken the place of innocence or malignantly lurks within a shell of innocence, then it is unfathomably terrifying; but if it is merely laid on top of innocence, then it is just like a scary costume that needs to be taken off or a bad dream from which one just needs to awaken. There is, after all, a great deal of very tangible evil in *Ghostbusters*, but it's really not that hard to get rid of. Even in *The Exorcist*, as suspenseful and terrifying as the evil is when it's around, once it's gone, there are no lasting scars on the previously possessed little girl (which, of course, never happens in a real experience of something evil). But in the hands of an artist of more subtlety and profundity, this depiction of evil achieves the deepest understanding of evil's power, pervasiveness, attractiveness, and malignancy. Augustine's contemplation of childhood evil in books 1 and 2 of his *Confessions* points to how evil is ridiculous and self-destructive but also inescapable.[42] Flannery O'Connor's (1925–1964) evil children characters achieve much the same effect:[43] no matter how unbelievably overdone they may be, they are utterly compelling as well as potentially apocalyptic in their destructiveness. And the grotesque, fetuslike cherub/demon creatures that populate the drawings of Aubrey Beardsley (1872–1898) convey the cloying attractiveness and sentimentality of evil: significantly, a drawing of one of these creatures is supposed to represent Judas.[44] Such depictions do not trivialize evil: they ruminate on its depth with utter seriousness, awe, and terror.

Projecting Judas's evil back into his childhood carries both the conflicting valences of these depictions of evil. On the one hand, it comes close to making his evil appear comical and superficial, almost like a childish prank: the devil made him do it. But on the other hand, it points to his evil being something much deeper than one might have imagined otherwise. It was not just some decision or mistake that he made as an adult; like a congenital disease, it was a part of him his entire life. It was neither impetuous nor rational but instead part of a mysterious plan that was foretold, perhaps even fated.[45] Taken this way, Judas's story and others like it tread a fine line between making evil appear trivial or profound, accidental or essential.

Dante and the Middle Ages

The Middle Ages were perhaps the heyday for the depiction of Judas as the epitome of evil and the most powerful object lesson in the dire results of sin. Poets, playwrights, and preachers exhorted and frightened their audiences with the image of Judas as the arch-sinner who reaps the terrible rewards of his actions.

Medieval passion plays (fourteenth to fifteenth centuries) took the hanging from Matthew's version and combined it with the bursting from Luke's to turn Judas's suicide into an orgy of violence that is both farcical and frightening. When Judas hangs himself, demons come to tear open his stomach in order to remove his soul, at which Judas cries out:

> "Oh! All of you demons of Hell,
> do you wish to be at my side?
> Come, all of you, be here at my death,
> my soul is leaving, my neck is breaking!
> Oh! I feel my stomach bursting!
> Oh! The devil is inside me,
> tearing up my guts,
> because I was so disloyal
> and betrayed my Master."[46]

The theological reasoning for the bursting was that Judas's soul could not be allowed to leave his body through the normal avenue of the mouth, as his mouth had both betrayed Jesus and treacherously kissed him.[47] The demons and Cerberus then boil his soul to make a "roasted-boiled stew" for Satan.[48] Again, the tone combines a low comedy of the grotesque with a real dramatic desire to scare the audience into fearing sin and its consequences. It would be the same kind of uneasy laughter we would express at Haman in the book of Esther, or at the evil characters in the movie *Ghost* as they are dragged away by hellish wraiths: derisive delight at their punishment coupled with fear at the awesome power of God.

Once Judas's punishment and suffering were extended and elaborated by Luke and the traditions that followed him, such punishments could of course be extended infinitely into the afterlife. This is exactly what Dante Alighieri (1265–1321) does with Judas.[49] Dante's *Divine Comedy* describes his journey through all three realms of the afterlife—hell, purgatory, and paradise. He is led through the first two realms by his literary hero, the pagan Latin poet Virgil (ca. 70–19 B.C.E.). As they descend further and further into the pit of hell, we see that Dante has ordered the sinners by the increasing level of their evil: the lower he goes, the more evil he considers the people he meets, and the more inhuman and destructive he considers their sins. When Virgil and Dante reach the bottommost center of hell, they find a three-headed Satan chewing on three sinners:

In each of his three mouths he crunched a sinner,
with teeth like those that rake the hemp and flax,
keeping three sinners constantly in pain;

the one in front—the biting he endured
was nothing like the clawing that he took:
sometimes his back was raked clean of its skin.

"That soul up there who suffers most of all,"
my guide explained, "is Judas Iscariot:
the one with head inside and legs out kicking.[50]

For Dante, Judas is the worst example of the worst sin possible, betrayal, and therefore he places him at the center of hell, the worst of human sinners. (The other two being chewed are Brutus and Cassius: although Dante knows of Caesar's rumored homosexuality and does not place him in paradise with Trajan,[51] he regards his murderers as responsible for all the misery of civil war and chaos that followed Caesar's death, and that, indeed, Dante still sees all around him.)[52] Besides the physical violence that is often concomitant with betrayal, Dante sees it as the perversion and rejection of the highest good, which is love. If acceptance and surrender to love is what finally redeems human beings, then its hellish opposite is not just hate but the rejection of all love and the perverse use of love and trust to destroy the very people who have loved one. This is what places Judas and the others at the *anus mundi*, the nadir, the spiritual rectum of the universe, where all the filth of sin slowly trickles down in the river Lethe to be forgotten forever. It is the point as far removed and insulated as possible from the demands of God or love: here one is free to hate forever, but such freedom is ultimate, total enslavement to sin and self-annihilation through isolation.

Judas's placement makes perhaps more sense than his punishment, however. For all other betrayers (and, indeed, for Satan himself), the punishment is to be encased in ice: the sinners are eternally cut off from light and heat, symbolic of human and divine love, just as they had cut themselves off from love during their lives by betraying those closest to them. Indeed, the only relationship the sinners have with one another is to increase their pain and punishment, as we see here with Satan eternally chewing on them. The worst betrayer, the one who knowingly destroyed his relationship with the Son of God, thereby rejecting the greatest offer of love, is surely the most icy, the most cut off from love, and should be punished accordingly. But I think Dante lets his desire for grotesque imagery get the better of his desire for consistent imagery: Judas needs a worse punishment than mere freezing, even if that is the most appropriate. The punishment of being eternally gnawed on might have suggested itself to Dante, however, because of the other places it occurs in the *Inferno*. Surely the most memorable of these is another betrayer, Count Ugolino (canto 33), who is eternally chewing on his former partner in sin, Archbishop Ruggieri. The other examples of nonhuman residents of hell chewing on sinners are Cerberus chewing on the gluttons (canto 6) and the hellhounds and harpies tearing apart the profligates and suicides (canto 13). All three of these previous scenes would fit Judas well. According to Luke, Satan was in league with Judas in the betrayal (Luke 22:3), so their relationship would be exactly like that of Count Ugolino and Archbishop Ruggieri: coconspirators who devoured each other in life and now continue their sinful relationship eternally. All three sinners being chewed on by Satan are also suicides, and Judas at least was vilified in some medieval legends as a glutton, so the punishments of those groups might have suggested themselves to Dante when he composed the final scene in hell. (Further, since the three-headed Satan is a grotesque parody of the Trinity, Dante may also have thought of the Eucharist: God lets his believers eat him while the anti-God, Satan, eats his followers.) Although inconsistent with the punishment of other betrayers, Dante has created his image of Judas to include the other sins of which he was accused.

In all of this, Dante has, as he has at so many other points in the *Comedy*, created one of the most influential and lasting versions of an ancient tale. This is the final vision of the complete futility and self-destructiveness of sin: it is without passion, heat, light, or nourishment, eternally gnawing on itself in the insular, frozen darkness that it has itself created. Judas and Satan are the final object lessons in sin, epitomizing both the worst sin and the combination of all sins, and Dante must indelibly etch their memory in his mind before he can ascend, accept, or even understand God's love, truth, and light.

Finally, though he comes at the beginning of the modern period, we should include here the work of Abraham a Sancta Clara (1644–1709), for his work epitomizes so much of the medieval spirit of amalgamation and embellishment of these traditions,[53] as well as their use of Judas as a symbol of horror and exhortation.[54] An Augustinian priest who became the court preacher in Vienna in 1677, Abraham used Judas as the basis for his preaching and writing for years. Judas was the basis of his teaching only in the sense of a starting point or touchstone for Abraham's thoughts, which could quickly move in practically any direction by means of catchword, wordplay, or some other association. While incorporating every biblical and apocryphal detail of Judas's life—including the Oedipal legends associated with him,[55] his red hair,[56] and his death by swelling and decay taken from Papias's version[57]—Abraham then uses each detail as the occasion to harangue his audience about any subject imaginable, including the proper raising of children,[58] the woes of an unhappy marriage,[59] and the evils of talking too much.[60] Abraham does not really talk about Judas (for Abraham, nothing really needs to be said about him), but he uses Judas to talk about all the evils against which he wants his audience to fight: "For the sort of preaching that Abraham represents, nothing is more useful than a palpable point of departure for inveighing against sinners, to paint in the brightest colors their evil ways and consequent damnation; and for this purpose no figure is better adapted than Judas."[61] For Abraham, there is not some point to Judas's story that he is trying to extract or elucidate but rather a myriad of points he wishes to convey, and Judas's story can be the vehicle or starting point for any one of them.[62]

Judas's Name in Charms, Curses, and Popular Celebrations

Another manifestation of these depictions that is perhaps more powerful, enduring, and widespread than literary versions is the use of Judas's name in popular culture in Europe, Africa, and North and South America. References to Judas can be found in charms and curses,[63] and they are also widespread in popular celebrations around Easter.[64] Although these usually do not qualify as depictions of Judas but only references to him, they often do show the kind of depiction they presuppose, and this depiction most often fits into our category of Judas as deservedly punished sinner.

In curses, Judas is first mentioned in Christian epitaphs, although they find their way into many formal documents as part of an official oath that is binding on the parties to the document.[65] Violators of tombs or contracts call down on themselves the same horrible fate as Judas (usually mentioned along with other biblical villains such as Cain and Ananias and Sapphira). Most of these threaten the oath breaker with Judas's punishments in hell,[66] though one very early one (possibly third century C.E.) seems to refer to his death: "The tomb of Andrew and Athenais and their child Maria, those who finished life virtuously. And if anyone should dare to open (this tomb) also to (the) sun, he will share the lot of Judas, all things will become darkness to him, and God will destroy him on that day."[67] Since the threatened "lot" is to occur either before or simultaneous with God's destruction of the sinner, it cannot very well refer to hell-ish punishments, and the mention of "darkness" may well mean that the author of this inscription assumes the Papias tradition of Judas's death by horrible disease, in which Judas's "eyelids swelled so much that he could not see any light at all."[68] If one can assume that Judas was punished as all sinners are justly punished, then one can assume that other sinners will be punished as Judas was punished: indeed, to remind God of one's wish that this should occur hardly seems like a curse but simply an affirmation of one's belief in God's justice.

A closely related phenomenon is the use of Judas's name in charms, where it is curiously invoked as part of a cure for a variety of diseases and mishaps, most of which involve heat or flame: these include inflammation, fever, burns, lightning, warts, toothache, and theft.[69] Most of these involve the typical magical practice of the conjurer drawing an analogy between an event that has occurred and the one that he or she wishes to occur. Judas is invoked in formulae that run thus: "O fever [or whatever appropriate disease], lose your heat as Judas lost his color when he betrayed our Lord."[70] Judas is only regarded as evil and deservedly pun-ished, but his story provides an analogy that can be used to eliminate another evil in the present: Judas may not participate in any blessing, but he ironically provides the believer with an opportunity to obtain blessings.[71]

Judas figures in many celebrations around Easter throughout Europe, Africa,[72] and the Americas. It is part of the irony of these festivals that their origin is almost certainly pagan, either as a spring purificatory rite or as a type of imitative magic to induce fertility, but their celebration, which in many places continues until today, is now promulgated and fostered by the church.[73] Almost all of these involve the burning or exploding of effi-gies of Judas; some instead beat the figure to pieces. All of these celebra-tions are intended either to imitate Judas's punishment in hell or to contribute to it. This is shown explicitly in another of the practices of the celebrations, in which a great deal of noise is made with large rattles; this noise is variously explained as either the "rattling of Judas' bones, that will not rest in his grave,"[74] or as the participants actually "breaking Judas' bones."[75] Whether the celebrants imitate Judas's punishment or partici-pate in it, however, they clearly enjoy and approve of it. Although in Europe these celebrations often have become scenes of anti-Semitic vio-lence, as the people turn to burning or beating real Jews when they have finished with the effigy of the arch-sinner who bears the name of the Jew-ish nation,[76] the life of folklore is not so simple and clear-cut: the effigy is often made to look like whatever individual or group is hated by the local population,[77] and the celebration is popular in many places where there is no Jewish population.[78] The celebration is clearly an unleashing of violence—either individual, communal, or cosmic—but it is not specifically anti-Semitic. Judas may represent the historical person who betrayed Jesus, or he may be the local mayor, or "the Jew," or "the Brit," or sin, or winter, or death. But whatever he is, the participants in these celebrations clearly revel in his defeat and punishment and celebrate it as reestablishing justice and equilibrium to their lives, society, and nature.

Conclusion

There is, then, even in these most negative portrayals of Judas, something deeply positive and redemptive. From Luke's and Papias's simple (though deeply satisfying) reveling in another person's (deserved) misery, to the scathing sermons preached for years by Abraham a Sancta Clara, the tradition used the image of Judas as a powerful lesson against evil and its effects. Along the way, others also developed the deeply disturbing image of Judas as a child being unable to control his participation in evil. While certainly not as effective for exhortation, the image is a sincere and provocative meditation on the nature of evil. But from these profoundly negative, frightening, and scolding images, the tradition also evolved into the positive visions of Dante using Satan's body as a ladder to ascend to God, people using Judas's ill-favored name to rid their own lives of diseases and mishaps, and Easter revelers all over the world defeating and rejecting sin from their own lives. Although Judas is eternally trapped on the other side of the abyss, his story has been used to lead people from the darkness of the cross to the hope and light of the resurrection. Unable to benefit from the lessons of his own story, Judas nonetheless benefits others.

Chapter Three

Judas the Villain:

Object of Hatred and Derision

John

As in Luke, John has Judas possessed by a devil, but he moves it up to the first introduction of Judas in the Gospel: "'Did I not choose you, the twelve, and one of you is a devil?' He spoke of Judas the son of Simon Iscariot, for he, one of the twelve, was to betray him" (John 6:70–71). Judas's character is simplified and made more uniform, portrayed as unregenerately evil throughout his life: "With singular harshness the author of the Fourth Gospel consigns Judas to the realm of the demonic."[1] The final, cosmic battle between Jesus and evil that Luke portrays at the end of his Gospel, John projects throughout Jesus' ministry. We know from the very beginning of John's Gospel that Jesus has come from heaven into the world of darkness, and the world cannot accept this: "He was in the world, and the world was made through him, yet the world knew him not" (John 1:10). For John, there cannot be a turning against Jesus or increasing hostility to him, because all hostility to Jesus is innate, unchangeable, and eternal in a person from the beginning: "He who believes in him is not condemned; he who does not believe is condemned already" (John 3:18). Judas simply personifies the forces that cannot accept Jesus, and therefore he has to be portrayed as Jesus' implacable and cosmic foe throughout.[2] In this Judas is exactly like Jesus' other enemies in John, "the Jews," who are also representatives of the demonic: "You are of your father the devil" (John 8:44),[3] and the coincidence of their names and their evil will figure in this strand of the tradition down to the present day.

But while a cosmic, demonic opponent is theologically necessary for John, he also insists on Judas as an intimate companion of Jesus,[4] and in this part of his portrayal, John accentuates Judas's participation in the pettiest of human behavior. It is only in John that Jesus' anointing is objected to by Judas, rather than by an unspecified group of "some" people (Mark 14:4–5) or by "the disciples" generally (Matt. 26:8–9). John makes Judas the sole objector not only to show an incomprehension of Jesus' person and mission but to blacken Judas's character further as a skulking, hypocritical thief: "But Judas Iscariot, one of his disciples (he who was to betray him), said, 'Why was this ointment not sold for three hundred denarii and given to the poor?' This he said, not that he cared for the poor but because he was a thief, and as he had the money box he used to take what was put into it" (John 12:4–6). Here John is using the character of Judas carefully to strike a balance in his portrayal of evil (much as we saw in the last chapter on the Arabic infancy gospel): on the one hand, he wants to depict it as cosmic and awesome but, on the other hand, as empty and trivial. It is both demonic and all too human.

The Johannine Jesus' confrontation with the demonic and human evil within Judas reaches its climax at the Last Supper:

> Now before the feast of the Passover, when Jesus knew that his hour had come to depart out of this world to the Father, having loved his own who were in the world, he loved them to the end. And during supper, when the devil had already put it into the heart of Judas Iscariot, Simon's son, to betray him . . . Jesus said to him, "He who has bathed does not need to wash, except for his feet, but he is clean all over; and you are clean, but not every one of you." For he knew who was to betray him; that was why he said, "You are not all clean." "I am not speaking of you all; I know whom I have chosen; it is that the scripture may be fulfilled, 'He who ate my bread has lifted his heel against me.' I tell you this now, before it takes place, that when it does take place you may believe that I am he." . . . When Jesus had thus spoken, he was troubled in spirit, and testified, "Truly, truly, I say to you, one of you will betray me." . . . Jesus answered, "It is he to whom I shall give this morsel when I have dipped it." So when he had dipped the morsel, he gave it to Judas, the son of Simon Iscariot. Then after the morsel, Satan entered into him. Jesus said to him, "What you are going to do, do quickly." Now no one at the table knew why he said this to him. Some thought that, because Judas had the money box, Jesus was telling him, "Buy what we need for the feast"; or, that he should give something to the poor. So, after receiving the morsel, he immediately went out; and it was night. (John 13:1–2, 10–11, 18–19, 21, 26–30)

On the one hand, the poignant and human element of betrayal by an intimate tablemate is brought out one more time in verse 18: "He who ate my bread has lifted his heel against me" (cf. Ps. 41:9).[5] But at the same time, the demonic is reiterated at verses 2 and 27, as well as in the final statement that Judas left the world of light and went out into the world of darkness.[6] It is further stressed by John's removal of any deal between Judas and the chief priests for money, even though this would fit perfectly with his depiction of Judas's greed and theft in the previous scene,[7] so that we have here not a human actor with motivations but an instrument of Satan, or indeed, Satan himself: "John portrays not a man acting here, but Satan himself."[8] In the end, Jesus' confrontation with his enemy is the confrontation of the divine with the demonic, thereby making Jesus' command to Judas/Satan in verse 27 all the more striking: "Ultimately, Judas is not in control, nor is the devil; Jesus directs everything."[9] God uses his friends and enemies alike to accomplish his own goals. Evil ultimately has no power, perhaps not even any existence, just as darkness is merely the absence of light.

Having Jesus authoritatively command no one less than Satan himself, John makes two other references to Judas that are anticlimactic. At John 17:12 (cf. 6:39; 10:28; 18:9), Jesus reports back to the Father on the success of his mission: "While I was with them, I kept them in thy name, which thou hast given me; I have guarded them, and none of them is lost but the son of perdition, that the scripture might be fulfilled."[10] Judas was a devil all along, outside of Jesus' realm (though completely under his control). Jesus could not have lost any of his own, because those who are his own are impossible to lose and those who are not his own are impossible to gain because they are completely and utterly different, just as darkness cannot become light.

Similarly anticlimactic and inevitable is John's version of the arrest, in which Judas almost completely disappears from the action:

> When Jesus had spoken these words, he went forth with his disciples across the Kidron valley, where there was a garden, which he and his disciples entered. Now Judas, who betrayed him, also knew the place; for Jesus had often met there with his disciples. So Judas, procuring a band of soldiers and some officers from the chief priests and the Pharisees, went there with lanterns and torches and weapons. Then Jesus, knowing all that was to befall him, came forward and said to them, "Whom do you seek?" They answered him, "Jesus of Nazareth." Jesus said to them, "I am he." Judas, who betrayed him, was standing with them. When he said to them, "I am he," they drew back and fell to the ground. . . . So the band of soldiers and their

captain and the officers of the Jews seized Jesus and bound him. (John 18:1–6, 12)

Judas and the evil he represents have literally become only bystanders to the divine plan that is unfolding. The kiss of Judas, perhaps the most human and poignant part of the tradition, has completely disappeared because of John's higher (almost dualistic) Christology: "For him the realm of darkness cannot touch the Lord of Light."[11]

In the Gospel of John we have the most villainous, demonic depiction of Judas in the New Testament. All attempt to understand him as a human character has dropped out, and he becomes merely an illustration of John's ideas about evil, which for John is both cosmic and powerful but also utterly creaturely and paltry. It is also completely under the control of God, whose plans it cannot alter or influence in the least, though God also cannot change any evil person or being into good, since they are eternally and ontologically opposed to him. Judas's representation of evil is shared in the Gospel by "the Jews" as a group, a connection we will see fatally elaborated on in later anti-Semitic adaptations of John's more cosmic confrontation.

Judas: The Beloved Disciple?

Although John has the most negative portrayal of Judas and of "the Jews" in general, the theory that Judas in fact wrote the Fourth Gospel keeps recurring.[12] It can be based on the common speculation that Judas was the only Judean among the otherwise Galilean disciples, and there was long tension between them. The Gospel of John may have been written by the "beloved disciple" who is described in it and who seems to be somewhat separate from the other disciples, perhaps because he was a Judean. This is reinforced by the observation of the Fourth Gospel's disinterest and even hostility towards the other disciples, especially Peter, who are more central in the Synoptics. Now, who would be more hostile towards the other disciples than Judas, whom they had always alienated and maligned? Therefore, Judas is the beloved disciple and the author of the Fourth Gospel, and all the negativity in it towards him is the work of later editors.[13] Such a twisted line of reasoning is not only amusing but further confirmation of exactly how plastic the tradition is: if an author's goal is to exonerate and even lionize Judas, then he or she can use even the most damning traditions to do so. Indeed, using such a source might be seen to make one's final point even more compelling.

Judas as Avaricious

The fact that in the Synoptics Judas was paid for his act of leading the authorities to Jesus, together with the further accusation in John that he stole from the common funds, has been seized on in many portrayals as a motive for his seemingly motiveless act. In part, this has been an attempt to render his story more believable, but it has also had a profound and tragic impact as part of the rhetoric of Christian anti-Semitic stereotyping: Judas was a Jew (as were Jesus and the other disciples, but this is easily overlooked in the anti-Semite's twisted world), and he was a money-grubber, thief, traitor, and Christ-killer, just like all Jews have been throughout time. All of these portrayals might imply anti-Semitism, as the author and his audience assume that any money-grubbing fiend must be a Jew just as every Jew must be a money-obsessed monster. I have treated separately, however, those depictions that seem to have the propagation of an anti-Semitic stereotype as an integral part of their message and those that treat Judas as a misguided or loathsome individual without singling him out for his religion or race.

Explicitly Anti-Semitic Portrayals

The anti-Semitic elements present in many versions of Judas's story are clearly elaborations of John's version, in which both Judas and "the Jews" are painted as implacably evil. Although anti-Semitism predates Christianity, the standard pagan accusations against Jews were that they were barbaric (circumcision was especially loathsome to non-Jews) and aloof (dietary and Sabbath laws prevented them from socializing with their non-Jewish neighbors), but not that they were thieves, swindlers, or avaricious;[14] this was the peculiar contribution of Christianity, and of the Gospel of John in particular. Avarice and theft through deceit and trickery became standard depictions of both Judas and Jews as a result of John's inclusion of them in his story of Judas, a telling witness to the undeniable and sometimes terrifying power of myth to shape our lives. Even a writer as critical of popular beliefs as Mark Twain easily adopted such conventional wisdom, saying that the Jew "has a reputation for various small forms of cheating, and for practicing oppressive usury, and for burning himself out to get the insurance, and for arranging cunning contracts which leave him an exit but lock the other man in."[15]

The simplest anti-Semitic use that Judas's story could serve is one of simple equation: Judas was bad; all Jews are bad. The equation can run both ways: Judas was evil because he was a Jew; Jews are evil, demonstrated by their similarity to Judas. This has certainly been the most frequent anti-Semitic use of Judas's story throughout Christian history. The eloquent (the surname given him means "golden-mouthed") John Chrysostom (ca. 349–407 C.E.) was virulent in his anti-Semitism and passionate in his denunciation of Judas. Sometimes Chrysostom uses Judas as a potent lesson against the evils of covetousness and greed:

> Hear, ye covetous, consider what befell him; how he at the same time lost the money, and committed the sin, and destroyed his own soul. Such is the tyranny of covetousness. He enjoyed not the money, neither the present life, nor that to come, but lost all at once, and having got a bad character even with those very men, so hanged himself.[16]

But Chrysostom is adamant that all Jews, in Jesus' time or his own, behave in exactly the same way, and indeed, in every other evil manner imaginable:

> What else do you wish me to tell you? Shall I tell you of their plundering, their covetousness, their abandonment of the poor, their thefts, their cheating in trade? The whole day long will not be enough to give you an account of these things. But do their festivals have something solemn and great about them? They have shown that these, too, are impure. Listen to the prophets; rather, listen to God and with how strong a statement he turns his back on them: "I have found your festivals hateful, I have thrust them away from myself." ... For I am persuaded to call the fasting of the Jews a table of demons because they slew God.[17]

And since both Judas and the Jews are avaricious, treacherous deicides, their punishment is the same and equally deserved:

> God compelled them to call the field in Hebrew "Aceldama" (Matt. xxvi. 24.). By this also the evils which were to come upon the Jews were declared: and Peter shows the prophecy to have been so far in part fulfilled, which says, "It had been good for that man if he had not been born." We may with propriety apply this same to the Jews likewise; for if he who was guide suffered thus, much more they. Thus far however Peter says nothing of this. Then, showing that the term "Aceldama" might well be applied to his fate, he introduces the prophet, saying, "Let his habitation be desolate." For what can be

worse desolation than to become a place of burial? And the field may well be called his. For he who cast down the price, although others were the buyers, has a right to be himself reckoned owner of a great desolation. This desolation was the prelude to that of the Jews, as will appear on looking closely into the facts. For indeed they destroyed themselves by famine, and killed many, and the city became a burial-place of strangers, of soldiers, for as to those, they would not even have let them be buried, for in fact they were not deemed worthy of sepulture.[18]

For Chrysostom and many Christians after him, the Jews as a people epitomize the avarice and treachery of Judas as an individual, and God has ordained and approved the punishments meted out to both. (And, they would add, who are we to question or disapprove of God's judgment? Indeed, are we not called upon as Christians to enact this just punishment?)

A similar equation between Judas's evil and that of Jews generally was demonstrated in the medieval passion plays (fourteenth to fifteenth centuries) by accentuating the ties and agreement between Judas and the Jewish authorities, as Judas addresses them:

> Sirs, listen to my words
> and do not take them as insane:
> Our Law has been violently cast down,
> day by day it is treated worse.
> You know how the son of Mary
> has done this by his babbling,
> turning the people from our Law,
> and many are with him.
> You do not believe this because you do not want to,
> but you have not given good counsel.
> Our Law will be confounded
> and in a short time everything will be lost,
> unless you take my advice,
> and let this sink into your ear.[19]

Whereas in the Gospels it looks as though the Jewish leaders enticed Judas, now it is he who lectures them on the danger posed by Jesus and the need to destroy him. He also shares with them a sadistic cruelty and delight at Jesus' suffering; which is prolonged and elaborated by his Jewish tormentors in lurid speeches and stage directions: it is the Jews who supply dull nails to maximize Jesus' suffering, they rip off his hair in clumps that still have flesh attached to them; they verbally abuse and threaten his mother; and in some versions, they finally take the place of the Roman soldiers so as to remove any remaining doubt as to who were the real killers of Christ.[20] And since the performers on stage were immune from physical punishment for their misdeeds, but real Jews were not, the performances of these plays were almost certainly the occasions for real violence against Jews.[21] Judas's role in these orgies of violence is to instigate Jewish evil as well as to epitomize it while the Jews mirror and accentuate his cruelty, and the image of both Judas and the Jews is used to encourage the audiences to hate and abuse their Jewish neighbors.

But all of this shows Judas and the Jews as participating in the generally repugnant evils of violence and cruelty. Something more specifically Jewish was needed in their depiction, so Judas also epitomizes what the audience believed to be the quintessentially (perhaps uniquely) Jewish evils of avarice and treachery in these versions. This is done most notably by their ubiquitous inclusion of a haggling scene between Judas and the authorities, in which they each try to cheat the other and destroy Jesus while getting the best "deal" possible. In these, Judas sometimes counts the coins and finds he has been cheated by his fellow Jews[22] or discovers they have paid him in counterfeit coin.[23] Even if he gets the agreed-on amount in legitimate coin, Judas shows how he both conforms to and perpetuates the stereotype of the obscenely greedy Jew that his medieval audience had come to expect,[24] as he gloats over the payment he has received for the death of his friend and master:

> Although I am full of spite,
> I have fooled everyone here.
> So kill him when he comes near!
> In my bag I will put my cash:
> Oh thirty denarii, you I will stash!
> One, two, three, and four—
> great desire to beat Jesus more!
> Five, six, seven, eight—
> and crucify him before it's late!
> Nine, ten, eleven, twelve, thirteen—
> oh such evil's never been seen!
> Fourteen, fifteen, sixteen, seventeen, eighteen—
> the evil day before the night will be seen!
> Nineteen, twenty, twenty-one, twenty-two, twenty-three, twenty-four—
> Jesus we can beat some more!

Twenty-five, twenty-six, twenty-seven, twenty-eight—
Him we will exterminate!
Twenty-nine and thirty, then—
Mary's heart will be broken![25]

Clearly the original audience was meant to laugh at the comic villainy of the scene.[26] But the unconcealed, derisive hatred in this kind of humor is so revolting that it should be difficult for us to imagine how one could laugh. How could any Christian laugh at Christ's betrayer spitefully making up a funny rhyme about his suffering? What legitimate part could such laughter play in one's faith? And how could any Christian laugh at a stereotype that contributed to centuries of violence and hatred against innocent people? As profound as medieval piety clearly was, there are points on which it should be incomprehensible to us, or, at the very least, where the medieval mind's ability to hold dichotomies and extremes simultaneously takes us to a breaking point: "Their laughter was the last trace of the play's medieval past, a past that was as comfortable with the vulgar and the brutal as it was with more elevated spirituality."[27]

An unusual holdover from medieval piety has been shown in the passion play of the Bavarian village of Oberammergau.[28] The legend of its genesis and history runs as follows. In 1633, plague was ravaging the area during the Thirty Years' War (1618–48). When the plague came to the village of Oberammergau and began killing people, the villagers took a vow that if they were spared, they and their descendants would perform a passion play there once every ten years. The village was spared further deaths; the villagers gratefully staged the play for the first time in 1634, and they have faithfully put on the play once each decade ever since. The play itself, the myth holds, has "always been free of the offensive impurities and scurrility that characterized other surviving Passion plays."[29] And the villagers who have put on the play have always been free of ideological influence from outside, piously living and producing their passion play in "a Christian Shangri-La, a missing link to a simpler, purer religious past."[30]

Another version of this story is not nearly so tidy or positive. Deaths from the plague did not stop abruptly but seemed to have tapered off (rather unimpressively) for some time before the supposed vow.[31] Further, the performing of the passion probably did not originate in Oberammergau with the vow of 1633 but had most likely been enacted (probably not with regularity) for years before that. More important for our study, a look at how the play evolved over the centuries shows how medieval anti-Semitism, and medieval piety in general, changed over time. Until 1750, the play was probably much like the other medieval passion plays, full of violence and low humor, with the crowds' violence to Jesus being portrayed graphically and elaborately and with many devils tearing apart both Judas and the impenitent thief.[32] A revision in 1750 by a Benedictine monk, Ferdinand Rosner, made the play more poetic and musical, though the devils were retained for their lively entertainment. It was apparently a huge success, with crowds of eleven thousand at the performances of 1750 and 1760.[33] The devils were apparently a little too popular, as the Catholic Church suppressed the play in 1770, complaining that it was debasing to the mystery of Easter to stage it in such rowdy scenes.[34] A revision in 1780 began to move the play away from its medieval roots, curtailing its devilish excesses, a trend that was completed with the rewrite of 1811 by Otmar Weis, who removed everything nonbiblical, as well as "all the devils and allegorical figures."[35]

It is with the removal of the devils that we see an amazing transformation in the way that the play presents its anti-Semitism. Previous plays perpetuated their anti-Semitism by portraying Judas and the Jews as in league with the devil. But the Oberammergau passion removed the devils and blamed the Jews *instead* of them, elaborating and accentuating Jewish evil as completely human but utterly and irredeemably evil. They are, in their own way, demonic and obsessed with destroying Jesus, and it is in this rewrite that the problematic line "His blood be on us and on our children!" (Matt. 27:25) becomes crucial, both dramatically and theologically: "the retention of the blood curse from Matthew was now charged with far greater emotional intensity."[36] A final revision in 1860 by Joseph Alois Daisenberger provided the ultimate version of modern and "enlightened" anti-Semitism. In his version, Judas and the Jews are much more psychologically plausible, and their opposition to Jesus is reasoned and based on their differing and conflicting worldviews: they are greedy, materialistic, nationalistic capitalists, and Jesus is a selfless, spiritual, peaceful romantic.[37] To call down God's judgment on these materialistic murderers is not vengeful but pious:

> God! annihilate this impious band
> Who have risen up defying Thee,
> And in murderous cov'nant joined the hand
> 'Gainst Thine only Son in mockery.
> Let them crash—the thunders of Thy might,
> Let Thy right hand's lightnings glow,
> Let Thy terrors on the guilty light,
> In the dust to lay them low.[38]

No longer was anti-Semitism something superstitious and irrational, believed in by the same people who believe in werewolves and vampires: now it was a perfectly rational decision made against people who hold an opposing worldview that could not and should not be tolerated.

It is hardly surprising, therefore, that the Nazis saw the usefulness of this portrayal and that many of the people who put on this play were sympathetic to the Nazis' ideological and racial agenda. On the Nazi side, the play offered a centuries-old anti-Semitic spectacle that they didn't need to manufacture or even fan into flame, for it was already there in all its virulence and hatred. It is a deep irony and mystery that after so much Nazi fanfare around the 1934 production, they canceled the 1940 performance.[39] On the villagers' side, the productions of both 1934 and 1950 had a highly disproportionate number of Nazis in the cast; in a further irony, only the actor who played Judas in the 1934 production was known to be an anti-Nazi (though practically all the villagers subsequently claimed to be so).[40] The Daisenberger version was kept more or less unchanged through the 1990 performance, despite worldwide protests from 1960 on.[41] Only the 2000 production saw substantial changes, creating a version that finally seems to take notice of the change in Christian attitudes towards Jews.[42]

But if the play's continued anti-Semitism almost fifty years after the Holocaust is disheartening, its attempt to understand and even to sympathize to some extent with Judas is more surprising. The Daisenberger version gives him a long soliloquy after the anointing at Bethany in which he describes his motives and disappointments:

> "Shall I follow him any longer? I do not much care to do so. The Master's conduct to me is very inexplicable. His great deeds allowed us to hope that he would restore again the kingdom to Israel. But he does not seize the opportunities that offer themselves, and now he constantly talks of parting and dying, and puts us off with mysterious words about a future which lies too far off in the dim distance for me. I am tired of hoping and waiting. I can see very well, that with him there is no prospect of anything but continued poverty and humiliation,—and instead of the sharing, as we expected, in his glorious kingdom, we shall perhaps be persecuted and thrown into prison with him. I will draw back, whilst there is yet time. It is a good thing that I was always prudent and cautious, and have now and then laid aside a trifle out of the bag, in case of need."[43]

Although the depiction retains the Johannine accusation that Judas pilfered from the common purse, the image here seems less of greed than of a petty, craven fear of insecurity, together with an understandable incomprehension (shared by the other disciples) of Jesus and his mission. Judas seems to be more of a weak man than an evil one. Indeed, at the actual betrayal scene, although he is stereotypical in his eagerness for the money, it is not the motivation for his action but rather a weakness that the evil Jews of the Sanhedrin can exploit:

> "Hear that, Judas?" cried Dathan, "thirty pieces of silver, what a gain!" Before Judas could reply, Nathanael sprang to his feet, saying, "And mark well, Judas, this is not all! If thou executest this work right well, thou shalt be cared for still further." "And thou mayest become a rich and famous man," added Ezechiel. . . . Josue said, "Don't trouble thyself, Judas, about the speech of this zealot [Nicodemus], let him go and be a follower of the false prophet. Thou dost thy duty as a disciple of Moses in serving the rightful authorities." Then came in Rabbi with the silver in a dish. "Come, Judas," said he, "take the thirty pieces of silver and play the man."[44]

And in Judas's final despair, there seems to be real sympathy with his guilt and repentance:

> "Oh! Where, where can I go to hide my shame, to escape the torments of conscience? No forest is dark enough! No rocky cavern deep enough! O earth, open and swallow me up! I can no longer exist. O my dear Master! Him, best of all men, have I sold! . . . I, how have I repaid him? Accursed avarice which led me astray and made me blind and deaf."[45]

Even in one of the most virulent and longest-lasting relics of anti-Semitism, the author and the audiences have more sympathy for Judas than one might have expected. Overall, their depiction seems to have been driven more by the considerations of drama than those of theology or ethics: a villain who is more rounded, nuanced, and conflicted is more compelling and interesting than one who is a flat representation of a racial stereotype.

The equation between Judas's evil and the evil of all Jews could be shown in later literature through avaricious and deceitful Jewish villains such as Shylock or Fagin who also imitate and perpetuate Judas's evil. It could also obscenely surface in public accusations against Jews, such as in the infamous Dreyfus affair: "The affair of Captain Dreyfus . . . is simply another episode in Jewish history. Judas sold the God of mercy and love. . . . Captain Dreyfus has sold to Germany our mobilization plans and the names of our intelligence agents. This is all just a fatal running to type, the curse of the race."[46] It is just this parallelism or "coincidence" that serves as the impetus for Maccoby's work, as he shows how in Christian culture "Judas was chosen for a baleful but necessary mythological role precisely because of his name."[47] Again, the myth has influenced us as much as we have shaped or used the myth.

But beyond a simple equation that all Jews are evil in the same way that Judas was evil, it is possible for the influence to run more in the other direction. Such depictions do not equate Judas with Jews generally and then transfer his guilt and evil to them, but rather they transfer the presupposed evil of "the Jews" to Judas. The myth of Jewish evil that Judas's story helped to create can also be used to shape the way Judas is depicted in a literary work.

Such a dynamic is found in the nauseatingly evil and overt anti-Semitism displayed in books such as Telemachus Thomas Timayenis's *Judas Iscariot: An Old Type in a New Form.*[48] Timayenis (1853–1918) immigrated to the United States in about 1869 and lived in Massachusetts and New York.[49] He taught and published extensively throughout his life in the United States. Although Timayenis always had intellectual pretensions far beyond his abilities, his writings were mostly just lively rewritings and popularizations of previous historical works. If not the height of scholarship, they were not offensive or scandalous—except, that is, for his three anti-Semitic screeds, all published by his own publishing house in just two years, 1888 and 1889.[50] There is no clear reason to suggest why Timayenis became a rabid anti-Semite for precisely two years and then just as suddenly stopped (at least publicly). It is certainly possible that his motives were purely financial—to make a quick buck and then get out of the anti-Semite "business"—but there is no way to know for sure.[51] Although *Judas Iscariot* is considered the most sophisticated of the three tracts,[52] it is a barely readable, freewheeling amalgamation of every anti-Semitic canard from nineteen centuries of Christianity that lacks any attempt at organization or analysis. One after another, slanderous accusations against Jews are just thrown out without proof or comment: Jews are cowardly and deceptive;[53] although they secretly control all modern governments and economies,[54] they are simultaneously plotting the overthrow of all these governments and the catastrophic crash of all these economies;[55] they were responsible for the terrible conditions at the Andersonville prison camp during the American Civil War;[56] they are sterile and must therefore marry people from other "races" if they are to reproduce;[57] they are lazy, greedy, and rapacious;[58] they produce liquor to get rich while destroying other people through its consumption but also for the more direct killing of people through the introduction of poisons such as "carbolic acid" into the liquors;[59] they control the press;[60] they murder children for ritual sacrifices;[61] they perform abortions;[62] they are thieves and murderers.[63] In a particularly frenzied set of accusations, Timayenis paints his portrait of the monomaniacal "Jew," who is at all places and all times paranoid, vain, self-centered, uncreative, unimaginative, shameless, weak, diseased, dirty, smelly, drunk, debauched, and promiscuous.[64] Despite his gutter-level racism, Timayenis's prescience is chilling, as when he states that "the solution of . . . the Jewish question" will not be "civilized"[65] and that "Israel will get a blood bath."[66] (Given Luther's call for the burning of synagogues 350 years before, such prescience may be chilling but hardly surprising.)[67] Even in some particular details there seems to be a diabolical, prophetic look into the future: more than fifty years before the Nazis would propose to deport all European Jews to the desolate, malaria-ridden island of Madagascar, Timayenis proposed to resettle all American Jews to the equally inhospitable desert of New Mexico.[68] Timayenis made a small but significant contribution towards anti-Semitism becoming "acceptable and respected to the American public,"[69] and in this he and others sadly succeeded, as the end of the nineteenth century "witnessed the emergence of a full-fledged antisemitic society" in America.[70]

So what does all this have to do with Judas Iscariot, the biblical character? It turns out, absolutely nothing. After the title page, Judas is not mentioned once, nor are the accusations against Jews supported or illustrated by examples from the Gospels, even when these would seem to be ready to hand. There is indeed a subtle (by Timayenis's standards) antipathy to Christianity. Old Testament passages are ridiculed by him for their barbarity,[71] but he does not (as would a more typically Christian anti-Semite) then contrast these with the kinder, gentler New Testament word of truth. Rather, he mocks Christians for the excessively sentimental and self-destructive feelings of sympathy that they have for others.[72] Nor does he slander Judas or the Jews with the typical Christian accusation that they were the killers of Christ. (Indeed, Timayenis probably would have felt that the founder of such a weak, effeminate movement got what he deserved from the more virile Romans.) In phrases that are again chilling because of their reappearance in Nazi rhetoric, Timayenis attacks Jews as barbaric parasites and Christians as weak sentimentalists who are to blame for their own destruction. It would take a more virile, scientific, and "enlightened" kind of anti-Semitism to rid Western civilization of its ancient enemies, the Jews. In all this there is then an irony that Timayenis names his book by the quintessentially Christian anti-Semitic label of "Judas Iscariot." The Gospel story of Judas may have given us the image of "the Jew" as greedy, deceitful, and treacherous, but it could not give us the image of one who is malodorous, promiscuous, or cannibalistic. These slanders come from the intervening nineteen centuries (and, indeed, are part of every racist's repertoire, hardly being unique to the anti-Semite's), but they can then be used to fill in the empty label of "Judas." Exactly the same development can be seen much earlier in Christian art.[73] Part of medieval anti-Semitic belief included the idea that Jews smelled different from Christians—they had a peculiar "Jewish stench"—and in some visual depictions Judas is portrayed as having the "Jewish stench" as well by showing the disciple nearest him holding his nose. No longer does "Judas" mean the "betrayer" (who is, for anti-Semites, a betrayer just like all other Jews): now the name simply means "the Jew," who embodies each and every slander that has ever been pronounced against him.

To see how plastic the tradition and its related bigotry really are, it may be worth considering another nineteenth-century American appropriation of the label "Judas." Immediately after Abraham Lincoln's assassination, John Wilkes Booth was called a "Judas," who, "worse than his namesake, went out from the presence of the chief priests and counselors of treason and himself committed the murder."[74] On the surface, the label appears to be a poor fit, as Booth never knew and certainly never loved Lincoln personally: he was guilty of treason but not betrayal. But the idea that Booth was another "Judas" had wide and lasting appeal.[75] Although Booth's life was subsequently embellished and romanticized in ways quite similar to what we will see done with Judas's—the addition of his romantic exploits,[76] his unusual closeness to his mother,[77] and the idea that he had mysteriously lived on and had not been killed at Garrett's barn[78]—his story was not used to advance anti-Semitism, even though it would seem as convenient for that as the infamous Dreyfus case would be thirty years later. (And lest one think that this was because Booth was not, in fact, Jewish, one need only consider the absurd fictions constantly spun by anti-Semites: accusing Booth either of being Jewish himself or of being the pawn or dupe of a Jewish conspiracy clearly would not have been beyond them.) Instead, however, American mythmakers, led by Edwin Stanton, the Secretary of War himself, simply accused the new "Judas" of being a member of another despised religious group, this time one to which neither Judas himself nor Booth belonged: Roman Catholics.[79] Taken as an empty label of hatred and contempt, "Judas" could be used to justify and furthermore more than just anti-Semitic violence: it could serve the rhetorical ends of any religious bigotry by branding the person so named with the worst and broadest of accusations.

Other Portrayals

James W. T. Hart's *Autobiography of Judas Iscariot: A Character Study* portrays Judas as possessed by evil all along, though it clearly increases through the course of the book: ". . . no man ever reached the highest point of excellence, or sank to the lowest depth of degradation—suddenly. . . . The causes which led up to the crisis had been surely, perhaps slowly and almost imperceptibly, maturing."[80] His patriotism is nearly nonexistent, as he holds his fellow Jews (and most everyone else) in contempt. And his longing to lead a revolution stems from purely individualistic desires for personal power, honor, and wealth: "But if my Gaulonite namesake had deeper ends in mind, aims for *himself*, then I cease to scorn him. Great, great indeed, would be his prize, who could lead forth our people against the eagles of Rome. . . . For him who broke her chain, what place of power! what lavish wealth!"[81] Judas is therefore very enthusiastic about Jesus' words that the disciples will later receive "thrones" (Matt. 19:28).[82] Only for one moment, after the Sermon on the Mount, do Judas's motives elevate somewhat: "But afterwards, after his teaching on the Mount, *that* moved my heart. . . . I feel the new heart, with higher aims than I had ever before. I am conscious of the new spirit, with nobler wishes than I thought I could experience."[83] In a somewhat artful irony, Hart makes Jesus' miracles into what leads Judas astray: after the elevated vision of peace and love offered in the Sermon on the Mount, Jesus' increasingly powerful acts mislead Judas back into expecting that Jesus will establish an earthly kingdom and to lusting after the power and wealth that he believes will come with it. When these hopes are disappointed, Judas decides to cut his losses and realize at least some material benefit by betraying Jesus for money. For some reason, though, he is surprised and revolted by Jesus' death and kills himself in despair, saying that he "had sinned—sinned past the hope of pardon."[84] All in all, the portrayal is a believable, though dreary, portrait of a man who is narcissistic and short-sighted, the evil counterparts to the boldness, confidence, and decisiveness that we will see in more heroic portrayals of Judas.

The explicit accusation of avarice and deceit survives in the poem *Judas* by Harold Monro (1879–1932),[85] though its anti-Semitic elements are subdued. The Jewish stereotype is hinted at with the description of Judas as having "a red beard. . . . Curved nose, thick eyebrows."[86] In the poem

Judas is doomed eternally to count his thirty silver pieces, be drenched in a thunderstorm of blood, drop the bloody coins, then pick them up and begin the process over again.[87] Like the usurers who in Dante's hell still clutch their money pouches,[88] this ghastly vision is accentuated by the fact that Judas shows no remorse and sees nothing wrong in what he did. He brags that it was he who thought of the publicity stunt of telling people that Jesus had raised Lazarus from the dead when he had really only been ill, not dead.[89] He still describes himself as a man of "honest thrift"[90] and maintains that he has always been right:

> I know that he [Jesus] eternally was wrong,
> I, right: and it is proved in the event.
> For now, 'mid those who traffick in the world
> How many dream like him? Is not the race
> True to the human standard? When in this
> Sequestered haunt I hear afar the loud
> Shrill wail of splendid suffering, the deep
> Strong laughter of ambition; when I feel
> The blood of human labour nobly shed,
> And all the struggle of it: the robust
> Inherent vigour of aspiring man—
> Oh, then I know, I know that he was wrong.[91]

If one could overlook the anti-Semitic overtones of the work, one could see it as a revealing depiction of how addictive and blinding sin is: one is truly under the power of sin when one is no longer able even to identify it, when one even praises and loves the very things that are loathsome about oneself. Or perhaps one should see the subtle anti-Semitism as part of Judas's litany of human evil: "When I see Jesus' life used to justify murder and hatred, then I know he was wrong."

One of the most dastardly modern depictions of Judas is that of *Judas* by Eric Linklater (1899–1974), a Scottish novelist known for his historical fiction.[92] In it Judas is an effete, condescending man who holds everyone in contempt and disgust. He sneaks off from the other disciples whenever he can so that he can stay at his wealthy parents' home and take a bath to wash off the grime from all the smelly, ignorant, offensive crowds who follow Jesus. Although he never steals from the communal funds, he is obsessed with the security of possessions: he yells at a contributor who claims to have donated more than he did,[93] at his sister when she takes something of his,[94] and at a servant for giving away too much of the family's leftover food to the poor,[95] and he completely turns against Jesus because of the wastefulness and impropriety of the anointing.[96] His motives are not insincere or evil; they are just pathetic and petty, as is his vision of the kingdom that Jesus is trying to establish: "I loved him because I thought he could turn the world into what I want it to be. A clean and happy place."[97] Although his real reason for hating Jesus is the anointing, he tries to justify it by the increasing violence of Jesus and his followers, but even this reason is completely self-centered, as Judas imagines that he will be praised for saving the people from the bloodshed that would have been instigated by Jesus: "The people would hail him in the streets, he would walk in the sunlight of their gratitude. They would say: Like Joshua who bade the day stand still, he held forth his hand and commanded that war should not come upon us. They would turn to bless him, the multitude crying with one voice, Our Saviour!"[98] Although Mary suggests at the end that perhaps he was saved,[99] she is focusing on the power of Jesus' love and forgiveness rather than on Judas, for there is nothing in his thoughts or words in the book to indicate that he would ever become capable of more than the basest vision of himself or others. Judas is like one of Flannery O'Connor's protagonists, who are often people who confuse gentility and respectability with goodness and truth, though they are usually granted an epiphany in which they see their error[100] while Judas remains and dies in the world of untruth and self-deception.

These depictions of Judas as avaricious that are not overtly anti-Semitic essentially take up the purpose of Chrysostom's eloquent preaching without taking up his anti-Semitism. They use the figure of Judas as a terrifying example of how powerful and addictive the sin of avarice can be as it pervades our lives not only in the actual seeking after money (both through lawful and unlawful means) but in the idolatrous security we hope possessions will bring and in the smug self-righteousness that we feel over others who are less wealthy than we are. The modern, consumerist motto "He who dies with the most toys wins" is empty and self-destructive because the toys are hardly worth dying for and they blind us to the things that are.

Judas's Red Hair: Anti-Semitic?

Both in verbal descriptions and in pictorial representations, Judas has often been depicted with red hair, beard, or skin,[101] and this is usually thought to be a part of his depiction as a caricature of Jewish features.[102] However, the connection between Judas's red hair and his Jewishness does not seem strong: when he is depicted with red hair, his face is not always a caricature of Jewish features, and when his face is a caricature of Jewish features, he often has dark hair.[103] Judas's red hair is thus not part of caricaturing him as a Jew. Rather, it seems first to be one of many signals used by visual artists to point out Judas in the otherwise indistinguishable crowd of disciples: others of these devices are to portray him in profile, or without a nimbus, or beardless,[104] or in a yellow robe,[105] or with a money purse.[106] But the reason for picking red hair as opposed to some other distinguishing characteristic seems to be part of an ancient and worldwide aversion to red hair, the origins of which are unknown but have been variously guessed at: the red hair of foxes is associated with trickery; it might have originated among Italians out of dislike for red-haired Germans, or among the English out of dislike for red-haired Danes; it might have originally been positively associated with the red-haired god Thor, but when his attributes were taken over by the Christian devil, it became negative; or it might have been considered "unnatural."[107] Physically speaking, this final point seems closest to the real reason: ". . . red hair is a minority feature within all societies and ethnic groups—including the Irish. . . . And minority features, like minorities, are suspect; antipathy to red hair is as simple, yet as complicated as that."[108] But symbolically speaking, it is the dual nature of color symbolism that makes the choice so interesting. Every color represents (or, more strongly, embodies) both good and bad qualities: "Yellow is the color of . . . splendor, nobility, wisdom; but also of jealousy, treachery, felony. . . . Green is the color of spring, youth, vigor, and of the Trinity; but also of envy and jealousy. Blue is the color of truth and faith; but sometimes the Devil in the mediaeval pictures has a blue body or Judas a blue robe."[109] It is such a duality that provides part of the driving force behind the allegory in *Moby Dick* and is fully elucidated in chapter 42, "The Whiteness of the Whale," in which Melville shows how the color white evokes "beauty, gladness, innocence, honor" but also "malice, horror, dread, annihilation." Judas's red hair may well represent malice, violence, and destruction, but it cannot help but carry other meanings: "Red is the color . . . of love, especially passionate love, of burning zeal, energy, courage."[110] These qualities are those that will be richly elaborated in the heroic depictions of Judas that we will examine in the next chapter, and they are unconsciously implied in his red hair in these traditions.

Judas and Theological Anti-Semitism

John most likely constructed his story and its theology (in part) in order to legitimize the hostility between his own community and Jews of his time. As we have seen, later appropriations of it usually move from taking his theology and turning it back into overt racism, depicting Judas as visually and personally possessing every anti-Semitic stereotype from the enormous arsenal Christians have at their disposal. But it is also possible in later works to have depictions of Judas that advance what could be called theological anti-Semitism. I use this term to refer to depictions that offer a negative portrayal and theological criticism of Judaism as a religion rather than as a race or as a collection of individuals. I am not suggesting that this kind of anti-Semitism is any less evil or destructive, and I have avoided labeling it separately as anti-Jewish as though this were different from anti-Semitic. Such a distinction has often been seized on by modern Christians to excuse themselves, their ancestors, and their scriptures by claiming that Christians have been anti-Jewish in a religious sense but never anti-Semitic in a racial sense,[111] as though one could hate and denigrate another person's religion without feeling any hostility towards that person. Such a mind-set of denial is powerfully portrayed in Elie Wiesel's *Trial of God*,[112] in which the priest constantly decries Judaism as evil and barbaric and then acts surprised, hurt, and betrayed when his parishioners go on murderous rampages against their Jewish neighbors. I therefore consider theological anti-Semitism a subcategory or species of anti-Semitism in general, one that feeds into and off of the more overt and violent variety.

The role that the character or figure of Judas can play in this kind of anti-Semitism is various. It could take the form of Judas as symbolic of Judaism from the very beginning:

> But are we sure that he was a man? To my mind he was surely not. *He stands for Jewry, for the Jewish people.* . . . I suspect that the oldest thought was of the surrender of the great Idea of the Jesus, of the Jesus-cult, by the Jews to the heathen. This, in fact, was *the supreme, the astounding fact of early Christian history, and engaged intensely the minds of men.*[113]

Such an idea of Judas would be repeated by no less a figure than Dietrich Bonhoeffer (1906–1945):

> Who is Judas? Shouldn't we ask here also about the name which he carries? "Judas," doesn't it stand here for that deeply divided people of Jesus' origin, for the elect people, which had received the promise of the Messiah and yet rejected it? For the people of Judah, which loved the Messiah and yet could not love him thus?[114]

In this depiction, neither Judas nor the Jews are thieves or traitors but rejecters of Jesus and his message. If it were not for the terrible and destructive history that Judas as symbolic of Judaism has had, I might hesitate to call this idea anti-Semitic. It is more like Paul's theology in Romans 9–11: the emphasis in both is on sadness not anger. In Romans, it is the grief felt by Paul for his fellow Jews, and in this reconstruction, it is symbolized by the overwhelming pain felt by Jesus at Judas' rejection of him.

A much more angry and disturbing version of this is found in the work of Protestant theologian Karl Barth (1886–1968), who repeatedly makes it clear that Judas is a symbol of the people of Israel:

> [Judas] obviously represents the Jews, the tribe from which both David himself and his promised Son sprang. When he reserves something for himself, and therefore in principle everything, in face of Jesus in this characteristic fashion, he merely does that which Israel has always done in relation to Yahweh. He merely does that which has always made Yahweh's rejection of His chosen people inevitable. . . . Israel always tried to buy off Yahweh with thirty pieces of silver. . . . And Israel itself delivers Him up to slaughter, to His destruction. What does it receive for this? What does it gain by it?—this Israel which rejected the protection of the Good Shepherd. What is left when it has refused this protection? The thirty pieces of silver, and therefore the modicum of religion with which it tried to buy off its God, a good enough contribution towards repairing over and over again the dilapidated temple![115]

This is not sadness at some people's rejection of the Christian message but undisguised and ugly hatred for a race that the author believes has "always" and "obviously" been unreprobate, ungrateful, and wicked for their entire history. The anger and revulsion that many readers feel for the character Judas, Barth has transferred and even intensified onto the entire people of Israel.

For a totally different sort of anti-Semitic story, let us consider the one-hundred-page poem *Judas* by Thomas Sturge Moore (1870–1944).[116] Although never highly popular, Moore was a respected and prolific poet, and his correspondence with Yeats shows the breadth of his thought; he was also a talented engraver. The subjects of his poetry were most often classical or biblical, so the topic of Judas is typical for him. *Judas* is also typical of his style: although always vivid and evocative, it is usually overwrought as well as tortured in its syntax. It also displays an encyclopedic knowledge of Judas traditions and an occasionally thoughtful and provocative use of them. Moore tells the events of the passion from Judas's perspective, interspersed with flashbacks to Judas's earlier career. Partly following the theory of Judas as disenchanted revolutionary, he mentions several times Judas's hope that Jesus will reveal his power and rout his ene-mies[117] and Judas's blaming of Jesus for not doing so.[118] Moore's depic-tion of Judas's faults is often subtle, even if totally speculative: Judas's pride and ambition are only hinted at by his slightly excessive satisfaction and enjoyment of the miraculous powers of healing that Jesus has given him.[119] (On the other hand, his speculations are sometimes merely porno-graphic, as in the completely gratuitous scene of Judas masturbating and then feeling guilty over it.[120]) Moore's main additions to the story, how-ever, would seem to be in granting extenuating circumstances to Judas's wrongdoing. This is done partly at the expense of the other disciples, who clearly envy Judas[121] and then wrongfully accuse him of theft because they have no "head for figures"[122] and who finally refuse to forgive him even when he asks them to.[123] But mostly Moore heaps on details of Judas's anguish and suffering at the tragedies of his life, especially the deaths of his parents, wife, and child.[124] The final extenuating circumstance is when Judas decides not to betray Jesus and attempts to lead the soldiers away from him, but as he nervously glances the other way (towards where Jesus really is), the soldiers notice this and get Jesus.[125]

The story's subtle anti-Semitism is in its depiction not of Judas but of the Jewish leaders and indeed of Judaism in general.[126] Moore does this by a typical nineteenth-century attack against religion as irrational and superstitious. Jesus and Judas came to reform Judaism by making it more reasonable, philosophical, and humane, and for this they were both destroyed. Judas himself saves a man who is being attacked by a mob of out-of-control Purim revelers,[127] and Moore even advances the theory that Jesus himself was killed as a part of Purim celebrations.[128] For Moore, Purim epitomizes Judaism as a nationalistic, unenlightened religion of orgiastic primitives, and it stands in direct and deadly contrast with both Jesus and Judas. The use here of Judas is the exact opposite of what we saw before: Judas's evil is not equated with the evil of all Jews, but rather his (and Jesus') goodness and enlightenment are contrasted with the sup-posed primitive barbarism of Judaism.

Finally, let us consider the kind of anti-Semitism found in *Judas the Betrayer*, by Albert Nicole, a traveling minister of the Free Church in Switzerland and the author of several books on New Testament themes.[129] This tiny book is a homiletic examination of Judas's story taken almost exclusively from John's version. Nicole grants some credence to the idea that Judas was first motivated by patriotism to follow Jesus,[130] but he does not allow this motivation for the betrayal: in the end he rules out the possibility of the DeQuincey theory that Judas betrayed Jesus in order to force him to reveal himself and defeat the Romans.[131] Since he relies so heavily on John's version, it is no surprise that Nicole makes John's unique additions to Judas's character the center of his analysis: Judas was obsessed with money, and he was a devil from the beginning, though still mysteriously free and responsible for his actions. All of this analysis is done not in order to understand the historical or literary figure of Judas but as an example to chasten the modern reader, as the author frequently reminds us that we all have the potential to succumb to such evil: ". . . this treachery does not remain isolated. It is being repeated through all the ages: only the outward manifestation is different. . . . This study, I hope, will enable us to examine our own hearts better, and serve to put us on our guard against the germs of evil."[132]

Although hardly the height of insight or sophistication in its exegesis, the book does try hard to make the reader appreciate the story's relevance and to use the story to see the sin within oneself, and not that of Judas or others. In this it is certainly following New Testament precedent and exhortation—"Why do you see the speck that is in your brother's eye, but do not notice the log that is in your own eye?" (Matt. 7:3; Luke 6:41)—and surely is to be commended. But because of its reliance on John's version, problematic anti-Semitic echoes remain. Especially telling is the author's description of Judas and the chief priests haggling over how much money is to be paid for Jesus[133] when such a scene occurs nowhere in any of the Gospel accounts. Nicole has fantasized it and probably believes it really is in the Gospels, not because he is an overt anti-Semite but because such an image has become the common assumption of every Christian reading the story for nineteen centuries.

That Nicole is not an anti-Semite is clear by the conclusion he repeatedly draws from his analysis: he does not say that Judas is greedy and evil like all Jews are but that Judas is evil like every one of us is. The problem I have is that an anti-Semitic addition to the gospel story (the haggling over the price) is still being retained, even if it is used to make a point that is not inherently anti-Semitic: that sin is powerful and insidious in all of us. To help understand my uneasiness, perhaps another biblical example would help. Certainly many men over the centuries have imagined (indeed, continue to imagine) that in the second chapter of Genesis, Eve is depicted as the epitome of stereotypically feminine vices of vanity, lack of intelligence, and unrestrained sexual appetite; many men have then used this supposed textual license to excuse and validate their own dominance and abuse of women. Suppose some exegete were to retain that depiction of Eve as vain, stupid, and licentious, but then showed that the vices Eve displays are not in fact peculiarly feminine but are ones to which all people are prone. Clearly such an analysis would be much less misogynistic than the previous, but is it not still misogynistic? And is it not still a violation and misrepresentation of the text? In the end, it is probably more intellectual rigor than anything else that makes me object to Nicole's reading. As insidious and powerful as I myself believe evil to be, I cannot endorse a reading that embellishes and falsifies the text (especially when these same embellishments have previously been used to such evil ends) in order to achieve this conclusion, and then claims this conclusion comes from the text. The medieval method of making new versions that claim no scriptural basis or authority seems to me much more honest.

We have seen, then, at least three different examples of the Judas story as a form of theological anti-Semitism. Judas can be used as a symbol of the Jewish people's rejection of Jesus; whether one is to take this as providential or unfortunate has been debated, but its history in Christianity has in general been one of triumphal smugness and superiority, frequently punctuated by murderous hatred. Judas can also be used by way of contrast, in which he is presented as noble and enlightened, and he is contrasted with the evil and barbaric Jews of his time: again, Christian superiority is clearly stressed. Finally, Judas can be portrayed as guilty of the stereotypically "Jewish" sin of avarice but then used as a chastening example to the audience of how even the best person can succumb to evil. In this final use, the anti-Semitic culture is again shaping the story, even if it is used to teach the audience a humbling message of their own sinfulness.

Conclusion

The villainous and usually anti-Semitic depictions of Judas we have examined in this chapter are perhaps most interesting for the interplay they show between culture and story. On the one hand, the author of the Gospel of John created his story partly in response to cultural influences of his time, as he wrestled with the painful rejection of Jesus by Jews, and the subsequent persecution of Christians by Jews. But his story then greatly shaped a Christian culture that became the dominant culture of

Europe and the Americas, and everywhere it spread, it brought along John's violently anti-Semitic message. But along the way, anti-Semitic images that had nothing to do with John's Gospel could infiltrate and shape how the Gospel story was presented and interpreted. Nowhere has the Gospel simply caused anti-Semitism, but nowhere has the Gospel not at least contributed to it. At the same time, nowhere in the world has the Gospel message simply been a transparent reflection of the culture's prejudices and values, but nowhere has the Gospel not been influenced by these forces. Indeed, exactly the same could be said of any work of literary merit: such works are powerful and survive precisely because they both epitomize and also influence the culture from which they come, and the Gospel, insofar as it is one of the greatest and most powerful of human documents, participates in exactly the same dialectic.

Chapter Four

Judas the Tragic Hero:
Object of Admiration and Sympathy

Judas the Hero: Admirable and Flawed

So far, we have seen portrayals of Judas that are either ambiguous or strongly negative. But there have been many depictions of Judas over the centuries that have been strongly positive, portraying him as the hero of the story. In most of these he is a tragic hero, flawed in various ways and ending in a horrible death, but still a hero with whom we identify and whose fate fills us with sympathy, admiration, and awe at our own vulnerability before the powerful forces of fate and God. But even in stories of Judas, some storytellers have found room for a happy ending, and Judas emerges victorious, a noble figure whose fate we would not mind sharing.

All of these more or less grow out of the tradition started by Matthew that sees Judas not as villainous, possessed, or depraved but that, in his suicide, allows the audience to feel sympathy for him. However, since the major development of Matthew's account has been to elaborate on the significance of Judas's repentance (Matt. 27:3), I have postponed discussion of it until the next chapter. In this chapter we will see several different versions of a heroic Judas: 1) the gnostic Judas, who was revered as the only enlightened follower of Jesus, the one who saw through the charade of the incarnation and crucifixion and proclaimed Jesus' real message of freedom from the fleshly world; 2) modern interpretations that similarly see him as the only obedient disciple, the one who was willing to obey Jesus' terrible command to hand him over to the authorities in order to complete his mission; 3) Judas as another Oedipus, another man doomed to commit unspeakable acts but who paradoxically always freely chose those horrible acts; 4) Judas as a nationalistic revolutionary who thought Jesus would help to cast off the yoke of Roman oppression but who became increasingly disillusioned and hostile to Jesus when he realized that this was not to be; and 5) finally, Judas the great lover, whose attachments to women either conflict with his loyalty towards Jesus or whose love of women is similar to his love for Jesus—passionate, violent, and destructive.

Judas the Misunderstood Gnostic

We have no direct evidence of what, if anything, gnostics might have thought of Judas or the stories of him they might have told. All we have are brief comments in the highly polemical works of Irenaeus of Lyons (ca. 130–200) and Epiphanius of Salamis (ca. 310–403) and the surmises that can be made from a knowledge of what Gnosticism in general favored or included.

Both Irenaeus and Epiphanius mention a supposed gnostic sect calling themselves the Cainites and possessing a book they call the *Gospel of Judas*.[1] Epiphanius's is the fuller of the two descriptions:

> They boast of being related to Cain, the Sodomites, Esau, and Korah. These, they say, are of the perfect knowledge from above. For this reason, they say, although the maker of this world devoted himself to their annihilation, he could in no way harm them, for they were hidden from him and transported to the upper aeon whence the strong power is. Wisdom let them come into herself, for they belonged to her. For this reason they say that Judas knew quite well what concerns these matters. They consider him their kinsman and count him among those possessing the highest knowledge, so that they also carry about a short writing in his name which they call the Gospel of Judas. . . . Now some of them teach this, but others say something else. Some of them say that it was because Christ was wicked that he was betrayed by Judas, because he, Christ, wanted to distort what pertains to the law. They admire Cain and Judas, as I said, and they say: For this reason he betrayed him, because he wanted to destroy sound teachings. But others of them say: Not at all; he betrayed him, although he was good, because of his [Judas's] knowledge of heavenly things. For, they say, the archons [naughty and ignorant lesser deities in gnostic cosmology] knew that if Christ were given over to the cross, their weak power would be drained. Judas, knowing this, bent every effort to betray him, thereby accomplishing a good work for our salvation. We ought to admire and praise him, because through him the salvation of the cross was prepared for us and the revelation of things above occasioned by it.[2]

Without granting the existence of the Cainites' (either as described here or otherwise) historical certainty, we must consider how and why these two Christian apologists *thought* gnostics might revere Judas. The specter of a gnostic Judas might only be a bogeyman of Christian polemics, but it is nonetheless a real *depiction* of him.

Both Irenaeus and Epiphanius believe that the gnostics revere Judas primarily as another member of a long list of what are (for the nongnostic church) biblical villains: both of them mention here Cain, the group's namesake, as well as the Sodomites, Esau, and Korah (leader of the unsuccessful revolt against Moses and Aaron; see Num. 16:1–50),[3] and to this could be added Eve and the serpent. The gnostics thereby do indeed seem to have deserved the label "mischievous" that was given to them.[4] Even though Cain, the Sodomites, and Esau could hardly be characterized as great pursuers of knowledge *(gnosis)*—they in fact seem rather too fleshly for gnostic tastes—gnostic reverence for them seems to come instead from the conventional wisdom that an enemy's enemy is a friend (or, in this case, spiritual ancestor). The gnostics believed that the God of the Hebrew scriptures is a spiteful and narrow-minded little deity, so anyone who is on his bad side can't be all wrong, and may in fact be on his bad side because they are followers of the "stronger power" that opposes him. Judas would be another member of this exclusive club. He was reviled in the overly Semitic Gospels because their concepts of God and Jesus were too narrow and low for him.

This much distances Judas from the God of the Hebrew scriptures and the Gospels, but it is clear even from the polemical descriptions of the gnostics that they thought of themselves as worshiping God as proclaimed by Jesus. How could Judas be seen as a worshiper of Jesus' God but also the betrayer of Jesus? Epiphanius's first suggestion, that Judas killed Jesus because Jesus violated "the law" and "sound teachings," makes no sense: "the law" held no interest or authority for gnostics, so this comment is either an honest mistake or just an attempt to discredit the gnostics by implying that they revere Judas *instead of* Jesus. His second suggestion, that Judas helped Jesus along on his way to the cross, makes much more sense in a gnostic context. Judas knew the real, heavenly reality that Jesus was not of the flesh, and he was just helping him to return to his spiritual, nonfleshly, heavenly home, thereby giving us a "revelation of things above." A further implication of this might be that by doing this Judas also tricked the other disciples, who were backward and completely fleshly in their thinking, into believing in a crucified, incarnate savior, one who was even in fulfillment of the misguided Hebrew scriptures: "Also Judas, the traitor, they say, had exact knowledge of these things, and since he alone knew the truth better than the other apostles, he accomplished the mystery of the betrayal."[5] By accomplishing "the mystery of the betrayal," Judas not only helped Jesus do what he had to do but also let the other disciples see exactly what their dull, clouded minds were capable of understanding while he and subsequent gnostics knew the full, spiritual truth.

Even where no direct dependence is likely, however, one can still find what would appear to be gnostic motifs in later versions of Judas's story.[6] For a modern version of such a gnostic depiction of Judas, we have that of poet Harry Kemp (1883–1960).[7] Kemp is known variously as the "Kansas Poet," for his early years in Kansas; the "Tramp Poet," for his tramping across the United States on freight trains; and the "Poet of the Dunes," for his later years of living among the dunes of Cape Cod. Kemp has Judas betray Jesus in order to force him into action:

> JUDAS: Thus at a single stroke I will betray him most
> gloriously into that Kingdom for which he came;
> for, caught at last in a trap from which there is no
> escape save by superhuman means, he will hesitate
> no longer; he will withhold his divine strength no
> more; he will pronounce the Mighty Word, the
> night will straightway flash everywhere with win-
> nowing wings of fire, and, at that moment, the
> Kingdom will have come![8]

But unlike the many other versions that have Judas do this because he has visions of Jesus establishing an earthly, human kingdom, Judas here does it so that Jesus will inaugurate the real divine kingdom and reveal his own real divine nature, freed from the flesh:

> JUDAS: I understand all now. Like a revelation it has come
> clear to me on the instant—why the Messiah, the
> Chosen of God, should flee from before the wrath
> of men. It is the care of the world, the clogging of
> the flesh in which his being moves, that weakens day
> by day the Power within him. So, Chosen of Jeho-
> vah though he be, day by day his light darkens and
> wanes in the night of the world's unbelief! . . . 'Tis
> the Flesh that his godhead moves in—'tis this that
> weaken his resolve—'tis this that makes him speak in
> parables! . . . That he might manifest himself over

the weakness of the flesh—that he might tarry no
longer, but blaze forth in all the splendor of his
God-head. In betraying him I do not betray him.[9]

If anything, in the stories in which Judas is a revolutionary,[10] his Christology is too low, causing him to have only human expectations and categories for Jesus, while here it is too high, causing him to think of Jesus' humanity as weakening and obscuring his divinity. Jesus' human life is something from which he needs to escape. Deliberately or unconsciously, Kemp has given extremely gnostic beliefs to his Judas. And one suspects that he sympathizes with these beliefs, as in the end, in a scene reminiscent of the ending of *Oedipus at Colonus* or of Goethe's *Faust*, angels appear and darkness falls, and when the light reappears, Judas and the angels are gone.[11] Whether they have gone to the same place or to opposite realms is left to the reader to decide, though the angels also affirm a rather gnostic interpretation of what has happened: "And, though man's body wither like the rose, / His soul at last her mighty nature knows."[12]

A different gnostic scenario is envisaged in *The Gospel according to Judas Iscariot* by American historian and biographer Ernest Sutherland Bates (1879–1939).[13] Bates first lays out a gnostic version of history, in which the God of the Hebrew bible is a naughty little deity who throughout biblical history has tricked and enslaved his "chosen people," blinding them to the knowledge of the true God.[14] When Judas sees how hostile Jesus is to the Pharisees and scribes, the representatives of this misguided religion, he is immediately taken with him and his preaching, which at first is quite compatible with gnosticism: "God is spirit, and they that worship him must worship in spirit and in truth. Needeth one to go into a temple to worship him? The whole earth is his temple. . . . Take of his strength and his peace, and build in your midst the kingdom of heaven."[15] But unfortunately, the enemies of the gnostic Jesus see the chink in his armor, attacking him by pointing out that there aren't many earthly benefits to being a gnostic: "Then the people, when they saw that he was silent, cried out to him, Speak, if thou art a prophet! What punishment cometh upon us if we heed not thy words? Jesus said unto them, Alas, my children, ye shall remain even as ye now are."[16] As many who teach first-year students know all too well, one already has to have some love of knowledge in order to appreciate the joys of getting more knowledge: ignorance is often quite content in itself. Disillusioned, Jesus begins following the Hebrew God, who now speaks to Jesus, further misleading him into believing he is his son. Jesus' preaching turns increasingly judgmental and apocalyptic, and the other disciples and the crowds respond enthusiastically. Judas faithfully tries to continue Jesus' original gnostic message, but to no avail: "Love God, that is life, for in life lieth every blessing. The joy of little children in their play, the joy of young men and maidens in the radiance of love, the joy of manhood in work, and the joy of old age in wisdom: think on these things, and praise God. Such were the words that I spake, but few hearkened unto me."[17] Judas turns Jesus over to be killed in order to save him from the delusion that the Hebrew God has perpetrated against him: "And in despair I said unto myself: Can nothing then save Jesus whom I love?. . . And a mad thought came into my bewildered heart. What if I should deliver up Jesus unto the priests?"[18] Better that Jesus should die than preach a lie: "For I loved my master whom I slew, nor would I have betrayed him but that I loved even more the truth."[19] Judas kills Jesus in order to save him from the lying promises of the Hebrew God and to save the Jewish people from Jesus' lies, keeping the world safe for Gnosticism to prevail one day.

The fleshliness and messiness of being human has troubled or even offended many people from the first century to the twenty-first, and they have constructed versions of Judas's story that reflect this. In these versions, Judas uses his insight to help Jesus leave this ungrateful and unredeemable mess of a world whether he wants to or not. Judas has become the real gnostic actor behind the misguided and misleading gospel story.

Judas the Only Obedient Disciple

Portraying Judas not as a disciple who misunderstood Jesus but as one (perhaps the only one) who understood him much better than the others is not confined to the gnostics and their literary descendants. Some have believed that Judas understood the necessity of Jesus' suffering and death much more than did the other disciples, and he accepted Jesus' commissioning of him to help enact that necessary though unpleasant goal.

This unconventional hypothesis was advanced by the equally unconventional Albert Lévitt (1887–1968) in his *Judas Iscariot: An Imaginative Autobiography*.[20] Like several of the other authors on Judas, Lévitt had interests and abilities in both religion and law, having a B.D. from Meadville Theological School and law degrees from Harvard and Yale. He was as restless as his literary subject Judas: he taught at ten different schools, served in the army twice, sat as a U.S. District Court Judge, and ran (unsuccessfully) for public office twice. Like other modern versions of Jesus' life, he has Jesus accidentally discover his superhuman powers late in life. While with Judas and John, Jesus picks up a beautiful dead bird and says, "I wish that I could see it fly."[21] The bird comes back to life and flies off. They then successfully test Jesus' powers on a dead lamb but agree to keep this a secret just among the three of them.[22] Jesus becomes a very popular preacher even without displaying his miraculous powers, but this puts him in conflict with the very pious and proud Saul of Tarsus. Judas becomes the creator of Christian theology by synthesizing the messages of Saul and Jesus:

> [Saul] also taught the coming of a Messiah who was to save all Israel from the just wrath of God and to set up the Kingdom of God upon earth.
>
> But Jesus taught that God was love and was tender and forgiving and that God did not desire burnt offerings and sacrifices but only purity of heart and gentleness of life. . . .
>
> Yet I pondered over the teaching of Saul that there must be a living infinite Sacrifice to atone for the sins of Israel and that the Messiah had to die that Israel might be reconciled to God and live under his eternal blessing. . . .
>
> As I pondered these things in the hours of the early dawn the Lord sent unto me the thought that the teaching of Saul and the teaching of Jesus were the same, that Saul taught the way to the salvation of God while Jesus taught the nature and spirit of God Himself.[23]

Jesus lacks a Christology, which Saul unwittingly provides, although he himself does not believe that Jesus is the Messiah. Jesus himself eventually comes to believe in this Christology, and he commissions Judas to act as the instrument that will begin the process of salvation:

> And you, Judas, still do question. Yet through you must redemption come to all Israel. Now am I as a lamb, a sacrificial lamb, decked in palm leaves and green branches, led to the slaughter. You, Judas, must open the gate that leads to the pathway where my feet must tread. I know that you believe in me; I know that you love me. Forgive me that I put this burden of my bodily death upon you. Yet so it must be.[24]

Judas reluctantly obeys Jesus, but in the end it is not clear to Jesus or Judas whether Jesus really was the Messiah. He does not rise from the dead, and the disciples eventually give up checking on his rotting corpse. Judas kills himself in confusion over what he has done but also in an attempt to be with his beloved friend:

Nor can I have peace in the knowledge that Jesus himself placed the burden of his death upon my soul. I was not sure then that he was not a vain sacrifice though he and John were certain that he was the Lamb of God and must be slaughtered to save all Israel. To destroy so lovely a spirit as Jesus was, is the uttermost of sin and evil. John believes that I was the necessary angel of death and that without my acts, and the acts of Saul, Jesus could not have saved Israel. I do not know what I have done nor truly why I have done it. I go to find Jesus and to help him . . . if he needs help.[25]

Judas accepts the terrible command of his friend, and he also imitates Jesus in his death, dying in an attempt to help his friend. Although the book ends on a note of doubt, there is some hope that the love and loyalty Judas steadfastly maintains for Jesus will save Jesus and himself: if people can be saved at all, it is through such love as this.

In a much more playful and lighthearted mode, this is also the presentation of Judas in the musical *Godspell*, with songs by Stephen Schwartz, made into a movie directed by David Greene, known mostly for his work on television.[26] Although clearly dated and at times silly, the work nonetheless presents some touching insights. Jesus first gathers his disciples in New York's Central Park, and they then frolic throughout a New York City that is miraculously empty of all people other than Jesus and his band. Along the way, Jesus pronounces many of his ethical teachings, and he and his disciples act out many of the best-known parables: the sower (Mark 4:1–9), the unforgiving servant (Matt. 18:23–35), the good Samaritan (Luke 10:25–37), the prodigal son (Luke 15:11–32), the rich man and Lazarus (Luke 16:19–31), and the Pharisee and the tax collector (Luke 18:9–14). Having been removed of all plot, the movie focuses on Jesus' teaching much more than other Jesus films. This creates some narrative difficulties, as there are no opponents for the final segment of Jesus' life, no one to kill him. This is solved in a strange scene in which some of the disciples build a large puppet that confronts Jesus and makes the accusations against him made by the Pharisees in the Gospels. Then at the Last Supper, Jesus simply commands Judas to betray him, Judas leaves, and then returns with police cars (the policemen never appear).[27] Judas cannot bring himself to kiss Jesus, so Jesus kisses him instead. Judas then ties Jesus to a chain-link fence, and as Jesus dies on the fence, Judas and all the other disciples assume similar crucifixion postures against the fence. All the disciples, including Judas, lovingly take Jesus' body off the fence and carry it through the city, which then magically repopulates after they turn a corner and leave our view.

In this version, Judas is in a way the epitome of the disciples, who as a group are completely faithful to Jesus throughout: Judas carries that faithfulness through to the unpleasant task of fulfilling Jesus' desire to be killed. Even if the puppet-opponent made by the disciples suggests "the presence of evil even in those closest to Jesus,"[28] it is significant that Judas is not one of the ones who builds the puppet. He stands alongside Jesus as he confronts it and is then shown running down the street with him in an especially upbeat sequence. And in the end, in absolute antithesis to the depiction of the disciples in Mark, Judas and the other disciples are willing and able to be crucified with Jesus, and they then do not run away from the tomb but bring Jesus and his message back into a "resurrected" city. The idea that the disciples take over Jesus' roles is shown clearly throughout: with his teachings as they put on the skits of the parables; with the foot washing as they wash one another after Jesus begins the process; and with their mass crucifixion together. But this elevated, Christ-like depiction of Judas and the other disciples is what disturbs some Christians about the musical. It might seem to imply that the disciples are not merely imitating Jesus but replacing him, as he loses his uniqueness by empowering them to do what he does: "His teaching is meant to free his disciples from what limits them and to allow them to free one another."[29] The idea that Jesus died for our sins has been reformulated slightly: Jesus commanded Judas to kill Jesus for our sins. For some people, this gives an uncomfortable amount of credit and approval to Judas and his actions.

This is essentially also the reconstruction of William Klassen, whose recent work on Judas has been so popular and influential. Klassen believes that Jesus directed Judas to lead the officials to him in order to facilitate his arrest and his necessary execution, and that Judas remained faithful, obedient, and loving towards Jesus in all his actions:

> The early sources do tell us that Judas "handed Jesus over" to the high priest, but that act came as no surprise to Jesus. Indeed, it is never described by him in any of the sources as a betrayal. . . . Above all, the relations between Judas and Jesus seem to have been warm and friendly. Even the most hostile portrait of Judas, provided by the author of the Fourth Gospel, explicitly indicates that Jesus sent Judas forth on his mission with the words: "Do what you need to do, quickly" (John 13:27). . . . The task of "giving over" is seen by the early church as fundamentally God-centered, initiated and carried out under the direction of God. It is, we would say today, a theological task.[30]

To advance this hypothesis, Klassen first shows that the verb usually translated as "betray" (παραδίδωμι) need not carry such negative connotations.[31] He then shows that in the earliest source, Mark, Judas's role is ambiguous and not at all necessarily negative[32] but that his portrayal became increasingly negative through the other Gospels, especially the Fourth.[33] Judas and his act were only considered negative as the early church looked for a scapegoat on which to heap its increasing hostility towards Judaism: "The emerging church began to see the need to draw boundary lines and found Judas a convenient figure—for he was both a Jew and had been a disciple."[34]

From many parts of my analysis it should be clear that I agree with much of Klassen's work: it is "the result of extraordinary research coupled with a real fascination and sensitivity to the subject."[35] As we have seen, two major trajectories—those begun by Luke and John—have portrayed Judas in increasingly negative terms, using him as a scapegoat and his story as a validation (even sometimes a cause) for the scapegoating and persecution of Jews. But it is when he attempts to get behind the earliest documents of these trajectories in order to find the real, historical Judas that I choose not to follow his methods or conclusions. People speculate all the time (indeed, they probably should), but it is still speculation, no matter how plausible or entertaining it might be and no matter how much we might want it to be equivalent to historical facts. Furthermore, I think this kind of speculation leads to a violation of the integrity and a distortion of the meaning of the traditions being examined:

> This points, I think, to a general problem with this type of work: an obsession with the historical facts behind the narrative often causes the author to distort or overlook the intentions or implications of the final work. . . . I would think we should compare Judas's "handing over" to Peter's denial, which Klassen almost never mentions. Klassen speculates that, in the case of Judas's "handing over," Jesus in fact advised him to do it, or at least approved of the action (p. 45). But such a conclusion would be seriously undercut by the parallel with Peter's denial: Jesus predicted both Peter's denial and Judas's "handing over," but surely no one would venture that Jesus thereby told Peter to deny him or approved of such a denial. The same would have to be said of Judas's "handing over," unless we privilege the historical-critical method to the exclusion of literary analysis, which we do only to the distortion of the Gospels.[36]

A depiction of Judas has a validity and a meaning that we lose or misunderstand if we regard it only as a mine or treasure-house of historical facts to be excavated. A depiction is a synthesis that is more real and meaningful than an abstraction that is derived from it by purely historical analysis.

Interestingly, *A Time for Judas*, one of the last novels of Canadian writer Morley Callaghan (1903–90),[37] arrives at much the same depiction of Judas for quite different reasons. Callaghan is known for his treatment of religious themes and for the sparse style he picked up from his friendship with Ernest Hemingway during the 1920s. He makes Judas into the obedient betrayer of Jesus because it is necessary *for the story*,[38] as Judas explains when he describes how Jesus asked him to betray him:

> Then my love suddenly lifted into a wild abandonment and though still nothing was said, flashes of perception seemed to enlarge my understanding of the word "betrayal." The story as it had been written, yes, the followers needed it. The law, its codes. But he himself had said, "Judge not." For him there was only one law—love. Then maybe only one source of evil—betrayal. The whole inner world swinging between love and betrayal—always first in a man's own heart. If it was time now for him to be betrayed, he would cause "betrayal" to be remembered with horror forever as the death of love.[39]

Jesus tells Judas to make the betrayal into a historical fact because it is necessary for the story to mean what Jesus wants it to mean: it is necessary for people to remember it this way, regardless of how it really happens. And this is what causes Judas to kill himself in despair: it is not because he betrayed Jesus to the authorities, since he didn't, but because he told the narrator of the book what really happened and undermined the story that Jesus wanted told. The narrator finds himself in an even more ambiguous situation by the end of the book, for besides knowing the "truth" about Judas, he also knows that he helped steal Jesus' body from the tomb, yet he is equally sure that he saw him walking around the next day. Which "truth" should he tell? In the end he decides to record the "truth" but bury it, allowing Judas's story to be told the way he wanted it to be: "There by the river he began to move me so profoundly that I wanted to clear him at once of the infamy heaped on him. Yet I understood that he did not want to be cleared; it was the last thing in time he wanted; he was where he wanted to be, he was where the Galilean needed him to be in the story—where he had agreed to be."[40] In the end, the novel is an intriguing look at the ambiguity of truth and the power of story.

Whether one lets historical fact overshadow literature or whether one lets literary needs shape the course of history, Judas can be seen as an obedient follower of Jesus. Viewed this way, it is his tragedy that he did everything out of love but has been remembered as the epitome of hate.

Judas and Fate

Wrestling with the problems of fate and free will is, of course, pre-Christian or even non-Christian. Even in a Christian context, it surfaces in many places other than Judas's story, and always with the same trade-off implicit in the stories: divine providence and human free will are in inverse proportion. If you increase your estimation of the one, you lessen the quantity or even threaten the existence of the other. Different stories play this balancing act with different proportions: the creation of Adam and Eve in a situation in which it seems that their free will will inevitably lead to their fall seems like very poor divine planning, while the repeated hardening of Pharaoh's heart in Exodus 7–14 seems to diminish or even eliminate human free will. Judas's story gives us no clear proportion between the two, but the implications of it have always been apparent. If Jesus chose Judas as a disciple and did not know or anticipate what he was going to do, then Jesus looks like a pretty poor judge of character, even by human, let alone divine, standards. But if Jesus chose Judas knowing that this choice would lead to Judas's betraying him, which would lead to Judas's being damned forever, then not only is Judas's free will threatened, but Jesus looks like a very cold, calculating, destructive man (or God) indeed.[41]

To theologize on this question usually results in bald assertions (e.g., divine providence is compatible with human free will because it has to be)[42] or in bemused invoking of a mystery.[43] But as these questions are usually implied in stories, their best (or at least, their most interesting) answers are also found in stories. What is an unsupported assertion in the hands of a theologian is, in the hands of a storyteller, a revelatory paradox or irony. As we will see, there are several literary ways to deal with the problems of fate raised by Judas's story, but for many centuries one of the most popular was to combine his story with that of perhaps the most famous wrestler with fate, Oedipus. Nor do these depictions end completely with the Middle Ages: echoes of them remain in modern works that reflect on fate or that still retain accusations of incest or parricide against Judas.[44]

Judas and Oedipus

Throughout the Middle Ages and well into more recent times,[45] Judas's story has been combined with that of another figure who committed abominable acts: Oedipus. Although Oedipus's story is clearly (and rather awkwardly) imposed on Judas's, it does follow on Matthew's depiction, both in its specifics of having Judas hang himself and also more generally in Matthew's depiction of Judas as less villainous. Clearly, Matthew's version would not suggest an analogy with Oedipus, but only Matthew's story is sympathetic enough to Judas that one would even think of depicting him in the same terms as a Greek tragic hero as appealing as Oedipus.

All of the medieval stories seem ultimately to depend on Origen's thoughts on free will and divine foreknowledge, and therefore show that they stem from a scholarly, or at least literate, background[46] though they end up in completely folkloristic traditions. In writing against his Platonist opponent Celsus, Origen (third century C.E.) raises a significant and influential comparison:

> We do not maintain that the one who has foreknowledge takes away the possibility of an event happening or not happening. . . . This holds good for all foreknowledge about matters controlled by free will, whether we are dealing with the divine scriptures or with Greek stories. . . . To make this point clear, I will quote from the Scripture the prophecies about Judas or the foreknowledge of our Saviour that he would betray him; and from the Greek stories I will quote the oracle to Laius, allowing for the moment that it is true, since its historicity does not affect the argument.[47]

Origen's intention is to show the compatibility of free will with both divine foreknowledge and with prophetic prediction by showing that neither Jesus' foreknowledge nor Psalm 109 caused Judas to betray Christ any more than the oracle given to Laius caused Oedipus to kill him and marry Jocasta: both merely warned or described; they did not cause or compel. But although it may not be Origen's intention to equate or make a direct comparison between Judas and Oedipus, that is exactly what happened in subsequent traditions.

The Judas legend that assimilated his life to Oedipus's was in existence by the twelfth century[48] and may be summarized here as it appears in *The Golden Legend* of Jacobus de Voragine (ca. 1270 C.E.).[49] Judas's parents are pious Jews, Reuben (or Simon) of the tribe of Dan (or Issachar) and Cyborea. Cyborea has a dream that their son will be so evil that he will destroy their race. When the son is born, the parents are terrified but cannot bring themselves to kill the infant. In some versions the child has identifying and ominous birthmarks while in other versions the parents mutilate it, sometimes on the ankles, sometimes elsewhere, thereby leaving identifying marks on it. They put it in a basket, box, boat, or barrel and set it adrift in the sea. Judas is carried thus to the island of Iscariot (hence his name) and is raised by the queen of the island, who misleads her husband the king into thinking the child is his own (in some versions, the king finds the infant and this deception is unnecessary). The king and queen later really do have a son of their own, and Judas abuses his supposed younger brother. Judas finds out that he is not the king's son, kills his adoptive brother, and flees the country. He ends up in Jerusalem and becomes the friend and servant of either Pilate or Herod, depending on the version. His evil master desires the fruit of Reuben's orchard, and Judas attempts to satisfy him by stealing some of the fruit. Reuben catches him, and Judas kills his father. He escapes undetected, and Pilate or Herod gives the widow Cyborea to Judas. Eventually, either through Cyborea's recognition of the identifying marks on Judas's body or by her telling him about the dream and the setting adrift of her infant, they recognize the parricide and incest that have occurred. Judas goes to Christ, repents, and is forgiven for his sins; the rest of the story can then follow the Gospel account. The legend not only existed on its own but was also incorporated into mystery and passion plays,[50] as we see in a French passion play that has Judas recollect his awful crimes and fate:

> New sadness, new pain,
> new frenzied violence around me!
> Ever since I killed my father
> and married my own mother,
> though my guilt is pardoned,
> for I was truly ignorant
> that I had done this crime.
> But nonetheless, nothing follows me
> like this damnation.
> It always returns at every step
> to bring me sorrow and confusion.
> I am more than any other person trapped!
> I am of all men the most accursed!
> Why was I born for all this misery?![51]

As incompatible as a strict idea of fate or doom might be in a Christian context, the power and pathos of it were irresistible to Christian writers and audiences, and versions of it circulated into the nineteenth century.[52]

On the one hand, such accounts, with their heaping of even more crimes on Judas's head and the parallels they draw between him and Adam and Cain, clearly seem intended to disgrace him as much as possible.[53] The one who committed the worst crime of all history could be expected also to be guilty of any other crime imaginable—parricide, fratricide, incest, theft. But his equation with Oedipus goes beyond this, raising the issues of fate, free will, and repentance. Although the storytellers would not say that Judas was destined to betray Christ and they would not rob Judas of free will, by invoking Oedipus's story they were playing with the idea that a series of freely chosen (and therefore culpable) acts could add up to a fated, necessary, and unavoidable outcome. This is clearly what happened to Oedipus: could the same have happened to Judas?

Told this way, Judas's story can be seen as having two cycles of evil,[54] the first of which includes everything before his meeting Christ and everything Oedipal about his story; this ends with repentance and forgiveness, as even the crimes of parricide and incest are easily brushed away by the love and sacrifice of Christ. The second cycle includes the sins he committed in the Gospel account and ends with despair and suicide. By making Judas's life into two distinct parts, however, a certain amount of consistency was sacrificed. There was the characterological or aesthetic inconsistency of having Judas be so repentant and humble one minute (for things over which he had no control) and so unmitigatedly evil the next,[55] together with a moral or theological inconsistency of having one man be both fated and evil, innocent and guilty. Even if less consistent, this was probably felt to be a much more intriguing story than either Oedipus's or the Gospel's alone.[56]

But what if the two parts of Judas's life are more closely related than this analysis implies?[57] It is extremely noteworthy that several medieval saints' lives are also assimilated to Oedipus's story of mother-son incest and parricide,[58] and it has even been suggested that Christ's own life bears a resemblance to Oedipus's.[59] St. Gregory was depicted in medieval legends as leading an incestuous life.[60] In the legend of St. Gregory's life, a king (or count, or emperor) conceives of an unnatural sexual attraction towards his sister. The king impregnates her, then repents and goes to the Holy Land to expiate for his sin, dying while on the journey. Gregory is the child born of the incestuous union, and he is cast adrift in the sea with tablets that indicate his identity. Meanwhile, enemies attack the kingdom and drive the king's sister (now queen) into a fortress that they besiege for many years. Gregory is found by fishermen, raised by them, and educated by monks. When he finds out that he is a foundling, he takes the tablets and leaves in search of his parents and other knightly adventures. His ship is blown towards his parents' kingdom, where he disembarks and drives out the invaders. In recognition of his assistance, he is given the queen in marriage. They are happy until the queen discovers the tablets, horrifying them both with what they have done. Gregory wanders off as a penitent and has a fisherman chain him to a rock in the sea. The fisherman throws the keys to the chains into the sea, and Gregory lives on the rock for seventeen years. When the pope dies, an angel tells the people to seek for a holy man named Gregory. They find him, catch a fish that has swallowed the keys, unchain Gregory, and make him pope, an office that he executes most worthily in every respect. His mother comes to confess to the pope (not knowing he is her son). They recognize each other, he makes her an abbess, and they die after living happy and holy lives. Although parricide is not included in this version, it is clearly similar to the stories of Judas and Oedipus, with the elements of prophecy, abandonment, and mother-son incest.

St. Andrew was also believed to have been abandoned and then to have committed parricide and incest.[61] A man (or his wife) receives a warning that their son will kill his father, marry his mother, and violate three hundred nuns. When the baby is born, they name it Andrew, slit open its stomach, and set it adrift (in the sea or a river). He is rescued, sewn up, and raised by nuns. When Andrew grows up, the devil puts sinful ideas in his mind, and he goes on to violate all three hundred nuns in the convent, some by rape, some by seduction. They drive him away, and he returns to his homeland and begins to work as the guard of his father's vineyard. His father unwisely decides to test his ability as a guard by sneaking up on him at night, and Andrew kills him, thinking that he is a thief. Andrew marries his mother, but when she sees the scars on his stomach, she realizes he is her son. He runs off and confesses to a priest. When the priest refuses to forgive him, Andrew kills him; this happens two more times (in one version he kills his mother as well). He finds a priest (or bishop) who does forgive him but orders Andrew chained and locked up in a cell for penance, the keys to the cell being thrown into the sea. Twenty-five or thirty years later, a fish is caught with the keys inside of it. They unlock the cell and find Andrew inside, still alive (not having been fed the whole time), still repenting furiously. He (and his mother, if he hasn't killed her) live happily ever after. This story overlaps in several ways with the others: the parricide and incest of Oedipus and Judas are included, as well as the setting adrift found in the stories of Judas and Gregory, as well as the keys in the fish from Gregory's story.

St. Albans was also thought to have been the offspring of an incestuous union, as well as being himself guilty of incest, patricide, and matricide.[62] An emperor in the north has a child by his daughter. To avoid scandal, they send it away to Hungary. The child is raised by the king of Hungary and eventually marries the daughter of the northern emperor. When they discover their incestuous marriage, all three—father, daughter, and son/brother—are ordered to wander for seven years in sackcloth as penance. In the seventh year they joyously feel their penance is done and start their return, but the father is again seized with lust for his daughter, and Albans kills them both. He performs severe penance for the rest of his life. This is perhaps the most poignant of the group, as the cycle of sin is repeated and cannot be ended by repentance but only by violence.

Now, any one of these three (and especially Andrew) is arguably worse than Judas: if their stories can ultimately lift them up to heights they could not have achieved without the horror and humiliation of incest, then it is not impossible that Judas's does as well. With Oedipus, Christ, or the incestuous saints, the theme of exaltation is prominent[63] while in Judas's case it must necessarily be muted, but it cannot be wholly denied. Oedipus's discovery of the horror of his fate and the Christian confronting of innate and overpowering sin both function in a similar way: they both face the mystery, pain, and *undeservedness* of human existence. Oedipus does not suffer his fate because of something he did to deserve it but just because of who he is; likewise, I think, an honest appraisal of the idea of original sin would not say that a baby is born with it because of something she did but just because she is human. One must ultimately confront such a mysterious fate or God, and such a confrontation must end in either despair and destruction or in purification and revelation,[64] as one realizes that being fated can be exactly what empowers one to survive one's fate: "The corruption that was born in me / Has helped me live out all this woe."[65] Oedipus was first destroyed by his confrontation (at the end of *Oedipus Rex*), and later elevated by it (at the end of *Oedipus at Colonus*). Either ending is also possible for Judas, but as long as he is depicted as an Oedipal figure, he must be seen as tragic and heroic and not as simply villainous.

Further, it may not only be that Oedipus's story has influenced Judas's, but also that Judas has influenced the medieval conception of Oedipus. This appears in at least two ways: the description of Oedipus as sinful and the idea that he had committed treason, both of which would have been absent from Greek versions of the story. For the Greeks, Oedipus is doomed, polluted, and shamed, but he is not sinful or guilty, yet that is how he describes his acts in the twelfth-century "Lament of Oedipus":

> My sin nourishes my infamy,
> And my tale echoes through all the world.
> My eminence makes clear all that's happened
> And everlastingly my sin resounds.[66]

This could just be part of "Christianizing" Oedipus's story, but the more specific conception of Oedipus as traitorous seems to come from Judas's betrayal and the horror it held for the medieval mind: "The ideals and realities of feudal ties made treason the most hateful of crimes, whether capital treason toward the king, his queen (sexual intimacy was treasonous since it threatened proper succession by blood), or the immediate lord."[67] If Judas is like Oedipus, then Oedipus must be like Judas (and we must see in both of them something of ourselves).

A different incestuous scenario is described in a Middle English ballad of Judas.[68] The poem dates from the thirteenth century and has been of great interest because it is the earliest known Middle English ballad. In it Jesus gives Judas thirty silver pieces and sends him out to buy the food for the Passover feast. Judas meets someone on the way:

He met his sister, the treacherous woman:
"Judas, you deserve that men should stone you with stone,

Judas, you deserve that men should stone you with stone,
For the false prophet that you believe in."

"Be still, dear sister, may your heart break!
If my Lord Christ knew [what you said], full certain he would be avenged."

"Judas, go upon the rock, high upon the stone,
Lay your head in my lap. Sleep for awhile."

As soon as Judas was awake from sleep,
[He discovered] thirty pieces of silver had been taken from him.

He tore his hair until it was bathed in blood;
The Jews from Jerusalem thought he was mad.[69]

Fascinating is the fact that elements of the ballad have survived in Appalachian ballads still sung in the twentieth century:

> Now Judas had one sister,
>   An evil sister she,
> She hated gentle Jesus
>   For His Christianity
>   For His Christianity.

"Thou shouldst be stonèd, Judas,
  With large stones and with small,
Thou shouldst be stoned for trusting
  This false prophet of all, of all,
  This false prophet of all."

Now Judas took a little rest,
  He took a nap of sleep,
He laid his head in his sister's lap,
  And there he slept so deep, so deep,
  And there he slept so deep.

When Judas woke from sleep and rest,
  He sought his sister dear:
"Pray help me find my silver,
  'Tis lost, 'tis lost, I fear, I fear,
  'Tis lost, 'tis lost, I fear."[70]

Judas goes on to betray Jesus in order to replace the lost money. This is clearly a combination of the Oedipal incestuous theme with the theme of Judas as ill-fated lover that we will see later, in which a woman character is created to be blamed as much as possible, acting as the betrayer of the betrayer.[71] The sister's image is highly erotic as well as maternal, especially as the Middle English for "lap" can also be translated as "breast": Judas is simultaneously being scolded, sexually seduced, and cradled to sleep.[72] His hair tearing and betrayal by a woman are meant to recall a hero no less than Samson,[73] while his sufferings are made similar to Jesus' and even accentuated beyond them: he is betrayed by a more intimate betrayer than is Jesus; his head drips with blood; and he is mocked by the bystanders. He does, of course, then enact a very rash and self-destructive solution to the predicament in which he finds himself. While he is hardly heroic in the ballad, he also does not seem villainous:[74] he is, like most of us, just pathetic and desperate.[75]

For at least seven centuries of Christian history, Judas was portrayed primarily as a man like Oedipus. But what may have begun as another embellishment to make him seem even more shocking and inhuman instead resulted in versions that caused their audiences to sympathize with him deeply and invited them to see the fatefulness of his life reflected in all of ours. And with its many similarities to the stories of incestuous saints, whose lives were both fated and graced, Judas's story also became one of hope as well as horror. Although Dante's placement of Judas in the deepest pit of hell is well known, it is perhaps just as significant for us that he did not place Oedipus anywhere in the three realms: it is just this ambiguity and mystery that surrounds Judas in these versions.

Other Versions of Fate

Among the many strange developments that contemplate Judas's story as it relates to fate and free will, we also find in folklore speculations about Judas's birthday.[76] The most common date given is April 1, as part of a tripartite division of the year around three evil dates that recur at four-month intervals: April 1, Judas's birthday; August 1, Satan's banishment from heaven; December 1, the destruction of Sodom and Gomorrah. (It is interesting that of these, only Judas's birthday is the initiation of an evil life history, while the other two are the punishments for evil actions: Judas was doomed, not punished.) One minority tradition makes Judas's evil day recur more frequently, designating the seventh day of each month as a *Judastag*.[77] Both in its date and in some of its customs, Judas's birthday resembles April Fool's Day,[78] but another minority tradition surprisingly places it on February 14,[79] perhaps leaving a hint that either Judas's birth might not be completely ill-omened, or that Valentine's Day might not be so uniformly cheerful and positive.[80] What ties this tradition to Oedipus's is that whatever date is chosen, it is conceived of as a day of ill omen. Important actions are not undertaken on that day, and children born on that day are considered doomed (like Judas), even to the point of imitating his death: "Children born on Judas's birthday, for instance, were thought to have had little chance of escaping the hangman's noose. . . . Children born on this day of the month come to no good end."[81] If Judas's birthday dooms others, it makes sense that it also doomed him. Literarily, one can show that Judas was the victim of an unavoidable fate by depicting him like Oedipus. Calendrically, in the rhythms and cycles of life, one can show the same thing by designating a certain day or days as "Judas's Day," a day that repeatedly reminds us that we are all like Judas: we are all subject to fate, a force—like God—that we fear, respect, cannot control, and do not understand.[82]

Also, in considering the implications for fate and free will raised by these versions of Judas's story, we should mention the legends surrounding the thirty silver pieces. The earliest of these is from Godfrey of Viterbo (twelfth century),[83] though he may have had it from a version of the much earlier *Gospel of Bartholomew*.[84] With variations in detail, the legend is this. The coins were made by Terah, Abraham's father (Gen. 11:26). (Some versions take them all the way back to Adam.) They pass down through the patriarchs and on to Pharaoh. They then end up in the temple, sent to Solomon either directly by Pharaoh or by the Queen of Sheba. They are later taken away by Nebuchadnezzar to Babylon. They are part of the gifts brought to Jesus by the magi, but Mary loses them during the flight to Egypt, and they end up back in the temple treasury (in some versions, the magi lose them; they are given to Jesus when he is an adult, and he sends them to the temple), where they are subsequently paid to Judas for the betrayal, after which they are dispersed, reappearing individually hundreds of years later as relics.[85] The legend is part of the development of ideas of fate because, like the convoluted actions and accidents that combine to form Oedipus's terrible fate, we see the coins kept as a unit and providentially guided all across the Near East for thousands of years until they have fulfilled their "predestined object."[86] The coins are as predestined as Oedipus or Judas, though ultimately to a much more cheerful end: even duplicates of them were thought to possess curative powers.[87] They serve as a symbol of the mystery of fate and free will, as each person who possesses them freely disposes of them, but the ultimate destination of the path they take is unchangeable, predetermined, and necessary.

Necessity and Free Will Again:
Judas in Shakespeare

It is beyond the purview of this work to consider the overtones of Judas that may be implied in any character who is depicted as committing treachery or betrayal; it is also beyond this work to consider Shakespeare's anti-Semitism apart from Judas, either in general or as it is manifested most overtly in *The Merchant of Venice*.[88] Nonetheless, there are several more specific echoes of Judas's story within Shakespeare's work.[89] There are explicit references to Judas in *As You Like It* and *Love's Labours Lost*.[90] The former is in a playful exchange on Orlando's inconstancy, and the latter plays on the confusion between Judas Maccabeus and Judas Iscariot for comic effect as the characters ineptly stage the pageant of the Nine Worthies.[91] There is also an implied reference to Judas in *The Winter's Tale*, one that may show Shakespeare's knowledge of the apocryphal versions of Judas's death as it connects Judas with disease and stench.[92] There are also two places in *Timon of Athens* that use the image of ingratitude and betrayal by dinner guests to denigrate Timon's unfaithful friends as Judases.[93] But besides these, there are several other places where

Shakespeare may attribute heroic characteristics to Judas and where he uses the figure of Judas to wrestle with the problems of fate and free will.

First, there is the textually suspect but highly suggestive line at the end of *Othello*, when Othello refers to himself as "one whose hand, / Like the base Indian, threw a pearl away / Richer than all his tribe."[94] With the mention of a very precious pearl, it seems hard to believe that some reference to the Gospel story of the pearl of great price is not intended here (Matt. 13:45–46), but that makes the "Indian" appear out of place. This problem is solved in folio 1, which reads "Iudean" instead, but this has raised further debate as to whom that would indicate. Although the suggestion that it refers to Herod the Great has merit,[95] I still think that Judas Iscariot is Shakespeare's intended reference, because of the specifics that this scene shares with Judas's story: Othello has just learned that Desdemona was innocent and he is therefore guilty of shedding innocent blood (act 5, scene 2, lines 123, 200);[96] Iago has repeatedly been called a devil (act 5, scene 2, lines 287, 301), analogous to Satan's influence on Judas; Othello kills Desdemona with a kiss (act 5, scene 2, line 15); and he commits suicide immediately afterwards (act 5, scene 2, line 356). If this is the correct reference, then Shakespeare is here using the image of Judas as a paradigm of the self-destructive fury that consumes him in Matthew's version and that has now destroyed Othello. As is usual when I read Shakespeare, I find here an analogy that I would never have thought of on my own but that makes perfect sense, both psychologically and aesthetically: Othello, the "one that loved not wisely, but too well" (act 5, scene 2, line 344) sees himself as Judas, the one who killed with a kiss, who gave in to hellish influence and destroyed everything around him, and who now feels he must punish himself with death. And to compare a hero as attractive as Othello to Judas is also to invite us to compare Judas to him. As with the parallels with Oedipus, once one sees Judas as like Othello, it is impossible to see him as unambiguously evil; instead, he is conflicted, doomed, or tragic.

Shakespeare's use of Judas in his histories seems to me much less ambiguous. The king's murderer in *King John* seems clearly intended to invoke Judas by the manner of his death:

> HUBERT: The king, I fear, is poisoned by a monk:
> I left him almost speechless and broke out
> To acquaint you with this evil, that you might
> The better arm you to the sudden time
> Than if you had at leisure known of this.

BASTARD: How did he take it? Who did taste to him?
HUBERT: A monk, I tell you, a resolved villain,
           Whose bowels suddenly burst out.[97]

Working from preceding plays and the biblical text, Shakespeare has made the assassin's death obviously reminiscent of Luke's version of Judas's death (Acts 1:18). The identification is especially deliberate, as Shakespeare and his predecessors have transferred John's death by intestinal swelling to his assassin by having the monk act as taster of the drink he knows is poisoned.[98] The critics' hesitation to note this parallel is because John's character hardly bears comparing to Christ: he is "weak and morally culpable"[99] as is Richard II, whose killer is also compared to Judas. Twice earlier in the play Richard has compared his disloyal followers to Judas,[100] and in Bolingbroke's denunciation of the killer I think we can also hear an echo of the terrible interplay between freedom and necessity that has characterized many of the medieval depictions of Judas:

HENRY BOLINGBROKE: They love not poison that do poison need,
                      Nor do I thee: though I did wish him dead,
                      I hate the murderer, love him murdered.
                      The guilt of conscience take thou for thy labour,
                      But neither my good word nor princely favour:
                      With Cain go wander through shades of night,
                      And never show thy head by day nor light.[101]

Clearly present in these lines is the idea that the king is God's anointed and therefore should be immune to murder and revenge. Regicide is sacrilegious in these plays,[102] although Shakespeare shows that this need not always be so: Gloucester's murder of Henry VI is done without any sense of sacrilege, and he playfully and gleefully applies the name Judas to himself at the end of the play.[103] Indeed, the total absence of shame and awe in this play and in *Richard III* is what makes their violence more shocking and degrading than that of plays with similar amounts of carnage.

     But the regicides in *King John* and *Richard II* go beyond this and take us back to the idea that Judas or Exton are necessary tools who nonetheless can be held accountable for their actions. (Also, the comparison to Cain is one we have seen previously applied to Judas.) John and Richard had to die, but woe to him who accomplished this act. While legend combined Oedipus's and Judas's stories to show that free will and necessity are not incompatible, Shakespeare has combined Judas's story with events from

English history to make a similar point, showing that in both history and theology necessity is not incompatible with either free will or guilt, and something may be lawful and determined but still be evil and punishable, as the murderers contemplate in *Richard III*:

FIRST MURDERER: What, art thou afraid?
SECOND MURDERER: Not to kill him, having a warrant for it; but to be damned for killing him, from which no warrant can defend us.[104]

Necessary evils are still evil, and justice may still exist in a world that is ruled by a combination of fated and freely chosen violence.

Judas the Misunderstood Revolutionary and Patriot

For at least the last 250 years, the most popular depiction of Judas has been that of a revolutionary and patriot who became disillusioned with Jesus' otherworldliness and his refusal to lead the disciples and the rest of Israel in a violent uprising to cast off the yoke of Roman oppression and establish a real, worldly kingdom.[105] This kind of depiction offers at least two advantages to the modern mind that other versions lack. First, it offers a psychologically plausible motive for the betrayal.[106] No longer is one asked to believe in a mysterious, motiveless evil or in a venality that is so absurdly petty it defies believability.[107] (Though it is perhaps important to note that all of these searches for Judas's motives—whether greed or patriotism—are similar in their opposition to depicting evil as mysterious: some describable "reason" must be found for what happened.) Now one can see the betrayal as a tragic but understandable misunderstanding over the nature of the kingdom that Jesus preaches. Second, it is a more or less secularized version of a religious tale. No longer does one need to think about the disciples' disbelieving in the theology of the cross or contemplate the depth and difficulty of Jesus' ethical and religious demands. Rather, in these versions, Judas—and to some extent Jesus as well—has had enough of all this God-talk: Jesus preaches health, prosperity, freedom, love, and happiness to the people, so he ought to give it to them. Anything else makes his preaching into a cruel tease, a numbing opiate, or a lying promise that he will not or cannot fulfill.[108] On the other hand, some of these versions transfer the role of violent agitator completely onto Jesus, in which case Judas as his opponent becomes the advocate of peace and seeks to defuse the more violent aspects of Jesus' ministry.

Although all these versions share an overall similarity in their depiction of Judas as a nationalistic revolutionary who expected Jesus to reestablish a Davidic kingdom in Israel and who became disillusioned when Jesus did not, there are two separate strands regarding his motivation for the betrayal. The first is that Judas betrayed Jesus out of frustration and anger at his refusal to lead a revolution.[109] These versions would still regard Judas as more or less villainous in the end, for his motivations are still bad though more understandable. However, up until the betrayal, Judas is regarded as a noble follower of Jesus who is understandably mistaken in his messianic expectations. But in the other versions of Judas the patriot, even the motivations for the betrayal are regarded as positive and well-intentioned. In these, Judas thinks that Jesus' arrest will force him to reveal himself and his power. No longer will Jesus be able to postpone or avoid violence: it will be forced on him by the authorities, and he will respond with divine violence that will sweep away his enemies and usher in the earthly kingdom that Judas expects. Since these two strands of tradition are so different regarding Judas's motives, we will examine them separately. Then we will look at those depictions that portrayed Jesus as the misguided revolutionary and Judas as the one trying to stop him.

Judas the Disillusioned and Vengeful Patriot

In the early eighteenth century, John Bonar (1722–1761) offered his version of Judas's story.[110] Bonar graduated from the University of Edinburgh in 1742 and was ordained in 1746. He published several pamphlets, including one responding to the new philosophy of fellow Scotsman David Hume. With Judas, Bonar is mostly interested in using his story as support for Christian claims. By declaring Jesus "innocent," Judas admits that he is the Christ; Judas is a hostile and therefore reliable witness. The same goes for the miraculous powers received by the disciples: if they had been fake, Judas would have admitted this when he became disillusioned with Jesus.[111] Along the way, though, Bonar several times analyzes Judas's motives for his initially following Jesus and finally becoming disillusioned with him.[112] He concludes that Judas must have had conventional, worldly messianic expectations for the restoration of Israel. He initially thinks that these will be fulfilled in Jesus, but when he sees that this is not to be, he abandons him as a disappointment and a sham.[113]

The poet Frank Kendon (1893–1959) gives more detail, complexity, and selfishness to Judas's motives in his *A Life and Death of Judas Iscariot*.[114] In incidents from Judas's early life, Kendon shows a character who oddly combines impetuousness with indecisiveness. In an echo of the Oedipal story, as a boy Judas knocks his father down (dead?) for unjustly whipping a servant, and then flees the country.[115] Two more episodes describe his flirtation with a girl, unsuccessful because he does not pursue her vigorously enough.[116] Judas takes up with Jesus, and Kendon manufactures incidents that show how the other apostles are unfairly hostile and antagonistic towards Judas.[117] But when they are in Jerusalem, a priest takes Judas aside and suggests to him that Jesus, having stirred up the people's emotions, is now doing more harm than good to the nation:

> But one thing lacks—a leader.
> Now hear me out with reason. This one need
> Outvies all others, and I think, to serve
> So great a cause, if we should seem to do
> A little evil by necessity,
> The sum of all, our freedom, makes all just.
> This Jesus has a power that he may use
> With men against the oppressor. Will he use it?
> You say he will not. Yet the power he wields
> Must find some exercise; it is a wind
> Blowing, a tide marching, that must assist
> Or hinder our adventure, if we launch.
> We need the passions of the men he sways—
> The labouring, unthinking multitude,
> But all his personal force is bent against
> This rousing up of angry loyalties;
> He cries content, and bids them cherish the foes
> And spoilers of their garden's liberty.[118]

Although Judas seems uninterested in the priest's suggestion that Judas could be that leader, when the priest goes on to mention the other disciples, Judas's envious resentment of them overwhelms him: ". . . stole / A snake of envy, black and venomous, / Into the secret heart of Judas."[119] Ultimately, the political and patriotic argument against Jesus is superficial and incidental to Judas, whose motives are completely personal: although he loves Jesus, his hatred of the other disciples is even greater. He betrays Jesus more to spite them than anything else, but spite is usually self-destructive. When Jesus is really taken and killed, the pain it inflicts on the other disciples is of no comfort to Judas, whose sense of loss is greater than theirs: "Revenge is never sweet, but it seems so / Beside the bitterness and maddening draught / Of active anger."[120] Judas is a man of violent anger coupled with almost paralyzing thoughtfulness and introspection, which causes his anger to flare up more violently in reaction against his vacillation. Kendon has created him as a curious and compelling combination of the worst characteristics of Othello and Hamlet, and one that is just as unhappy and self-destructive as they are.

An even more attractive and heroic version of Judas the revolutionary is seen in *Jewish Flower Child*, by Coral Topping (1889–1988).[121] Topping was a sociologist and criminologist by training, as well as a frequent writer of fiction and poetry, though this was his only published fictional work.[122] In this version, Judas is extremely ambitious and power-hungry though he is not untouched by Jesus' message of compassion and love. Judas merely seeks to temper his master's kindness with righteous anger directed against the Romans. Judas wants to be king of Judea, with Jesus as high priest, as part of an overall revolt against both the Romans and the corrupt, collaborationist Jewish hierarchy. In the end, Topping completely exonerates Judas of wrongdoing. He never really betrays Jesus: he only reveals his whereabouts to Annas and Caiaphas.[123] They proceed to betray both Jesus and Judas to the Romans. To the very end, Judas plans on leading a Zealot raid to break Jesus out of jail and is shocked that they have already executed Jesus and are now after him.[124] When he hangs himself in the end, it is not out of regret at his sin, for there has been no sin on his part; rather, it is out of despair at God's absence:

> But it was the thought of how the God of Love had let down the man who proclaimed him that finally broke the spirit of the proudest of the Hasmoneans and forced him to search out a limb on the redbud tree strong enough to bear his weight and to order Saul to bring him a stout rope.
>
> "How could a God of Love," he asked himself, "permit the noblest of men to die the most ignoble of deaths? And why should any man of spirit remain alive in a world where courage ranks so low and cunning so high?"[125]

This story of Judas is thus not one of human sin and repentance but of theodicy. He does not sin; he does not even make a mistake as in most other versions of a revolutionary Judas; he just cannot accept God's silence and acquiescence to the injustice and violence he sees around him. If he is guilty of anything, it is despair. It is not, however, despair that God may be unable to forgive but despair that God is anything but just: he is either absent or a sadist. Judas is made almost into a Job figure though without Job's faith and redemption: Judas only curses God and dies (cf. Job 2:9). Further,

Topping's point may also be Christological. If one sees Jesus as only a man, as Judas clearly does in the book, then Judas's position here seems unavoidable: unless one believes that God died on the cross, it is hard not to see Jesus' death as merely another of God's sadistic and unjust acts.

Even though they share the depiction of Judas as disappointed with Jesus' refusal to establish an earthly kingdom, these versions can still present his character in quite different ways, from someone bent on self-destructive revenge to a man hopeless in the face of divine absence and apathy. Although Judas may be equally self-destructive in these versions, his message to us is vastly different.

Judas the Instigating Revolutionary

From his first publication, *Confessions of an Opium Eater* (1821), Thomas DeQuincey (1785–1859) had a literary career that is fascinating for its length, breadth, and sometimes melancholy: his collected works run to fourteen volumes of essays on literary criticism, biography, history, politics, economics, and theology.[126] He advocated and made widely known in the English-speaking world the theory that Judas's intentions towards Jesus were misguided but noble.[127] He was such a well-known proponent of this theory that it was often referred to later as simply "The DeQuincey Theory." First, according to DeQuincey, Judas's ideas of Jesus' mission were probably no different from the other disciples. He probably shared with them the same messianic expectations as others of their time: "Judas Iscariot, it is alleged, participated in the common delusion of the apostles as to that earthly kingdom which, under the sanction and auspices of Christ, they supposed to be waiting and ripening for the Jewish people."[128] But while the others were too unambitious and ignorant to act on their beliefs, Judas thought he could force Jesus to be the kind of messiah that they wanted:

> Simply and obviously, to a man with the views of Judas, it was the character of Christ himself, sublimely over-gifted for purposes of speculation, but, like Shakespeare's great creation of Prince Hamlet, not correspondingly endowed for the business of action and the clamorous emergencies of life. Indecision and doubt (such was the interpretation of Judas) crept over the faculties of the Divine Man as often as he was summoned away from his own natural Sabbath of heavenly contemplation to the gross necessities of action. It became important, therefore, according to the views adopted by Judas, that his Master should be *precipitated* into action by a force from without,

and thrown into the centre of some popular movement, such as, once beginning to revolve, could not afterwards be suspended or checked. Christ must be *compromised* before doubts could have time to form.[129]

So Judas's plan was not one of avarice or treachery. He was, like the other disciples, profoundly mistaken about who Jesus was, but he did not mean him harm: "His hope was, that, when at length actually arrested by the Jewish authorities, Christ would no longer vacillate; he would be forced into giving the signal to the populace of Jerusalem, who would then rise unanimously."[130] He was, however, much more arrogant than the others, in that he thought he understood Jesus' intentions better even than Jesus and thought that he himself had the kind of bold decisiveness that Jesus lacked:

> But, whilst the other apostles had simply failed to comprehend their Master, Judas had presumptuously assumed that he *did* comprehend him; and understood his purposes better than Christ himself. His object was audacious in a high degree, but (according to the theory which I am explaining) for that very reason not treacherous at all. The more that he was liable to the approach of audacity, the less can he be suspected of perfidy. He supposed himself executing the very innermost purposes of Christ, but with an energy which it was the characteristic infirmity of Christ to want. He fancied that by *his* vigor of action were fulfilled those great political changes which Christ approved but wanted audacity to realize.[131]

As proof of all this speculation, DeQuincey offers the evidence of Judas's suicide. If Judas had been motivated by baser motives, it would seem unlikely that he would suddenly have become high-minded and killed himself:

> That neither any motive of his, nor any ruling impulse, was tainted with the vulgar treachery imputed to him, appears probable from the strength of his remorse. . . . Read under the ordinary construction as a life exposed to temptations that were petty, and frauds that were always mercenary, it could not reasonably be supposed to furnish any occasion for passions upon so great a scale as those which seem to have been concerned in the tragical end of Judas, whether the passions were those of remorse and penitential anguish, or of frantic wrath and patriotic disappointment.[132]

Finally, DeQuincey proposes that Judas probably believed that the Romans and the Jewish crowds would effectively protect Jesus from any harm the Jewish leaders might intend. As part of this, he is especially concerned to show Pilate's sincere desire to save Jesus.[133] So for DeQuincey, Judas was neither a traitor nor a thief, and the worst thing he was guilty of was impudence and miscalculation.

DeQuincey claims that the basic outline of his theory is not original to him, but that it has been described and discussed for some time.[134] This would seem confirmed by the fact that, although the first known publication date for DeQuincey's essay on Judas is 1857, the first artistic version of the theory actually preceded its publication. Richard Hengist Horne (1802–1884) was a professional writer who traveled throughout North America and Australia and published widely from 1828 on. He first published his play *Judas Iscariot: A Mystery* in 1848.[135] The play is an occasionally artful melodrama in which Jesus is kept from ever appearing onstage. Judas's character is overwrought—constantly shrieking, biting, frothing, or glancing wildly about—while the other disciples are flat and pious, and the Pharisees, scribes, and priests are flat and sanctimonious. Like DeQuincey, Horne believes that one of his chief purposes is to excuse Pilate: "If any judge ever did the most he could safely do to save the life of one brought before him, certainly Pontius Pilate was that judge."[136] Judas does not seek to destroy Jesus, but to force him to save his people:

> JUDAS: . . . Why doth he wait?
> Would he were seized!—condemned to instant
>   death—
> Set on a brink, and all his hopes for man
> Endangered by his fall—till these extremes
> Drew violent lightnings from him![137]

Nor does Judas ever think that this could result in Jesus' death: "I never thought of death to him—/ Never believed in it."[138] Horne does, however, seek to blacken Judas's motives somewhat by accusing him of idolatrous ambition and pride. At the end of act 1, Judas soliloquizes:

> JUDAS: . . . and while his Chosen Priests
> Shall with exalted trumpets pierce the sky,
> And Scribes and Pharisees, scorched with
>   inward flames,
> Sink into heaps of ashes, will the name
> Of JUDAS echo from an angel's voice,
> Crying, "Behold, the one ordained of heaven
> To urge the great work of redemption on
> Commencing with Christ's Kingdom upon earth!"[139]

Here we also see Judas's expectation of divine assistance when Jesus reveals himself, an element not included in DeQuincey's reconstruction, which had Judas imagining a purely earthly uprising and kingdom. In his final agony, Judas again admits his ambition: "I dreamed of nothing / But power's surpassing glory."[140] Horne places Judas near enough to Golgotha to see what is happening, and to beg for Jesus' forgiveness:

> JUDAS: . . . —Oh mercy, Christ!
> Mercy! for thou canst hear me from afar—
> Hear me scream "Mercy!"
>   . . . He prayeth for them—
> Forgiveth them!—me, too, Lord! I have ever
> Loved thee—but I grew mad—and now I wake![141]

Blinded by ambition and patriotism, Judas makes a terrible mistake. But, unless we believe that Jesus' ability to forgive is limited by his physical ability to hear the petitioner, in this version it is not an irreparable mistake.

A misguided, nationalistic Judas is also kept close to Jesus throughout the crucifixion in the film *King of Kings* (1961), directed by Nicholas Ray,[142] best known for his classic *Rebel without a Cause* (1955), which was nominated for three Academy Awards (including one for the screenplay by Ray) and in 1998 was named one of the One Hundred Greatest American Movies by the American Film Institute.[143] Here we see a Judas (played by actor Rip Torn) exactly like that portrayed in Horne's play. The film adds several scenes between Judas and Barabbas as they plot an armed uprising against the Romans. During these meetings, Judas even tries to convince Barabbas to listen to Jesus' alternative way of opposing the Romans' oppression. When this fails and Barabbas leads an unsuccessful uprising that kills many people (in one of two vivid battle scenes that Ray uses to liven up the Gospel account), Judas then hits on the idea of turning Jesus over to the authorities in order to force him to use his divine powers to call down the violence of heaven on his earthly persecutors. In a bold move, the film omits any mention of Judas's being paid for his information, so the act is portrayed as purely one of principled calculation. Judas seems to maintain his hope that Jesus will resort to divine violence right up to the end, closely following Jesus to Golgotha and witnessing his execution. But when he sees that his plan has failed, Judas hangs himself in sadness over his miscalculation, and Barabbas rather lovingly and poignantly takes his friend's body down from the tree. Judas is tragically portrayed as torn between two charismatic leaders and ultimately destroyed by their competing and contradictory visions of the good.

William Wetmore Story (1819–1895), a Harvard graduate and the son of Supreme Court Justice Joseph Story, went on to become a successful lawyer and writer on the law himself. But he is also known for his poetry, and his greatest and most lasting fame is from his later years, when he devoted himself to sculpting full time.[144] His work on Judas combines his interests in literature and law into an imaginative letter from a Roman lawyer, Marcus, writing to his friend, Caius, in Rome, relating the story of Judas as told to him by Lysias, the leader of the soldiers who arrested Jesus and also a friend of Judas.[145] The letter describes both Jesus and Judas as nascent socialists: "What most aroused the wealthy Rabbis' rage was that he set the poor against the rich."[146] Lysias believes that Judas thought to himself that "they shall go, all armed with swords and staves, strong with the power of law, to seize on him,—and at their touch he, God himself, shall stand revealed before them, and their swords shall drop, and prostrate before him shall adore and cry, 'Behold the Lord and King of all!'"[147] Neither money nor spite was the motivation, but Judas wanted to force Christ to reveal his true nature and inaugurate his socialist kingdom. Story explicitly cites DeQuincey as the source for his depiction.[148] Like other versions of this depiction of Judas as instigating rebel, Story leaves open the possibility of his forgiveness, or at least gives his sincere expression of his desire to be forgiven: "O Christus! Master, Lord, Forgive me, oh, forgive me!"[149]

Another typical appropriation of Judas as a revolutionary seeking to force Jesus' hand is *The Diary of Judas Iscariot or The Gospel according to Judas* by Gregory A. Page.[150] Judas repeatedly (almost tediously) expects Jesus to lead his followers in revolt.[151] And when Jesus makes it clear at the confession at Caesarea Philippi that this is not to be, Judas's thoughts turn from expectation to disappointment, doubt, and hostility.[152] He regains hope at Jesus' triumphal entry into Jerusalem,[153] but when Jesus retreats to Bethany, Judas once more despairs. This time, however, he conceives of a plan:

> Truly, there is but one way whereby he can be made to put forth all his strength. And himself hath shown me that way!
>
> Did he not say unto us, even while we were yet in the land of Galilee, that the Son of Man shall be betrayed into the hands of men, and we would not believe the saying? But, verily, the word had a meaning whereof no man dreamed, but which beginneth in these latter days to shine in upon my mind.

Wherefore should the Son of Man be betrayed, and cast bound into the hands of his foes, if it be not that he may thereby the more abundantly make manifest his glorious might in the eyes of all the world? . . .

What, then, can be done to such a one?—Verily, there is but one way: he must be compelled to show his power. The crown must by might be forced upon him, and the sceptre thrust violently into his hand.

Notwithstanding, I tremble while I think on these things, and sorely doth my heart misgive me.[154]

Judas betrays Jesus only reluctantly and with misgivings, which is repeated in the payment scene.[155] He does so in order to satisfy what he thinks is Jesus' desire as well as his own. He is mistaken and misguided, but there is no evil or malice in his actions. Even at the arrest, he takes the soldiers falling to the ground (cf. John 18:6) to be the first sign that Jesus will finally use force.[156] And when he realizes his mistake, he begs God for forgiveness, the outcome of which readers are left to fill in on their own.[157] In a postscript, the author adds a provocative suggestion: "There are few trials harder to bear than that of base ingratitude; and here we see how Christ deliberately put Himself in a position to suffer this trial in its worst form, so that He might better sympathize with all human souls smarting from a like temptation."[158] Although "base ingratitude" hardly fits his depiction of Judas, it is an insightful solution to the question of why Jesus would pick his betrayer. Whereas we often focus on the problems of foreknowledge and predestination this causes, from another perspective it makes sense as part of Jesus' overall mission to be fully human: although he could easily have avoided it, he willingly had to suffer the pain of betrayal and loss of a friend, a pain that most of us do everything in our power (unsuccessfully) to avoid. This is also captured in the song "Judas' Kiss," by the Christian rock band Petra:

I wonder how it makes you feel when the prodigal won't come home
I wonder how it makes you feel when he'd rather be on his own
I wonder what it's like for you when a lamb has gone astray
I wonder what it's like for you when your children disobey
It must be like another thorn stuck in your brow
It must be like another close friend's broken vow
It must be like another nail right through your wrist
It must be just like
Just like Judas' Kiss[159]

Jesus was as tempted by Judas's betrayal as he was tempted to avoid all the other pains of the incarnation: indeed, he was tempted more than Judas was.

DeQuincey's theory is fully adopted in *I, Judas*, one of the last novels of Taylor Caldwell (1900–1985), a popular writer of historical fiction.[160] The book is riddled with gaffes, from having Jesus anachronistically studying the Talmud,[161] to the repeated equation of reincarnation with resurrection,[162] to having Jesus somehow drop a crumpled-up piece of parchment while nailed to the cross.[163] Judas first turns Jesus over to the authorities because Annas and Caiaphas promise that if he cooperates, Jesus will not be found guilty.[164] When the trial turns out to be rigged in order to find Jesus guilty and execute him, Judas then hopes that this will cause him to reveal himself, believing this up to the very end at the foot of the cross: "But I had believed, I of all had believed. Why else had I challenged him? For I loved him as none of the others. My love was greater, for I demanded more of him. . . . I held his gaze, beseeching him to save himself and show himself mightier than Rome."[165] Caldwell's work does point to an inherently unsatisfying aspect of these depictions. If Judas just made a mistake, then it is hard to depict him as either heroic or repentant. Heroes have flaws, penitents have sins, but Judas does not seem to have either, just a mistake: "But first one must repent, and how did one repent what was only a mistake?"[166] Judas kills himself out of overwhelming sadness at what has happened, not out of remorse, and it seems not to show a flaw in his character but only an error he made from misleading information.

These versions lack some of the mystery or drama of others, but their weakness is also their strength: they present Judas as normal and ordinary. While he may not be as noble as in some portrayals, he is a familiar, fitting, and sympathetic figure with whom the audience can identify. His mistake and the possibility of his forgiveness is reflected in the experience of all of us.

Judas the Anti-Revolutionary

On the other hand, perhaps it was Jesus who succumbed to temptation. Such a possibility has long been entertained in polemical Jewish literature that sought to malign Jesus as a sorcerer and rabble-rousing revolutionary. Along the way, they sometimes elevate Judas as a loyal Jew who seeks to discredit and disarm the dangerous and destructive Nazarene. Such legends circulated throughout the Middle Ages and were popular at least up until the nineteenth century. The best-known written version is the *Tole-*

doth Yeshu.[167] Its precise origins are unknown, but it existed at least as early as the tenth century.[168] The exact status of Judas in the legend is unclear, as up to three different Judases are mentioned, and they may or may not be the same person.[169] In the first instance, Judas is engaged by the elders to combat the wicked charlatan Jesus, in a scene that is typical of the off-color humor of the *Toledoth:*

> Then went the elders of Israel and took a certain man whose name was Judas Iscariot, and brought him into the house of the holy of holies; and he learned the letters of the Ineffable Name which were engraved on the foundation stone, and wrote them upon a small parchment, cut open his thigh and spake the Ineffable Name that it pained not even as Jesus had done at first. As soon as Jesus with his company had returned before the queen, and she had bidden the wise men attend, Jesus answered and said, "Of me it was prophesied and said, 'For dogs compassed me about.'" When the wise men entered and Judas Iscariot with them, they began vehemently to accuse him, and he them, until he said to the queen, "Of me it was said, 'I will ascend into heaven'; and it is written, 'For she shall receive me.' Selah." Then lifted he up his hands as the wings of an eagle and did fly, and the world was amazed before him, "How is he able to fly between heaven and earth!" Then said the elders of Israel to Judas Iscariot, "Do thou make mention of the letters and ascend after him." And straightway he did so, and flew in the heavens, and the world was amazed, "How are they able to fly like eagles!" Until Iscariot gripped him and flew in the heavens; but he was not able to force him down to the earth, neither one the other by means of the Ineffable Name; for the Ineffable Name was with each of them. Now when Judas saw that it was so, he acted foully and polluted Jesus, so that he became unclean and fell to the earth, and Judas also with him. And for this deed they weep bitterly on their night, yea, for the deed that Judas did to him. In that hour they seized him, and said unto Helene (the queen) . . . Let him be destroyed.[170]

Although the exact pollution is not specified, this perhaps makes the possibly scatological humor of the story even more noticeable. Judas does not seem to be a disenchanted disciple of Jesus, and he clearly is not a betrayer. Instead, he is the loyal instrument of the pious Jews in their fight against the impious Jesus. Judas is the rather comical figure who shows that Jesus' powers are illegitimate and can easily be imitated and defeated.

The *Toledoth*'s version of the betrayal is also told to Judas's credit, in which he is again an obedient and faithful Jew:

Then came one of them whose name was Judas, and said to the wise men, "Would you pay off the wicked one?" They say, "But where is he to be found?" He saith, "He is in the temple." They say unto him, "Show us." He saith unto them, "We, his three hundred and ten disciples, have already sworn by the ten commandments that we will not say who he is; but if ye will come in the morning and greet us, I will come and make him obeisance; and to whom I make obeisance that same is the wicked one." And they did so. And when (they that were with) Jesus were gathered together, they went and greeted (the disciples of) Jesus that were come from all parts to pray on the feast of the Passover on the mount of Olives. And when the wise men had entered into the temple where those were that came from Antioch, and the wicked one also with them; then entered Judas with them, left the whole congregation and made obeisance to the wicked Jesus. Immediately the wise men perceived this, they rose up against him, and seized him.[171]

Either this is a different Judas who was a follower of Jesus, or the original flying Judas who fought Jesus has gone on to infiltrate his group. Either way, his indicating the "wicked one" is another of his obedient and pious acts.

Finally, the *Toledoth* makes (the same?) Judas responsible for extinguishing the pernicious lie of Jesus having risen from the dead. Jesus is first killed by being hanged on a carob (or cabbage) plant, for he had used the Ineffable Name to command all other trees not to bear his body. His body is then buried. Judas the gardener piously steals the corpse in order to prevent Jesus' wicked disciples from doing so: "This day shall joy and gladness be in Israel, for I stole him on account of the insurgents, that they should not take him away and have an open mouth for ever."[172] Judas's plan temporarily backfires, for the empty tomb is taken as proof of Jesus' resurrection, but when he produces the body (which is then subjected to further humiliation by being dragged through the city by a horse), this lie is definitively refuted and put to rest.

In all of these episodes, both Jesus and Judas are lowered to the overall tone of the story, which is one of parody and low humor, a burlesque religious polemic.[173] As a persecuted religious minority, the Jews often did not engage in real criticism or refutation of Christianity, but instead kept up their spirits by making fun of their persecutors:[174] one of the clearest examples of this is the book of Esther and the *Purimspiel* that followed it in the Jewish tradition. For Christians, Judaism was often the object of hatred and attack, both physical and theological. Although this could include the kind of savage humor that we saw in the passion plays, the fact that this humor came from the persecutors rather than the persecuted puts quite a different valence on it: for Christians, this humor was part of an overall propaganda campaign that both justified and contributed to phys-ical violence and genocide. But for European Jews, with physical retalia-tion an impossibility and theological controversy an irrelevance (since it would most likely neither convert nor restrain their persecutors), making Christianity the butt of off-color jokes was not part of an anti-Christian campaign but simply a matter of surviving and making the best of an awful and dehumanizing experience. Many Holocaust survivors also testify to the self-defensive value of humor in Auschwitz, whether it was directed towards the persecutors or was self-deprecating.[175] Christians told anti-Semitic jokes in order to justify killing Jews; Jews told anti-Christian jokes in order to tolerate being killed without going mad or losing their faith. So in the *Toledoth*, Jesus is lowered only to the level of a comic villain, vain and shallow, much like Haman in the book of Esther; and Judas is raised only to the level of a bumbling, comic hero like Inspector Clouseau. Although he often doesn't seem to know what he is doing, he is able to defeat Jesus' magic powers, bring about his lawful death despite his sor-cery, and finally put an end to the pernicious rumor of his resurrection. All of this is possible not because of Judas's great virtue but because of Jesus' impudent baseness.

The poem "Dear Judas" by famed American poet Robinson Jeffers (1887–1962)[176] envisions a more serious, but nonetheless similar sce-nario, in which Judas turns against Jesus because of the latter's pride and his complete lack of concern for his followers. Jeffers often wrote on clas-sical and biblical themes, and his thought was deeply influenced by Schopenhauer and Nietzsche.[177] The level of Jesus' arrogance and lust for domination in the poem is truly shocking. He admits that his "love" for humanity has reached some new and terrible level on which he wishes to "possess" them, to dominate and reign within them in a way far beyond what any mere mortal tyrant could ever hope to achieve.[178] Whether this is human or divine arrogance is debatable, as Jesus' mother repeatedly calls his parentage into question (Jesus' illegitimacy being another simi-larity to the *Toledoth*),[179] but it is shocking either way. It shocks Judas, who cannot consent to the brutal, inhuman violence that Jesus callously seeks to bring upon himself, his persecutors, and his followers. Judas poignantly accuses himself of never having really helped to alleviate any human suf-fering in his life, and he now believes that stopping Jesus' monomaniacal suicide is the one unambiguous chance he has to do so.[180] Judas never

believes that harm will come to Jesus, and he turns him over to the priests
in order to stop Jesus from killing himself and others. As shocking as Jeffers's depiction of Jesus may be to us, his depiction of Judas is imminently
sensible: he is essentially a man trying to stop his friend from committing
suicide. As we will see in the next chapter, Jeffers also adds to his depiction a profound meditation on how this portrayal affects Judas's ability to
be forgiven, and to forgive himself.[181]

A similar scenario, but without the negative portrayal of Jesus, is envi-
sioned in *Judas*, by the journalists Anton and Elly van Heurn.[182] (Indeed,
Jesus does not receive much characterization at all, the focus being almost
exclusively on the disciples.) In it, Judas again seeks to save Jesus by turning him over to Caiaphas, who has promised that they will not harm
Jesus.[183] As DeQuincey observed in his reconstruction, Judas's essential
flaw in this portrayal is not faithlessness towards Jesus but presumption
that he can solve problems that Jesus cannot:

> Then a voice cut across his thoughts. It was the voice that he
> had never tried to silence, the voice of his own will.
> "Iscariot, it was I who made you proud, who set you apart
> from other men. When you clenched your fist in indigna-
> tion, it was I who did it. I made you feel superior, fit to pass
> judgment on others. And it was I who sowed the seed of blind
> passion in you. It grew luxuriantly, like a weed. I alone have
> been your guide and teacher, and you have been my splen-
> did pupil—willful and stern. And you have been ever faith-
> ful to me."[184]

Judas loves Jesus, but in a way that is proud and self-centered: "There had
not been the humble offering of himself, which alone constitutes true
love. He had not truly placed his hope and faith in the Master."[185] Judas
cannot fully give himself to Jesus, and therefore he is lost.

The exact same depiction of Judas is found in *King Jesus* by English poet
and novelist Robert Graves (1895–1985),[186] who is perhaps best known
for his historical novel *I, Claudius* (1934). *King Jesus* is an especially turgid
novel, being often simply an excuse for the author to engage in syncretis-
tic speculations about the identities of Hebrew, Canaanite, Egyptian,
Greek, and Roman gods, or in historical speculations, the most notable
being the identity of Jesus' father, who is Antipater, the murdered son of
Herod the Great, making Jesus literally the rightful heir to be King of the
Jews. Judas is Jesus' first disciple, and his most loyal throughout. In a par-

ticularly nice irony, Graves not only does not make Judas the one to object to Jesus' anointing at Bethany, but he makes him Jesus' most vocal defender: "The disciples hotly defended Jesus. Judas said: 'The poor are always at your gates. Why do you grudge this honour to one who has renounced all worldly possessions?'"[187] Judas only has his doubts when Jesus' preaching turns increasingly violent: "Why had Jesus broken the principles which he had strictly laid down for them?. . . And worse: why had he, hitherto a quietist and prophet of peace, stood up to incite the Zealots and Anavim to passionate thoughts of military glory?"[188] Judas then realizes the terrible turn Jesus' ministry has taken: "Clearly, he had resolved upon self-destruction, upon becoming the scape-goat that should bear away the sins of the whole people."[189] At the Last Supper, Jesus orders the disciples to kill him: "'One of you shall kill me!' . . . Judas alone understood that Jesus was issuing an order, not leveling an accusation."[190] Judas cannot bring himself to accept this awful responsibility: "His instructions were clear: he was to buy a sword with which to kill his master. How could he obey? How could he take the life of the man he loved best? And why had Jesus chosen him as the assassin?"[191] Nor can he refuse it, for he fears that Jesus will then simply designate one of the other disciples to be his killer. So Judas meets with Nicodemus and they decide to turn Jesus over to Caiaphas to prevent his death, not cause it. When things turn out differently, Judas persuades Nicodemus's son to kill him, so that he will not be technically guilty of suicide: again echoing DeQuincey, he confesses in his final prayer only to "presumption,"[192] to fatally disobeying the awful command of his master. Graves concludes his depiction of Judas with an interesting meditation on the similarity of Judas and Peter, and the possibility of Judas's redemption: "But whether Judas's fault, which was cowardice rooted in intelligence, was graver than Peter's, which was pugnacity rooted in unintelligence, and whether he made full amends for it by his death, that let our God decide."[193] Both are guilty of weakness and disobedience, but neither is guilty of malice. Indeed, Judas's mistake seems far more admirable than Peter's: Judas weakens when called on to kill Jesus, while Peter weakens when called on to die for him.

The acclaimed rock opera *Jesus Christ Superstar*, by Andrew Lloyd Webber and Tim Rice, also depicts Judas as loving Jesus to the very end and as acting against him only in an attempt to prevent violence to his friend and their followers.[194] Despite some rather dated dance numbers and costumes, there are still frequent moments of brilliance in the musical and the movie version (1973), directed by Norman Jewison. Jewison recently won the Irving G. Thalberg Memorial Award by the academy of Motion Picture Arts and Sciences for a lifetime of achievement in film making (1998), and he directed many acclaimed movies, such as *Fiddler on the Roof* (1971), *The Thomas Crown Affair* (1968), and *In the Heat of the Night*, which won the Oscar for Best Picture in 1967. In *Superstar,* the other disciples practically disappear, only appearing prominently to display their shameful self-serving attitude at the last supper and Peter's cowardice at the denial. Instead, Mary Magdalene and Judas rise to prominence: their songs are haunting or jarring, and their depictions are passionate, much more so even than that of Jesus, who seems rather too passive, confused, and weak, except for some annoying falsetto screams.[195] This is also part of the convoluted context that makes choosing Carl Anderson, an African American, for the role of Judas so provocative.[196] Whether one is a racist who is quite comfortable thinking of a black man as the world's worst villain or whether one reacts in the opposite way of being appalled that a black man would be cast as a villain, the portrayal here will undermine and call into question one's expectations. Either way, our expectations are subverted by having a black man as the problematic hero of the story, a character we know we are "supposed" to hate but who is quickly shown to be the most appealing and powerful character of the story. In a racially charged context, the simultaneity of both hating and admiring a black man has to call into question the whole idea of race, as well as the whole idea of Judas's villainy. Jewison effectively used racial stereotypes to undermine the racism that lay behind them: "The 1970s interest in the black performer was still driven by white constructions of African American stereotypes, but the newly revised image of many minorities, including women, provided them with an active, even angry voice, a way to speak out against long years of repression."[197]

The story is told almost completely from Judas's perspective. The very first song is sung by Judas, as he laments the turn that Jesus' ministry has taken. In contrast to the other disciples (and Jesus himself?), who blandly have "Heaven on Their Minds," Judas's tone is strident and compelling as he lists all the obstacles and dangers that are in the way of Jesus and his followers and that threaten the life of both. Jesus does not appreciate the danger into which he has put himself, his followers, and even his message by letting them think he has militaristic ambitions (even if he rejects these in the song "Simon Zealotes"). But Jesus won't listen to Judas, as indeed he does not seem to listen to anyone. But while anger and confusion at Jesus' inability to see what is happening push Mary Magdalene into singing the most beautiful song in the work, "I Don't Know How to Love

Him," Judas's feelings push him (after being chased by tanks and fighter planes that may be real or imagined) to try to stop his friend's self-destruction by going to the chief priests, who he hopes can stop Jesus. They only offer him, however, the "Blood Money." When Judas sees that he has lost control of the situation, he realizes his mistake and the terrible, mysterious love that Jesus had for him. Judas also admits that he doesn't know how to love Jesus, echoing Mary's song, and goes on to see that his friend knew all along what would happen. This prescience makes Judas even more angry at Jesus, and he accuses his friend of murdering him when he commits suicide. But as final as Judas's despair and suicide may appear, he surprisingly returns for one more number, with no less than a heavenly chorus (at least, they are dressed all in glittering white pantsuits) backing him up. They acclaim Jesus Christ as "Superstar" though Judas continues his accusatory questions right up to the end. His tone, however, has changed from despair: it ends as wonder, doubt, or criticism—a criticism that perhaps implies hope or confidence that the criticism can be accepted and the situation and relationship improved. In the end, Judas does seem to be saved, even if his angry questions are still unanswered. He remains critical of Jesus (and God), but repeatedly asks him not to "get me wrong": his questions come from love, not hate, as accusatory as they remain to the end. As in the book of Job, the human need to question and even accuse God is affirmed, even if such a need must ultimately go unfulfilled in this life.

The most Othello-like of these depictions of Judas is that given in *The Man Born to Be King* by Dorothy L. Sayers (1893–1957).[198] Sayers was perhaps most popular for her detective novels, but she is also known for her theology, her friendships with T. S. Eliot and C. S. Lewis, and her translation of Dante's *Divine Comedy*. In her play, Judas and some of the other disciples begin as disciples of John the Baptist before they follow Jesus; Judas stays with John during his imprisonment but eventually joins the others with Jesus. Judas completely rejects the proposals of the Zealots and never wavers from this position.[199] He alone among the disciples understands the necessity of suffering, both Jesus' and their own: "The way to salvation is through suffering and death. . . . so he laid our burden upon us—sorrow and humility and torment and shame, and poverty and peace of heart. God's salvation. And we were filled with a strange happiness. Then he blessed us."[200] But like Othello's obsession with his idealized Desdemona that turns love into hate as soon as a doubt is introduced, Judas's single-minded devotion to the ideal that Jesus has taught dooms him as he begins to suspect a different kind of infidelity. He suspects that

Jesus is not true to his own message, that he has—or eventually will—succumb to the temptation to take up arms and a crown:

> JUDAS: About this journey. *Why* do you want to go to
> Judaea? To weep at the grave and console the bereft?
> Is that all?—Or do you mean to come out boldly—
> to leave this pleasant backwater and face the flood-
> tide of events? *(passionately)*—I wish I knew what to
> make of you? Sometimes you speak as though you
> meant to dare everything and take the consequences.
> But which way—which way? You have made the way
> of the Kingdom plain to my eyes and my heart. But
> there is another way and another kind of kingdom—
> and there are things going on that I don't under-
> stand. Or perhaps I understand too well. . . . For
> God's sake, Master, are you honest? Or do your
> words say one thing and your actions another?[201]

Like Othello, once Judas is suspicious, everything seems to fit into his twisted, paranoid view of Jesus: when he hears that Jesus replied to the inquiries of the Zealot leader Baruch by saying, "Tomorrow he shall have the sign he looks for,"[202] all his suspicions of Jesus seem confirmed. (Baruch tells him later that the appointed sign was for Jesus to enter Jerusalem on a horse if he agreed to lead the rebellion, on an ass if he did not.)[203] Judas turns Jesus over to Caiaphas in order to save him from himself, to keep him from betraying his own message:

> He *was* the Messiah, if only he had been true to himself. Indeed, my
> Lord Caiaphas, there was a great man lost in Jesus of Nazareth. The
> noblest dreams I ever dreamed, the holiest prayers my heart could
> utter, all my hopes, all my ideals, seemed incarnate in him. Yet he has
> lowered himself to the measure of little minds, eating the applause of
> the ignorant, and bartering his heavenly birthright for the mess of
> pottage which he despises even while his mouth waters at the thought
> of it.[204]

Like Othello, once the ideal has been corrupted by suspicion, there is no turning back: everything contributes to increasing Judas's suspicion and destroying his idea of the beloved, until there is nothing left but hate for the one he thinks has destroyed his ideal and resentment for the pain and humiliation this (supposed) betrayal has caused him. The object of his love is pure, but the love itself is completely self-centered. Othello's love for

Desdemona or Judas's love for Jesus are ways to ratify and increase their own self-worth: when the love threatens their self-worth, when it threatens to humiliate rather than uplift them, then it is turned into hate, destroying both the beloved and the lover. As with Jeffers's portrayal of Judas, this self-centeredness also affects Sayers's idea of repentance and forgiveness in the story, as we shall see in the next chapter.[205]

Besides the *Toledoth*, which plays all this for comedy, the more serious of these depictions of Judas do not base their evaluation of his character on whether he is seeking to provoke violence or prevent it, as these are two sides of the same coin. In either case, it is neither his motivations nor his goals that are base, as these are completely noble in these scenarios: it is his attitude towards himself that can become sinful and self-destructive. If he cannot imagine relying on God, Jesus, or any other human being, then it means that he cannot love, trust, or obey anyone. It also means that in the end, without some enormous transformation of his outlook, he cannot let himself be forgiven, as this is the ultimate act of letting oneself be vulnerable to another.

Judas the Lover

Besides the stories of mother-son or brother-sister incest, there are other stories that take a very different interest in Judas's romantic and sexual life. These are clearly based on Matthew's depiction of Judas, and especially on his death by suicide, as they depict him as an intensely impetuous and obsessive man: his attraction to women as well as his attachment to Jesus are both passionate and violent. Even within this category, however, a wide range of emphases and meanings can still be found.

Judas Iscariot by Ernest Temple Thurston (1879–1933) has Judas's love of a woman, Huldah, conflict with his ambition to follow Jesus and benefit from his establishment of his messianic kingdom.[206] Along the way, the author plays with the idea of fate we have seen repeatedly in the Oedipal versions of Judas's story by having the magi visit Judas's parents and warn them of their son's terrible fate in a passage that tries to reconcile this with free will:

FIRST CHALDEAN: Shepherd, our destiny is only in the sight of God—all that a man doeth in the eyes of man and of himself, he doeth of his will, but knows not the result. The sign I spoke of was that I should warn you of your infant's fate. If I speak more, only my will shall speak it.[207]

Having witnessed Jesus' raising of the widow's son,[208] Judas is convinced that he is the promised messiah who will deliver them from Roman oppression, and he leaves Huldah to follow Jesus: "He will march into Jerusalem with faith all armed in thousands in His steps and Herod and Rome shall vanish in a night."[209] Following DeQuincey, Thurston has Judas betray Jesus in order to force him to reveal himself: "Perhaps if they do arrest Him then he *will* declare himself."[210] But the addition of Judas's lover to his story makes his disillusionment with Jesus' message of non-violence resonate a little differently:

> JUDAS: Love our enemies! He has indeed said that. But how
> can you love the thing you hate? Of all men but
> Him I would say I did mistrust the man who could
> not hate. Will *love* call Herod from his sin? Will love
> drive Rome out of the land of Israel? Are they but
> sheep these vultures that feed upon us? Is it a shep-
> herd's voice that will call them from their prey?
> Love will not free this land of Judah, but hate that
> wields a sword to drive its enemies before it.
> Never—never—never will the name of Christ pre-
> vail with love! Rather His name will die before love
> has the power of victory. Has this explained it to
> you? You do not understand. You are a woman and
> love seems all to you.[211]

Ironically, having rejected his love in order to follow Jesus, Judas now rejects Jesus' message because it is one of love. This is not just the disillusionment of a revolutionary with a pacifist but the bitter disappointment of a man who has steeled himself to forsake love in favor of hate but then has found that his sacrifice was unnecessary, ineffective, and unappreciated.

Stories that blame everything (or as much as possible) on the woman are ancient indeed, going back in the Judeo-Christian tradition at least to the story of Eve and the serpent. The storytellers who created and passed on Judas's story also saw the usefulness of this theme: as early as the fifth century, one version had Judas's wife counsel him to betray Jesus, and "He listened to her as Adam did to Eve."[212] Following the betrayal, Judas's wife was also depicted as cavalier and dismissive of what had happened:

> And he went home to make a halter to hang himself, and he found
> his wife roasting a cock on the coals. And he says to her, "Rise, wife,

and get a rope ready for me; for I mean to hang myself, as I deserve."
And his wife said to him, "Why do you speak like that?" And Judas
says, "Know in truth that I unjustly betrayed my master, and that he
is going to rise on the third day; and woe to us!" And his wife says,
"Do not speak or think in that way. It is just as likely as that this cock
roasting on the coals will crow, that Jesus will rise, as you say."
No sooner said than the cock flapped his wings and crew thrice.
This decided Judas, and he immediately made the halter and hanged
himself.[213]

Whether she is talking him into betraying Jesus, or talking him out of
repenting, Judas's wife offered an irresistible possibility that "in the case
of the ultimate crime, the betrayal of Jesus, a woman might ultimately be
to blame."[214]

In 1932, Sybil Morley followed in this tradition by publishing *Judas, A
Poem*, which consisted of 1932 lines of rhymed couplets.[215] Rather than
have Judas's love of a woman conflict with his love of Jesus, Morley also
makes the woman's role more determinative and sinister, like that of Eve.
Judas's lover, Ireen, is greedy and vain. She actively taunts him that she
will leave him for another man and that this is Jesus' fault for not letting
Judas have more money. Judas therefore betrays Jesus to placate her. Judas
is portrayed as impetuous and quick to be made jealous, and much of the
blame for his betrayal is put onto his lover.

Almost exactly the same scenario takes place in *Judas Iscariot, A Poetical
Play*, by James Lewis Milligan (b. 1876).[216] Milligan was a fairly well-
known Canadian journalist and poet. In this play it is again Judas's lover,
this time named Shikona, who instigates the betrayal in order to satisfy
her own greed:

SHIKONA: The Priests are after Jesus. They are bent
            On breaking up His band of followers,
            And they have paid me to prevail upon
            Judas to help them bring the Nazarene
            Under arrest before the Passover.
            Poor Judas did not like the thing at first,
            But I have never failed to have my way
            With him, and so he yielded to my plea,
            And to the need of money.[217]

Milligan also works into his play some of the ideas of terrible predestination that we have already seen, having Judas refer to himself as "a pawn of

fate."[218] He also leaves some possibility that Judas's death was not completely in vain: the final line of the play has Shikona casting away the silver pieces as Judas's voice warns her to do so from beyond the grave. Milligan allows him to make the kind of warning that the rich man was denied in the parable of the rich man and Lazarus (Luke 16:19–31): Judas cannot save himself, but his love and loyalty powerfully outlive even his death.

Similar, but with more twists and with more elements integrated into it, is *Ish Kerioth* by George C. Alborn.[219] Alborn was a Baptist minister in Wisconsin and a frequent author, though few copies of his works survive. In his version, patriotic longings and personal ambitions, both of which are encouraged by both his mother and his lover, prompt Judas to follow Jesus:

> During the intervening time [his mother] had many long talks with Judah, from each of which he emerged with his ambition, his love of wealth and power, and his hatred of Rome all burning at a fever heat. Astar [his lover], too, inspired him with insatiable ambition. Her love of greatness and her disgust with common men made him long and scheme to be great. Her approval was very important and dear to him, and to win it he must rise above the level of common humanity. All his hopes centered in Messiah and the possibility that Jesus of Galilee might be he. In this possibility lay all his hopes for greatness.[220]

Here we see an elaborate combination of themes present in other heroic depictions of Judas. His patriotic hatred of Roman oppression is present in many modern versions, as well as its tendency to blend into or combine with merely personal ambition and greed. His unusual closeness to his mother and his eagerness to please her are clearly Oedipal, and she also takes on some of the instigating role that is often placed on his lover, for she is "his fiery and ambitious mother, who loved him and seemed to live only in the hope of one day seeing him great."[221] The author retains his lover as instigator as well, though it is mostly in the form of Judas's vivid imagination rather than her own, direct instigation: Judas feels that she will not accept him unless he is the powerful minister and follower of the Messiah. His relationship with her also foreshadows his betrayal of Jesus, for he leaves his former lover to pursue the exotic Astar: "Last night he had thought regretfully of Tirzah, and had dwelt in loving memory on her fancy-pictured face; tonight his fancy was entirely filled with the face of the fair Astar. Ah, Judah, art thou already false?"[222] The women both prompt Judas and resemble him, for their passion and ambition are reflected in the feelings he has for Jesus: "If Jesus prove to be Messiah, he shall have no more zealous and loyal supporter than I. But if he is not, he has betrayed me, deceived me, ruined my life, and he will have no more bitter enemy than Judah of Kerioth."[223] But while both his mother and lover give up their personal and nationalistic ambitions and accept Jesus' message of love and self-sacrifice, they are unable to convince Judas to have the same hopes. He kills Jesus and himself in frustration over the failure of his ambitions: "Disappointment and disgust filled his soul. The swift reaction which always follows high nervous tension set in strongly, and despair filled his heart."[224] In an inversion of the image from Milligan's story, their love for Judas outlives his death: "The neglected spot where unfriendly hands bestowed the remains of the false disciple, Judah, was visited often for the next few months by two women, upon whom their grief rested heavily."[225] Judas and the women he loves all start the story as passionate, ambitious, and mercurial, but the women make a passionate commitment for Jesus while Judas tragically and self-destructively directs his passion against Jesus, and then against himself.

Similar to these stories of Judas betraying Jesus at the instigation of a woman, there is the absurd scenario found in Urban Nagle's play *Barter.*[226] Nagle was a Dominican priest, and in 1931, together with Thomas Carey, he founded the Blackfriars Guild, a group dedicated to writing and producing plays with religious themes.[227] In the play Jesus is once again done in by star-crossed lovers, though in this version Judas is not one of the lovers, his role instead being transferred onto the newly created character of Varrus. In the play, Jobal of the Sanhedrin wants his daughter Miriam to marry Phanuel, who is eager to marry Miriam. But Jobal's second wife, Rhea, wants Phanuel for herself. Meanwhile, Miriam wants to marry Varrus, a Roman soldier. Rhea convinces Jobal to let Miriam marry Varrus, thereby spiting Phanuel and also keeping him available for herself. Jobal speaks to Varrus, offering him Miriam in exchange for Varrus's not interfering in the arrest of Jesus. Although Varrus is appalled that an innocent man will die as part of the bargain, he wants Miriam so badly that he agrees. Phanuel, however, is lurking around while Jobal and Varrus talk, and he double-crosses Varrus and turns him in for supposedly helping Jesus. So Varrus cooperates in Jesus' arrest and death but is ironically arrested himself on the false accusation of helping Jesus (which he wished to do but did not). Judas's role as conflicted and tortured lover seems moving in some versions, as his allegiance is understandably torn between a lover and a friend (or master), but to transfer it to someone like Varrus who is uninvolved with Jesus makes it a laughable part of a play that is overladen with melodrama and coincidence, as if one were to play Monty Python's *Life of Brian* with complete seriousness.

Cecil B. DeMille's silent epic *The King of Kings* (1927) also depicts Judas's attraction for a woman and the resulting jealousy as contributing to his betrayal of Jesus.[228] The film begins with a long sequence of Mary Magdalene cavorting in a palace somewhere. Played by Jacqueline Logan, she is perhaps the most beautiful and erotic Mary Magdalene of any Jesus film (with all due respect to the voluptuous Barbara Hershey of *The Last Temptation of Christ* and the waiflike Catherine Wilkening of *Jesus of Montreal*). She is jealous because her lover Judas has run off to follow some Galilean carpenter, and she leaves the palace in a huff on a chariot driven by zebras. (Mary's prominence in the film is part of its general emphasis on Jesus' relations with women: Mary Magdalene, the woman taken in adultery [John 8:1–11], and Martha and Mary [John 11:1–44] dominate the first half of the film, to the exclusion of any of Jesus' teaching.[229] They are augmented by two very touching, noncanonical scenes of Jesus with female children: Jesus is first seen through the eyes of a blind girl whom he heals, and later he repairs a doll for a little girl.) When she meets Jesus and Judas, she is mesmerized by Jesus and gives up her wanton ways. Judas looks quite disappointed at this. This disappointment clearly augments his frustration at Jesus' refusal to establish an earthly kingdom, a combination of Judas as lover and Judas as ambitious patriot similar to Alborn's portrayal. In the end he betrays Jesus because all his expectations of him and his kingdom are disappointed, and he is "bitter, panic-stricken . . . desperate . . . all hope of earthly kingdom gone." Judas loves his country and women more than he loves Jesus.

Rather than having Judas's love of Mary interfere with his love of and loyalty to Jesus, Philip Robert Dillon (b. 1868) has Judas's obedience to Jesus destroy his relationship with Mary.[230] Judas is wildly, violently in love with Mary Magdalene throughout the novella. At first it seems as though Judas is going to be represented as a revolutionary, as he is shown meeting with an all-powerful group of cabalistic proto-Masons.[231] But when Jesus does not agree to their plan, Judas follows what he thinks are Jesus' wishes and hands him over to the authorities, as he explains to Mary Magdalene:

> It will not matter, if only you know the truth!—how I believed in Him, that He was the Son of God and that the same Father commanded us both—He to die, and I to be an instrument for the Redemption. . . . Not in enmity, not in selfishness did I do this thing—No, No!! Never! He called me to do it, that the Redemption might be fulfilled—miracle of miracles![232]

Mary cannot accept this explanation, and she rejects Judas. This rejection, together with his confusion at Jesus' cry of dereliction on the cross and his failure to bring about the redemption immediately, cause him to kill himself in despair. The price of obediently following Jesus was high indeed, costing him his love and his life.

Judas and Mary Magdalene are also lovers in *Behold the Man* by N. Richard Nash (b. 1913).[233] Nash is best known for his play *The Rainmaker* (1954), which was made into a movie with Katherine Hepburn and Burt Lancaster (1956) and recently revived on Broadway (1999), but he later turned to writing historical novels. As with other fictional treatments of Judas, the sex scenes seem gratuitously perverse (a Roman orgy that includes bestiality, the attempted incestuous rape of Mary by her brother, and numerous scenes from her days as a prostitute), but overall this is a tightly wound story that alternates between the perspectives of Judas and Mary. Significantly, Nash deliberately distances Judas from any appearance of being a revolutionary: Judas's least favorite of the other disciples is Simon Zelotes, whose violence (which he continues to practice even after he becomes a disciple) Judas abhors. Instead, Nash focuses on the love of Judas and Mary, showing how they love each other and Jesus differently. Mary's love of Jesus is confused by the issue of reciprocity: she can never really be sure that he loves her, at least not in a way that is different from his love of everyone else. In the end, she must accept him only as her "beloved," not her lover: like God, it is the only kind of love he can offer. Loving God, Jesus, or, to some degree, any other human being means accepting their silence and their enigma and loving them in spite (or because?) of it. Mary is capable of this kind of love, and this allows her and her love to survive Jesus' death and witness his resurrection. On the other hand, Judas's love of Jesus and Mary is self-destructive, not because he demands reciprocity—he seems satisfied with the kind of love they can offer him in return—but because he confuses love with knowledge. He turns Jesus over to Annas and Caiaphas because he thinks their interrogation might finally be successful at finding out Jesus' identity, which question has plagued Judas throughout the book. (Also consider the Oedipal episode at the beginning of the novel: Judas tries to kill his father because he cannot understand why his beloved father collaborates with the Romans.)[234] He cannot love Jesus or Mary without knowing them, and in the case of Jesus especially, this kind of knowledge is impossible. Dante expresses a similar idea of the difference between faith and love, on the one hand, and knowledge, on the other, as the celestial eagle addresses him concerning the saved:

> [I]t raised its voice again: "And to this realm
> none ever rose who had not faith in Christ,
> before or after he was crucified.
>
> But then there are all those who cry, 'Christ, Christ!'
> and at the Judgment Day will be less close
> to Him than will be those who know not Christ.
>
> Such Christians shall the Ethiop condemn
> the Day those two assemblies separate,
> one rich, the other poor forevermore.[235]

For Dante, it is possible to believe in Christ without knowing him. Nash's depiction of Judas raises this possibility to a necessity: one *must* love without knowledge. In the end, the novel makes an important point, that one must love God, and to some extent, other human beings, both unconditionally and without any guarantee of reciprocation; otherwise, the love is flawed and self-destructive.

Finally, although it is one of the more unlikely scenarios, William Rayner's (b. 1929) *The Knifeman* is also one of the more entertaining.[236] Rayner is best known for historical fiction, especially novels set in the American West, as well as children's fiction. Rayner transforms first-century Jerusalem into a city resembling Cold War Berlin, in which spies and double agents carry on elaborate plots under the watchful eye of a nearly all-powerful police state, while Jesus is turned into a vacant but charming character like the protagonists of *Forrest Gump* or *Being There*. Everything Judas does is under pressure from Daniel, the sadistic and diabolical Chief of the Intelligence Service. Having forced him previously to betray Jesus, Daniel now wants Judas to find out if the Nazarene is still alive. Judas is vulnerable to Daniel's threats because Judas deeply loves his wife, Ruth, who is a model of piety and devotion and a convert from the Essenes to Christianity. Daniel shows Judas the dungeon and the tortured prisoners to make it clear what will happen to her (and him) if he refuses. Judas refuses direct payment but suggests that Daniel buy a field, which he names the "Field of Blood," of which Judas could later take possession. Judas attempts to find Jesus in Jerusalem, but while he is looking, Ruth is kidnaped by the underground, which is secretly led by the double agent Joseph of Arimathea. They have done this in order to force Judas to work for them, escorting Jesus out of Jerusalem together with two of Joseph's henchmen, Nathan and Moishe. For Ruth's sake, Judas has to go with them. When he meets Jesus again, he realizes that, as the saying goes, the lights may be on, but there is nobody home: Jesus is disoriented and unresponsive, aimlessly following his escort out of town. Jesus does, however, insist on going to Galilee, which alarms his handlers. Like a James Bond villain, Nathan then reveals the whole plan to Judas. Joseph's followers have been monitoring Jesus all along: it was they who met him at the transfiguration and duped the gullible Galileans into thinking they were angels. They drugged Jesus on the cross, resuscitated him later, then let him wander around in a daze to trick him and his Galilean followers into thinking he had risen from the dead. They had planned on having him then act as a figurehead for a Zealot revolt against the Romans, but since he continued to refuse to do this, they now ask Judas to kill him. Judas pretends to go along with their plan but ambushes and kills both Moishe and Nathan in bloody and graphic knife attacks after making sure that Ruth has been released and that Jesus has safely wandered off. He tries to get back to Jerusalem to escape with Ruth, but more of Joseph's henchmen attack and kill him in the Field of Blood, where he is found by one of Daniel's spies, Saul of Tarsus, who retrieves Judas's journal from his dead body.

The book is obviously too ingenious in its devices to make the story fit the details of the Gospel accounts and too eager to titillate with its gratuitous and prurient sex scenes, which range widely from sex between Judas and Ruth, to a vivid description of gang rape in Daniel's dungeon, to a flashback of a homosexual affair that Judas had, to an orgiastic scene of necromancy performed by Simon Magus. Nonetheless, the story is undeniably suspenseful, and the device of first-person narration from Judas's perspective does bring out his character quite effectively. In particular, the anger that is typical of all the heroic depictions of Judas is vividly conveyed in passages such as the following, which is given when Judas realizes that Jesus has been broken by his ordeal and is effectively lost to all human contact:

> I jumped up and rushed out of the room. What did I feel? Resentment? Despair? Disbelief? A spasm of malice? Yes, all those things. But my hatred and my anger, as they took shape out of the chaos of my feelings, weren't directed against that patient, bewildered man I'd left sitting alone in the room. No, they were directed against the cruelties of Fate. Because this was not indifference; this was God in the role of cruel jokester. This was a cynical abasement of goodness and sacrifice. Jesus, who'd been as gorgeous in his spirit as Simon Magus was in his outward appearance, was like a splendid butterfly who'd been outraged and despoiled by boys, his wings torn off and his being

brought down to struggling impotence. If this was God's work, then what kind of God ruled the affairs of men? All the cruelties and terrors I've witnessed in my life crowded in on me—a crowd of jostling, vile, malodorous phantoms. Rotten flesh and sleek blue flies, the ignominies of the cross, Mary of Shimael astride her log, the barking nonchalance of the Roman procurator, the eyes of Daniel. All the swamps of the spirit, the humiliation forced on men, the lies and treacheries the world demands and, at the end of it all, the grinning face of Death, God's final gift to the world.[237]

If not equal in overall artistry, the passage does effectively echo in imagery and emotion Gloucester's speech in *King Lear:* "As flies to wanton boys, are we to the gods. They kill us for their sport."[238] Such lines will always resonate with anyone who has seen a loved one suffer. But I think, for all its limitations, *The Knifeman* even goes beyond a meditation on theodicy to be as hopeful a story of human triumph as one of these heroic stories of Judas can be. In the end, in the face of sadistic human cruelty and equally sadistic divine indifference, Judas's love for Ruth and Jesus does prevail and saves both of them. In a remarkable role reversal, Judas's self-sacrifice becomes the truly effective, loving act in the book: "Greater love has no man than this, that a man lay down his life for his friends" (John 15:13).

Depictions of Judas as a great lover can carry quite different emphases and conclusions. His love of women can drive him to betrayal, or despair, or heroic self-sacrifice. But all these scenarios again emphasize the basic character we have seen in almost all of the heroic depictions of Judas: he is portrayed as a man of intense passion, at once loyal and decisive but also impetuous, enraged, and embittered. His desires and drives—whether for a woman, for Jesus, for his people's freedom, for knowledge, or for justice—are powerful and all-consuming. They drive him to greatness, but when they are not satisfied, they destroy him. Judas the hero shares in a truly captivating and terrifying way all the "hideous rashness,"[239] self-destructive rage, and inquisitiveness of his pre-Christian analog, Oedipus, and also that of Christian tragic heroes such as Lear or Othello.

Chapter Five

Judas the Penitent:

Object of Hope and Emulation

Judas before God:
The Most Hopeful Traditions of Judas

We turn finally to the most hopeful traditions about Judas, those that consider his final fate to be one of salvation. These consider him mostly from the divine rather than the human perspective. If Judas repented as Matthew reports, how could God deny this repentance and condemn Judas? This flies in the face of everything Jesus taught of repentance. Or from a different divine perspective, if Judas's act led directly to Jesus' salvific death on the cross, perhaps it was part of God's plan all along. It would then not be a horrible aberration of human sinfulness, selfishness, and shortsightedness but the ultimate surrender to a divine plan that is awful and inscrutable, but one that must be obeyed and must lead to redemption, not condemnation.

Matthew

Judas figures in five narratives in Matthew (10:1–4; 26:14–16, 20–25, 47–56; 27:3–10), the first four of which are taken over from Mark. Judas is again at the end of the list of the twelve disciples (Matt. 10:4), with the same designation as "the one who handed him over."

The last four episodes involving Judas occur in Matthew's passion narrative, where his wording is even closer to Mark's than in the rest of the Gospel.[1] Indeed, it has been estimated that 80 percent "of the Matthean Passion story is identical in vocabulary and content with its Markan counterpart."[2] All the more significant, then, are his changes in the Markan text in which he elaborates on Judas.[3] In the next episode with Judas, Matthew again follows Mark for the most part: Judas approaches the chief priests immediately after the loving act of the anointing woman. Matthew has made it "the disciples" who object to her act,[4] thereby implicating Judas in their general incomprehension, though in no way singling him out. Matthew has also elaborated on the Markan text: "Then one of the twelve, the one called Judas Iscariot, went to the chief priests and said, 'What are you willing to give me if I hand him over to you?' And they counted out thirty silver pieces. And from then on he sought an opportunity to hand him over" (Matt. 26:14–16). The change is slight but significant. It is Judas who initiates the exchange of money, not the chief priests. As we will see, this is not done to impugn Judas's character; nor does it really provide a believable motive, as the amount involved is so small.[5] It is done to give a scriptural allusion and especially to provide a link with the later story of Judas's death (Matt. 27:3–10).[6] The Scriptural allusion here is problematic, as the wording is so close to Zechariah 11:12 that some connection cannot be denied.[7] But on the other hand, the context hardly seems apt: what are we to make of Matthew portraying Judas as the good shepherd of Zechariah 11?[8] I think the problem arises from focusing too much on Judas and trying to make the allegory fit him, when the scriptural allusion is really intended to explain the money, not the role of Judas. The point of the thirty shekels in Zechariah 11:12 is that it is a paltry, insulting amount, with the added implication of it being the price of a slave (Exod. 21:32).[9] When put this way, the application to Matthew 26:15 seems clearer: Judas has sold his master as one would a slave, and at the same time he has ironically sold himself far too cheaply by accepting such a shameful sum for his services.

Matthew also adds dialogue in his account of the Last Supper. After predicting that one of the disciples will hand him over, and after pronouncing the "woe" upon that disciple (all in words almost identical to Mark's), Matthew adds, "Judas, the one who handed him over, said, 'It isn't me, is it, rabbi?' He said to him, 'You say so'" (26:25). It may be that "rabbi" in Judas's question is meant to set him apart from the other disciples who here address Jesus as "Lord" (26:22) and put him on the side of Jesus' enemies;[10] however, at one other point in Matthew Jesus does accept the title (23:8), so a negative connotation to the title cannot be certain.[11] However, Judas's use of the title here does anticipate his use of it at the arrest of Jesus, and in that sense it carries negative connotations. Judas's question and Jesus' response are clearly inserted here to heighten Judas's hypocrisy and guilt, as he is already in the employ of the chief priests.[12] Jesus' response is very similar to what he will offer his other enemies, Caiaphas (26:64) and Pilate (27:11), later in the passion narrative, as he agrees and submits to their correct but misguided perception of him.[13]

At Jesus' arrest (26:47–56) the major addition Matthew makes is to add the obscure saying, "Friend, do what you have come for" (26:50). Given Matthew's usage elsewhere (20:13; 22:12), "friend" (ἐταῖρε) seems ironically negative here, denoting someone who is behaving in anything but a friendly manner.[14] The rest of the saying is obscure,[15] and however translated, it does not give us any particular interpretation of Judas's act but rather shows Jesus' reaction to it. He submits to it, and this makes perfect sense in Matthew's passion narrative, where Jesus' submission and obedience are constantly stressed despite his desire (26:36–46) and power (26:53–54) to change the course of events.[16] The scene does not show us anything new about Judas but focuses squarely on Jesus.

It is in the next scene that Matthew adds new material about Judas. In a text unparalleled in Mark, Matthew tells of Judas's fate subsequent to Jesus' arrest:

> When Judas, the one who handed him over, saw that he was condemned, he repented and brought back the thirty pieces of silver to the chief priests and the elders, saying, "I have sinned by handing over innocent blood." They said, "What is that to us? See to it yourself." And throwing down the pieces of silver in the temple, he left; and he went and hanged himself. But the chief priests, taking the pieces of silver, said, "It is not lawful to put them into the treasury, since they are blood money." So they took counsel, and bought with them the potter's field, to bury foreigners in. Therefore that field has been called the Field of Blood to this day. Then was fulfilled what had been spoken by the prophet Jeremiah, saying, "And they took the thirty pieces of silver, the price of him on whom a price had been set by some of the sons of Israel, and they gave them for the potter's field, as the Lord directed me." (Matt. 27:3–10)

This is the largest block of material inserted by Matthew into the Markan passion account.[17] Since Matthew has been following Mark so closely in the narrative, such a sizeable addition as this seems all the more significant. What is Matthew's purpose in telling this story?

First, Matthew has carefully crafted this story to fit with the material he has taken over from Mark, including in it material that is the continuation or culmination of the previous stories of Judas:[18] the collusion of the chief priests with Judas (Mark 14:10–11//Matt. 26:14–16); the money paid for Jesus (Mark 14:11//Matt. 26:15); and Jesus' words about the one who would hand him over (Mark 14:21//Matt. 26:24). It is this last point that caused Matthew to make this addition, because in the Markan narrative,

Jesus' words about the one who would hand him over had never been fulfilled, unlike his words on the arrest or Peter's denial. Matthew thus found the following gap in the Markan narrative:

Jesus' words	Fulfillment
On his being handed over (Mark 14:18–20)	Jesus' arrest (Mark 14:43–50)
On the one handing him over (Mark 14:21)	
On Peter's denial (Mark 14:27–31)	Peter's denial (Mark 14:66–72)

Matthew was extremely interested that the words of Jesus be fulfilled within the Gospel itself, and he therefore included this story of Judas's death to provide just such a fulfillment.[19]

But this is only a beginning. If Matthew's only purpose were to narrate Judas's death, parallel to Peter's denial, then the story could have ended at verse 5. Also, a more gruesome death might have been deemed more appropriate, an interpretation that has led many to wonder whether Matthew intends an allusion here to the suicide of Ahithophel, the unfaithful counselor of David: "When Ahithophel saw that his counsel was not followed, he saddled his donkey and went off home to his own city. He set his house in order, and hanged himself" (2 Sam. 17:23). The verbal similarity is minimal—only the one word "hanged himself" (ἀπήγξατο)—though the fact that Ahithophel and Judas are the only two people in the Bible "to hang" themselves makes the similarity biblically unique and therefore more persuasive to many.[20] My own thinking on this has changed,[21] and I do not think now that Matthew had the story of Ahithophel in mind as he composed his story of the death of Judas. The verbal similarity is so slight as to carry almost no weight, and Ahithophel's situation would not seem to lend itself to Matthew's purposes. Although a parallel between Jesus and David would make perfect sense in Matthew's Gospel, Ahithophel killed himself because his advice was not followed while Judas kills himself because of regret that his advice was followed too well. Ahithophel killed himself out of fear of the consequences of his actions; in Matthew, Judas imposes the consequences on himself.[22]

In what sense Judas "repented" for what he did is another crucial point of interpretation in the passage. Since the verb used here (μεταμέλομαι) is not the usual one (μετνοέω) for repentance, it has often been taken to mean that Matthew is portraying Judas as not repenting in the full, religious sense but only as changing his mind[23] as the verb seems to mean in the other places that Matthew uses it (21:29, 32).[24] Again, my thought on this has changed.[25] In light of Judas's admission, "I have sinned" (v. 4), I do not see how one could take his repentance here as anything other than a complete acknowledgment and repudiation of his sinfulness.[26] He admits his sin publicly, casts away all gains he has made by it, breaks his connection with his collaborators, and punishes himself.[27] I do not think that someone who has only "changed his mind" about his sin would do all this: he would only regret the bad consequences of his actions, or at the most, regret his actions because of their bad consequences. But Matthew has Judas go much further and accept his guilt. I cannot think of what more would be required in order to say that he repented in the fullest sense, unless it is to ask for forgiveness and mercy (an act that Peter also is not yet capable of in the parallel scene of his denial [Matt. 26:69–75]). But is this strictly speaking a part of repentance, or is it an act of faith that follows repentance? I believe that Matthew gives us a depiction of Judas in which he repents completely but does not believe in the possibility that Jesus or God could forgive him.[28] And for Matthew this would clearly represent a faulty concept of God and God's forgiveness but not therefore an incomplete experience of repentance.

Although it is Judas's death that usually most interests readers, it is the silver pieces that most interest Matthew and that hold this narrative together[29] as well as tie this story back to the earlier story of Judas's agreement with the chief priests (Matt. 26:14–16). Judas's death is described in the first half of the story (vv. 3–5) and the purchase of the potter's field in the second (vv. 6–10), but the silver pieces figure in both parts (vv. 3, 5, 6, 7, 9, 10). Matthew uses the silver pieces to transfer guilt from Judas to the chief priests: the money is "blood money" (v. 6), and the blood it bought was "innocent blood" (v. 4), so the money carries the guilt for Jesus' death with it. Judas disposes of this guilt and gives it back to the chief priests.[30] For Matthew, Judas was only temporarily the instrument of evil while the chief priests, "some of the sons of Israel" (v. 9), are consistently and implacably opposed to Jesus (and to God). Therefore, rather than have the guilt rest with Judas or have it be expiated by his death, Matthew makes sure that the reader knows it is the chief priests who are really guilty of Jesus' death by having them symbolically accept their guilt in the form of the money; he may even intend this story to increase their guilt by blaming them with Judas's death as well.[31]

Matthew uses the chief priests' quandary over what to do with the "blood money" to connect the story of Judas's death with an independent story about a "Field of Blood" somewhere in Jerusalem. That the Field of Blood is an independent tradition seems likely, as it is not redactionally necessary to the story, and it is about the only detail Matthew shares with the story of Judas's death in Acts 1:16–20.[32] Matthew uses this independent tradition to end the narrative part of the story and link it to the prophecy-fulfillment text of verses 9–10.

Matthew begins this fulfillment text with an unusual connective (τότε instead of his usual ἵνα or ὅπως).[33] Matthew thus separates the two times in which one of Jesus' enemies are said to have fulfilled scripture (Herod at 2:17; the chief priests here), for they do so unwittingly and not in submission to divine purpose even though their actions still indirectly contribute to and become a part of the divine plan.[34] The divine plan does not force evil deeds, but neither can it be thwarted by them.

The prophecy to which Matthew is referring is problematic: this "conglomeration of words cited by Matt exists *nowhere* in the standard OT."[35] The clearest reference is to Zechariah 11:13, thereby tying this text back to the earlier mention of the silver pieces (Matt. 26:15). From Zechariah 11:13 Matthew took the reference to the throwing of the thirty silver pieces as well as a wordplay on "potter" (Matt. 27:7, 10; Zech. 11:13 in the Masoretic text) and "treasury" (Matt. 27:6; Zech. 11:13 in the Septuagint reads "foundry" instead of "potter," probably referring to the Temple treasury).[36] The thirty silver pieces are thrown by Judas into the Temple (v. 5) but cannot go into the treasury (v. 6), and eventually end up with the potter whose field is bought (vv. 7 and 10).

But Matthew attributes the prophecy to Jeremiah. This has led some commentators to describe Matthew's process here as a "slip or . . . confusion."[37] Others have hypothesized an apocryphal version of Jeremiah that contained this passage, but we have no evidence other than the Matthean passage to suggest such.[38] Finally, others have looked for passages in Jeremiah that would fit this context, especially ones that would fill in the final detail of the purchase of a potter's field that becomes a burial plot. This has caused many to suggest Jeremiah 18 and 32, the potter being from the former and the purchase of a field from the latter.[39] But there are no other connections between these and the Matthean text, nor are the two Jeremiah texts closely related. If Matthew is here referring to them, it is only in the sense that he lifted two unrelated details from them and inserted them into his story.[40]

This scenario is certainly possible. Indeed, under any reconstruction we will have to admit that Matthew combines two or more prophetic texts, at least one of which is not from Jeremiah. But I think that Gundry's reconstruction using Jeremiah 19 is the more likely one,[41] especially since it provides a catchword between all three texts: the "potter" (Zech. 11:13; Jer. 19:1, 11; Matt. 27:7, 10).[42] If we include the other Jeremiah texts, then there is no such catchword unifying Matthew's choice of texts, and he is making connections between texts in some unrecoverable way, a scenario that must mitigate against such a reconstruction. And if we make the connection to Jeremiah 19:1–13, the parallels with Matthew's story are considerable: besides the "potter," there is "innocent blood" (Jer. 19:4; Matt. 27:4); the prophecy is directed against "the elders and the priests" (Jer. 19:1; Matt. 27:3, 6), there is a burial ground in both (Jer. 19:11; Matt. 27:7, 10); and there is a similar renaming of the land ("Valley of Slaughter," Jer. 19:6; "Field of Blood," Matt. 27:8).

All in all, the most likely scenario would seem to be that Matthew composes this prophecy fulfillment text out of Zechariah 11:13 and Jeremiah 19:1–13 and ascribes it to Jeremiah because the parts drawn from Jeremiah are the less obvious ones.[43] And although the prophetic texts referred to may be obscure, Matthew's purpose seems much less so: as prefigured in the prophetic texts, the chief priests again unjustly bought the life of an innocent man for thirty silver pieces (Zech. 11:13), accepted back the tainted money, and bought a piece of land that symbolized their own sinfulness and the wrathful, deadly destruction it would bring (Jer. 19:1–13).[44] In all of this Judas has receded into the background, and the focus is on "the total and complete rejection of Jesus by the Jewish leaders, a rejection that fit perfectly into their sinful pattern in the Old Testament."[45]

Finally, Matthew makes his narrative consistent by referring to "the eleven" at the very end of his Gospel, giving us one last reminder of Judas and his death.[46]

To conclude: Matthew follows Mark's depiction of Judas for the most part, keeping and elaborating the painful irony of the failure of one of Jesus' disciples. Matthew also accentuates Jesus' knowledge of and submission to the divine plan. But Matthew is not wholly satisfied with Mark's story of Judas. In particular, it had left one of Jesus' sayings unfulfilled within the narrative. So Matthew constructs a story that shows how Jesus' words were fulfilled. He also constructs this story to show once again that Jesus' life and death fulfilled the scriptures; he even retrojects the scriptural allusion back to an earlier mention of Judas (Matt. 26:15) in order to tie the whole structure together. He also uses this story to implicate further the consistent villains of his Gospel, the chief priests: they more than Judas are guilty of rejecting and killing Jesus. Matthew carefully portrays their rejection as also in fulfillment of scripture.

But while doing all this consciously and deliberately, Matthew also creates the most memorable and influential depiction of Judas, one that makes Judas into more than just a cipher that fills a narrative role. By further implicating the chief priests, Matthew has significantly mitigated Judas's sin;[47] and by portraying his death as a suicide, Matthew has made it tragic, even noble.[48] In Matthew Judas becomes the repentant sinner who angrily and ineffectually tries to undo his sin, who cannot see the light of grace and forgiveness, and who dies tragically in despair. It is perhaps the greatest witness to Matthew's genius that he could almost inadvertently invent this story that embraces such extremes. Matthew's story is simultaneously the greatest example of repentance, showing that there is no sinner who is so far gone that he cannot reject and repudiate his sin, and also the greatest tragedy of human pride and despair being unmoved by divine grace, which cannot save unless it is humbly and absurdly believed in.

Judas the Ultimate Penitent and Universal Guilt

Matthew's story of Judas has been perhaps the most influential, since it is the most elaborate and nuanced. In it Judas is not a stereotype of "the Jews," nor is he demonized as a man of unmitigated evil. Instead, he almost rises to the level of a complete and rounded character in Matthew's story, and he is not simply a character of complete evil but one that Matthew has spent some care crafting and with whom he has some sympathy. In particular, in his account of Judas's death, Matthew has created the version that has most influenced later accounts, for it is here that we find the hint of the possibility of repentance and forgiveness even for Judas. Was even Judas forgiven? Is he, or could he be, even now dwelling in Abraham's bosom?

The earliest speculation we have on these questions is surprisingly optimistic in its evaluation of the possibility of Judas's salvation. Origen (ca. 185–254 C.E.), whose ideas about fate formed the nucleus of the Oedipal stories about Judas, also provided the beginning of a long tradition in which the betrayer is neither completely wicked nor completely lost:

> For he that betrayed Him gave to the multitude that came to apprehend Jesus a sign, saying, "Whomsoever I shall kiss, it is he; seize ye him,"—retaining still some element of respect for his Master: for unless he had done so, he would have betrayed Him, even publicly,

without any pretence of affection. This circumstance, therefore, will satisfy all with regard to the purpose of Judas, that along with his covetous disposition, and his wicked design to betray his Master, he had still a feeling of a mixed character in his mind, produced in him by the words of Jesus, which had the appearance (so to speak) of some remnant of good. . . . But if this covetous Judas, who also stole the money placed in the bag for the relief of the poor, repented, and brought back the thirty pieces of silver to the chief priests and elders, it is clear that the instructions of Jesus had been able to produce some feeling of repentance in his mind, and were not altogether despised and loathed by this traitor. Nay, the declaration, "I have sinned, in that I have betrayed the innocent blood," was a public acknowledgment of his crime. Observe, also, how exceedingly passionate was the sorrow for his sins that proceeded from that repentance, and which would not suffer him any longer to live; and how, after he had cast the money down in the temple, he withdrew, and went away and hanged himself: for he passed sentence upon himself, showing what a power the teaching of Jesus had over this sinner Judas, this thief and traitor, who could not always treat with contempt what he had learned from Jesus. . . . [These are] proofs which show that the apostasy of Judas was not a complete apostasy, even after his attempts against his master.[49]

Every detail of the betrayal—even including the treacherous kiss—is taken here as proof of some residual goodness and some continuation of Jesus' message. Even the fact that Judas stole proves his goodness for Origen, as it proves his avarice[50] and therefore proves the depth and sincerity of his repentance when he casts back the money. For Origen, Judas's repentance was sincere and complete: his fatal mistake was to follow this repentance with a futile act of passing "sentence on himself." Given how prominent Satan is in Origen's interpretation of the betrayal,[51] he may have thought that Satan prompted Judas to suicide, either by despair or by a misguided idea that he could precede Christ to Hades and there receive forgiveness (an idea that recurs in many subsequent versions of the story).[52] As the passage shows, for Origen all of this comes back to the power of Jesus' message and the power of God's love, all of it is an "expression of Origen's belief in the reconciliation of the cosmos."[53] If Judas cannot be saved, then it is not a sign of his failure but a much more problematic sign of the failure of divine love and forgiveness. As we shall see, this connection between Judas's fate and our own becomes the crucial point in these stories of Judas.

Such tantalizing ambiguities and questions about Judas's fate were further elaborated in the Middle Ages in versions that relied on that of Theophylactus (eleventh century C.E.):[54]

> Some say that Judas, being covetous, supposed that he could both make money by betraying Christ, and yet Christ not be killed, but escape from the Jews as he often did escape. But when he saw him now condemned and judged to die, he repented because the affair had turned out other than he supposed it would. And this was why he hanged himself, in order that he might get to hades before Jesus, and there implore him and obtain salvation. You must know, however, that he actually put his neck into the noose, having hanged himself on a certain tree; but the tree bent down and he continued to live, because it was God's will either to reserve him for repentance or for open disgrace and shame. For they say that he had the dropsy, so that he could hardly pass where a carriage could easily pass; and then he fell on his face and burst asunder, as Luke says in Acts.[55]

There are many interesting aspects to Theophylactus's version, not the least of which is his harmonization of the Papias tradition with Matthew's and Luke's, in which he seems to regard canonical and noncanonical versions as equally worthy of inclusion.[56] But besides this, Theophylactus elaborates on the idea that Judas killed himself in order to meet Christ in the afterlife and there beg him for forgiveness, a poignantly powerful image that still surfaces in some depictions of Judas.[57] Theophylactus depicts this attempt as unsuccessful and misguided because God wants full, unambiguous, and open repentance from Judas. But it is important that Theophylactus does not rule out this final possibility—that Judas attempted suicide, failed, and then lived a life of repentance and therefore must be saved—if everything Christ preached about forgiveness is to be taken seriously. Theophylactus's version is as coy as Matthew's about its meaning or conclusion, leaving it up to the audience to decide whether they want to believe Judas was saved or damned.

As we have repeatedly seen, the tradition likes to resolve ambiguities, and this is exactly what is done to Theophylactus's version by Vinzenz Ferrer (1350–1419) in a sermon from 1391:

> Judas who betrayed and sold the Master after the crucifixion was overwhelmed by a genuine and saving sense of remorse and tried with all his might to draw close to Christ in order to apologize for his betrayal and sale. But since Jesus was accompanied by such a large crowd of people on the way to the mount of Calvary, it was impossible for Judas

to come to him and so he said to himself: Since I cannot get to the feet of the master, I will approach him in my spirit at least and humbly ask him for forgiveness. He actually did that and as he took the rope and hanged himself his soul rushed to Christ on Calvary's mount, asked for forgiveness and received it fully from Christ, went up to heaven with him and so his soul enjoys salvation with all elect.[58]

Judas's story becomes unambiguously the greatest example of the triumph of the gospel over sin and death, as even the worst sinner is now with Jesus in heaven.

Even the late medieval passion plays, which we noted earlier for their virulent anti-Semitism, show some softening in their depiction of Judas, though they still tie him to what they believe is the typically Jewish sin of avarice:

> I have committed such a great act of betrayal,
> and for such a small amount of money.
> How could I have sold for thirty denarii
> my Lord, who was completely righteous.
> I gave him up for a small price,
> my sweet Master Jesus Christ.[59]

Here we are still closely tied to anti-Semitism, as Judas only reproaches himself for how low a price he demanded. But even within these anti-Semitic slurs, there is some attempt to understand and even sympathize with Judas. When Jesus calls Judas to be an apostle, the author adds these strange statements:

> "And now I grant this to you,
> for I wish you to be the purse-bearer
> henceforth, and to dispense
> everything that is given to us:
> the money will pass through your hands.
> You will be the banker of our common funds
> and from every ten denarii you will take one
> in order to support your family.
> So you may support yourself,
> but do your job carefully."[60]

John's accusation that Judas stole from the common funds is here explained away as a loving concession on Jesus' part to care for the family of his trusted apostle. One of the most significant, negative additions to the story has been turned into something positive.[61]

Some of the versions of the passion plays raise Judas's character and his repentance to an even higher level, in which he really confronts his evil and tries to undo it:

> Sir, Caiaphas, if you please,
> give me back my Lord,
> and I will return to you the denarii,
> for which I sold my Holy King,
> who is the Lord most righteous.
> I gave him up for thirty denarii.
> Oh! I am wretched, for I have done evil.
> I have betrayed my Lord,
> sold him and given him over to death.
> This was wrathful and mistaken,
> for He was my good Lord,
> Who gave me great honor.
> And I have paid him back with evil!
> Oh, the evil hour when I was born,
> cursed be the one who carried me!
> Better if I had been torn
> from her belly, than to have carried me.
> I have sinned most severely,
> that I cannot be saved.
> I will suffer for all the evil I have done.
> Sirs, what can I do?
> Everything confounds me!
> I cannot be in the earth,
> nor can I rise up to the sky,
> because I am full of sin.
> I am completely in despair.
> Of all people,
> I am the most wicked.[62]

In one version the author constructs a lengthy dialogue between Judas and a personified Despair, in which Judas defends and elaborates the qualities of his repentance:

> You make the conclusion
> that I must be taken away by death.
> But I have made my confession,
> in which I have said that I have sinned.

Then I made restitution
by giving back the denarii.
And then I felt such contrition
that just a little bit of it would break my heart.[63]

This is not the comic villain of earlier passion plays but a truly distraught, sympathetic, and reasonable character. Even these versions begin to show some sympathy for Judas and depict his repentance as poignant, sincere, and well thought out, even if they still believe it is not necessarily effective.

Theophylactus's version of Judas's suicide as unsuccessful because of the pliability of the tree he chose appears in many European legends about the nature and characteristics of various trees.[64] Among the species proposed as the one on which Judas hanged himself are the fig, sycamore, elder,[65] willow, grape vine (!), aspen, tamarind, oak, dog rose, poplar, and redbud.[66] (The idea that Judas hanged himself on a tree seems to have been more popular than his hanging himself on a man-made structure.)[67] Although these legends seek to explain some characteristic of the particular species—its size, odor, color, etc.—and therefore are only peripherally interested in Judas's story, they nonetheless leave tantalizing traces of his story. Theophylactus's story of the bending of the tree and Judas's desire to get to Hades before Christ figures prominently in several:

. . . when Judas hanged himself on an aspen the tree bowed its branches so that the traitor's feet touched the ground and he could not die. The tree did this lest Judas die before the Savior, and, arriving in Hell before him, be freed in the harrowing of Hell. Judas hung alive on the lower branch until his Master had returned to earth, when the tree straightened itself, tightening the cord about his neck so that he died. . . . Judas the traitor knew that Christ would bring out all those who were in Hell. So when he had betrayed his Master, he planned to leave the Garden and keep the money. Then he ran to hang himself in order to reach Hell before Christ. He ran to one tree to hang himself to its branches, but it bowed to the ground; and a second one did the same. He ran and ran, but no tree would take him. It meant that our Lord did not wish his suicide but his repentance; Judas had no desire to repent of his crime, but wished only to hang himself so that he might reach Hell as quickly as possible. He realized that haste was necessary. Finally he caught sight of a sunken road, and on the edge of it a tree which was on the point of falling over. Judas hastened to it and the tree fell on him with such violence that his eyes were squeezed out of his forehead. But he had failed to reach Hell before his Master, who had already freed the souls there. Thus Judas, still bearing his purse, was the first to come to Hell after Christ's visit.[68]

Although these two legends explicitly interpret Judas's desire to meet Christ as mere legalistic trickery and not real regret, there are some stories in which the availability of forgiveness, even to Judas, is prominent:

> Then Judas rose and rushed out to hang himself. Christ called after him, "Return, O Judas, your sin is forgiven, and your punishment remitted." But Judas did not hear, and ran until he reached a forest. To the pine he said, "Your wood is too soft, and my sin too heavy; you, pine, cannot bear me." He hanged himself on an aspen and from that moment it has quivered and trembled as it will do until the Day of Judgment.[69]

As brief and childlike as such a story may seem to us, one cannot help hearing some sympathy for Judas when the legend has him say, "Your wood is too soft, and my sin too heavy." It is, at the very least, a clear and unambiguous admission of guilt.

On the other hand, Judas's repentance can be turned into a story of mere hypocrisy and empty legalistic trickery, as in the short story "Judas Iscariot," by W. Doroschewitch.[70] Here it is not Judas's betrayal for which he is blamed but his repentance. He considers hanging himself but does not. Instead, he asks for the silver back. The servant of the high priest cheats him and only returns twenty pieces, which Judas uses to set up business as a money lender in Egypt.[71] At first, he intends to use the gains to help the poor, but this is quickly forgotten, and he lives a normal life of money-grubbing, a respected and successful member of his community. As he is dying a peaceful death at a very old age, he tells those around him that he has committed sins in the past and that he "shall bear them myself and bring them before the Throne of the Almighty. He will put upon one scale my whole life and upon the other one my only sin, an error of youth, a seduction of the Devil!"[72] Like a Nazi war criminal in South America, Judas never really repents in this story; he simply wishes to forget (and have everyone else forget) his terrible past while imagining (and having others imagine) that his life of complete normalcy is in fact a life of great and noble virtue and self-sacrifice. The story shows (in a rather heavy-handed way) that repentance is neither forgetfulness nor restitution. Either of these reactions is possible (and probably preferable to real repentance), but they leave the pollution of sin untouched: "Rain and wind have since washed away the tomb of Judas, erased it completely—as one washes away a dirty stain."[73] Here there is none of the profundity of real repentance, so vividly described by Michel de Montaigne (1533–1592): "It is not a spot, it is rather a tincture with which I am stained all over. I know no superficial, halfway, and perfunctory repentance. It must affect me in every part before I will call it so, and must grip me by the vitals and afflict them as deeply and as completely as God sees into me."[74]

But even without proper repentance, the popular imagination has long thought that Judas could be forgiven or his punishment at least mitigated, as seen in the tenth-century *Voyage of St. Brendan.*[75] While sailing with his monks southward in the Atlantic, Brendan finds Judas sitting on a rock in the middle of the sea, quite comfortable, with two hooks holding a piece of cloth in front of his face to protect him from the wind, though it annoys him by flapping in his eyes. He explains that he is allowed to sit there every Sunday and goes on to describe the rest of his week as considerably less pleasant: Monday, blown about by violent winds; Tuesday, dragged around and then bound on a bed of spikes; Wednesday, boiled in tar and then roasted; Thursday, frozen by terrible cold; Friday, skin flayed off, rolled in salt, and made to drink molten lead and copper; Saturday, locked in a stinking dungeon. (It is interesting that the torments on the two days adjacent to Sunday also seem to be ameliorated, so the relative amnesty really lasts for almost half of all eternity.) The objects providing him relief are relics of the only three good deeds he ever did: he put the rock in a ditch so people could walk over it; he gave the hooks to the priests in the temple; and he gave the cloth to a leper, though it causes him annoyance because he bought it with money stolen from the common purse. When it was rendered into English, the "hooks" became "tongs," and these were then mistaken for "tongues," as in the verse rendering of Sebastian Evans (1830–1909):

> For He whom the gates of the hells obey,
> Each winter hath granted me here to stay
> From Christmas Eve for a night and a day.
> And this is my paradise, here alone
> To sit with my cloth and tongues and stone,
> The sole three things in the world mine own.
>
> The cloth I bought from the Lord's privy purse,
> But gave to a leper. It hath this curse,
> That it beats on my skin, but it saves from worse.

These tongues I gave to the poor for meat,
In the name of Christ—and the fish that eat
Thereon as they list—forebear my feet.

This stone I found by a road where it lay,
And set for a step in a miry way:
Therefore sit I on stone, not ice, this day![76]

This part of Brendan's story has survived and is still well known long after the Middle Ages:[77] Matthew Arnold (1822–1888) and Rudyard Kipling (1865–1936) also wrote poems of Judas's day of rest, both putting him on an iceberg instead of a rock.[78] Although the tradition obviously delights in heaping numerous and grotesque punishments on the damned, at the same time, there has long been a belief that all the damned periodically receive some relief from their suffering. This belief goes back at least to the fourth century and was tolerated if not endorsed by Augustine: "But let them think, if they so wish, that the pains of the damned are mitigated to an extent at certain intervals of time."[79] Although Judas might be expected to enjoy this general periodic amnesty, Brendan's story seems to single him out as a special example of the power of divine forgiveness: "If there is nothing in the earliest versions of the Brendan legend to suggest a meeting with Judas at the Smoky Mountain, why did a tenth-century redactor add it unless to register a conviction that the lovingkindness of Jesus had embraced Judas?"[80] Judas's story becomes one not of judgment but of mercy, as divine love repeatedly (if not completely) triumphs over human sin and intransigence through all eternity.

In the early eighteenth century the Rev. Samuel Moodey (1676–1747) published a pamphlet on the fate of Judas.[81] Moodey (often spelled Moody) graduated from Harvard in 1697. He was a minister of the Congregational Church in New England and the great-great-grandfather of Ralph Waldo Emerson. He was also said to be a man of extremely violent temper, taking to wielding an axe against Catholic (he would have said "Romish" or "Popish") churches during the French and Indian War (Seven Years War), so his (relatively) kind treatment of Judas is perhaps surprising.[82] In *Judas the Traitor*, he begins by using Judas as an example of a terrible sinner, an example that he considers especially chastening, since if one who was so close to Jesus could fall, the danger is even greater for others. He then goes on to a vivid description of the torments of hell. It concludes with a *Dialogue* in which an unidentified questioner interrogates an unidentified sinner and the sinner is brought to repentance and salvation. Could the sinner be Judas? Moodey never says so explicitly, but the caption title of *Judas the Traitor* is *Judas' Fall Improved*, which is the title to which the later pamphlet refers. Moodey has at least invited the identification, and his description of the sinner's final step to salvation sounds oddly like Judas: "No sinner shall die eternally, that is bro't thus to justify God, and judge and condemn himself."[83] Judas's last act is one of self-condemnation, and it is one that comes awfully close to saving him, as noted also in the version of Samuel Pearce Carey (b. 1862), great-grandson of the famous Baptist missionary William Carey: "Little is permanently done for any man, till he has been empowered to know and to judge himself."[84] This possibility of Judas's salvation is also vividly portrayed in a painting by Sascha Schneider (1870–1927),[85] in which Judas offers the money not to the chief priests but to Jesus. Even with this change, however, the artist leaves us guessing, as in the painting a devil and an angel are standing beside Judas, each grabbing a shoulder, and it is not clear who will have him in the end. In these versions, Judas's story does not teach us about his damnation; it teaches us about the likelihood of our own damnation, for everyone is just as guilty as Judas, and our repentance is often just as imperfect.

Rev. Moodey's more famous contemporary Johann Sebastian Bach (1685–1750) also used the image of Judas to teach about repentance in his *St. Matthew Passion*.[86] Judas sings a dissonant tritone (known in the Middle Ages as "The Devil's Interval" and scrupulously avoided in composition) in the first and last recitative in which he appears in the *Passion*, a musical representation of his destructive abandonment of Jesus and finally of himself. Also in these recitatives, it is the accompaniment rather than Judas that moves the piece away from the key in which it is written, a signal that sin or fate now controls him, as the accompaniment controls him musically. But in two arias associated with Judas, 51 and 75, we hear a fuller appropriation of Judas's character. In aria 51, the bass soloist echoes Judas's words to the chief priests by singing over and over, "Give me back my Jesus!"—a line that echoes the medieval passion plays of three hundred years earlier. The piece is accompanied by violin and strings, which are usually associated with Jesus in the *Passion*, but here their sound is not soothing and ethereal but martial, furious, and completely human. Judas's self-destructive anger at the chief priests and at himself is powerfully and sympathetically conveyed here. And this anger is transformed and redirected in aria 75, the only aria after Christ's death and the last aria in the *Passion*. The piece is no longer angry and strident but mellowed by the oboe in the accompaniment and the slow, reverent tone of the music. But when the bass sings, "Make thee clean, my heart, from sin. . . . Unto Jesus give thou welcome. . . . World depart; let Jesus in!" it still sounds somewhat like Judas's angry command. This command, however, is not directed outward at some implacable and unalterable force, like the chief priests, or the past, or fate: it is directed inward to the human heart, the only object of one's control, and the essence of one's being and meaning. The bass soloist invites us to direct an anger like Judas's against our own sinful hearts in order to cleanse them and make them a home capable of receiving a divine presence. Although looking at his own sin destroys Judas, Bach's musical appropriation of it invites us to use his anger as a transformative rather than a destructive power in our lives.

The image of everyone sharing in Judas's guilt is also found explicitly in works such as D. B. Lutyens's play, *Judas Iscariot*.[87] Judas begins the play as a demonic figure. When asked whether he loves Jesus, he gives the following answer:

> JUDAS: I do.
>   As darkness loves light;
>   As cold loves fire;
>   Love I the Lord. . . .
>   Even so; would not the Devil
>   sing a Magnificat, if he could believe?
>   He
>   is condemned to deny, through all eternity. . . .
>   my heart is a cold fire
>   burns, gives no warmth,
>   hungers, and thirsts. I glorify the Lord.[88]

But Judas ends the play completely identified with the other characters and with the audience: "There is not one in the whole world, who can sustain the charge, and say, 'Lord, I am not guilty.' Upon that day, we assumed inexpiable guilt."[89] Perpetual antagonism to God has been lifted from the devil and placed on all of us: we are as much enemies of God as Satan or Judas is.[90]

The image of Judas and his guilt is also taken up implicitly in Fyodor Dostoyevsky's (1821–1881) *The Brothers Karamazov*. The suicide by hanging of the parricide Smerdyakov resembles Judas's death, as does the description of his frame of mind as one of despair without remorse:

> But why, why, asks the prosecutor, did Smerdyakov not confess in his last letter? Why did his conscience prompt him to one step and not

to both? But, excuse me, conscience implies penitence, and the suicide may not have felt penitence, but only despair. Despair and penitence are two very different things. Despair may be vindictive and irreconcilable, and the suicide, laying his hands on himself, may well have felt redoubled hatred for those whom he had envied all his life.[91]

And Dostoyevsky paradoxically offers the idea of universal guilt as the remedy to this despair in his brilliant character of Father Zossima, who believes deeply that "every one of us has sinned against all men,"[92] but in a way that brings joy, not despair:

> My friends, pray to God for gladness. Be glad as children, as the birds of heaven. And let not the sin of men confound you in your doings. Fear not that it will wear away your work and hinder its being accomplished. Do not say, "Sin is mighty, wickedness is mighty, evil environment is mighty, and we are lonely and helpless. Evil environment is wearing us away and hindering our good work from being done." Fly from that dejection! There is only one means of salvation. Make yourself responsible for all men's sins. As soon as you sincerely make yourself responsible for everything and for all men, you will see at once that you have found salvation. On the other hand by throwing your indolence and impotence on others you will end by sharing the pride of Satan and murmuring against God.[93]

It is the mutuality and interconnectedness that we have between ourselves, and between ourselves and God, that makes this thought liberating and not oppressive. As we shall see, this idea has been powerfully reaffirmed in several modern theologians' ideas on Judas.[94] Stories in which Judas cannot see his interconnectedness with Jesus, God, and others can only end with his death in despair.

Another version of Judas's story that stresses human interdependence in guilt, repentance, and forgiveness is the play *Spikenard* by Charles Edward Lawrence (1870–1940).[95] The play consists of just one scene of seventeen pages, in which Judas, Ahasuerus (the "Wandering Jew," who in medieval legend insulted Jesus while he was carrying his cross),[96] and Gesmas (the impenitent thief)[97] lament their sorry fates. All of them have been condemned to wander or be buffeted around the earth or the universe, never resting, never dying. Their conversation consists mostly of complaining that over the centuries, many others have behaved much worse, and some of them have been saved, so why should the three of them still be suffering? Then suddenly Mary Magdalene shows up and anoints their feet, and they all go to heaven.

With the unbelievable suddenness of their transformation and the almost magical (sacramental?) efficacy of the anointing, I was more than willing to overlook this work, but I think it bears a second glance. What struck me is that the depiction of Judas's attitude towards his sin is really very different from the usual depiction of his despairing over it. To despair is to look inward with an unforgiving attitude: in its deepest, most extreme form, an attitude that cannot even conceive of the possibility of forgiveness. But in his speeches here, Judas is always looking outward at others with an unforgiving attitude, accusing them of being worse than he and even less worthy of forgiveness: this clearly is not despair but sanctimony and self-righteousness. Rather than asking Judas to repent, which, as far as I can tell, none of the three sinners ever do, Mary's humbling act prompts him to forgive others, which he does do in his final line: "Brothers, let us love and pity all poor things."[98] Here repentance is not the necessary precondition for forgiveness, but forgiveness is. The ability to forgive leads to the ability to be forgiven, an idea with Gospel support (Matt. 7:1; Luke 6:37), especially in the parable of the unforgiving servant (Matt. 18:23–35). It is also echoed in the words of an African-American slave spiritual, "When you get to heaven, rub poor lil' Judas's head,"[99] and similarly again in Dostoyevsky, "If I have sinned against everyone, yet all forgive me, too, and that's heaven. Am I not in heaven now?"[100] The believer's ability to forgive even Judas shows that he or she must be in heaven, for nowhere on earth could such an incredible thing occur. It is not that by forgiving Judas one excuses oneself;[101] quite the opposite. By always blaming Judas we have tended to overlook our own sinfulness: "To the extent that Judas is traditionally the personification of pure wickedness, he tends to exonerate the rest of us from our share in Christ's sufferings."[102] It is by forgiving Judas that we begin first to blame ourselves and then to find our own forgiveness.

Sayers's version of Judas also illustrates another aspect of forgiveness: that an important part of it is to be capable of asking for it.[103] While we usually think of forgiving others as extremely difficult, it might be much more difficult to let oneself be forgiven. In his final agony, Judas realizes that he doesn't want to be forgiven, that he cannot allow himself to be forgiven: "Is God merciful? Can He forgive?. . . What help is that?—*Jesus* would forgive. If I crawled to the gallows' foot and asked his pardon, he would forgive me—and my soul would writhe for ever under the torment of that forgiveness."[104] Dostoyevsky also meditated on this aspect of forgiveness in his *Notes from Underground* (1864). In it, the narrator seeks to drive away the kind and loving Liza by humiliating her to the point where (he thinks) she could never forgive him and would run off. But something quite different happens:

> And what happened was this: Liza, insulted and humiliated by me, understood a great deal more than I had imagined. She understood out of all this what a woman, if she loves sincerely, will always understand before all else. She understood that I was myself unhappy. . . . She clung to me, embraced me, and remained motionless in that embrace. Still, the trouble was that the fit of hysteria had to pass in the end. And then (I am, after all, writing the loathsome truth), lying prone on the sofa, pressing my face into the wretched leather cushion, I gradually, involuntarily, distantly at first, but irresistibly began to feel how embarrassing it would be for me now to raise my head and look straight into Liza's eyes. What was I ashamed of? I don't know, but I was ashamed. . . . And then—I'm sure of it to this day—precisely because I was ashamed to look at her, another feeling suddenly flared up within me . . . the need to dominate and possess.[105]

His shame, like Judas's, is so great that he can never face her in a redemptive way, never let her forgive him, never let himself be vulnerable to her again: he can only twist his shame into a destructive loathing of her and of himself. Letting oneself be forgiven makes oneself more humbled and vulnerable than feeling shame, for it puts oneself completely in the other's power. While the other person does not have complete control over whether one feels or does not feel shame, the other does have total control over whether one is forgiven or not. And it is sometimes too painful to let another have this control: the pain of shame and loneliness might be preferable to the risk and vulnerability of forgiveness.

Turning from the human side of forgiveness to the divine, Ray Sherman Anderson (b. 1925), a professor of theology at Fuller Theological Seminary as well as a minister himself, devotes most of his work *The Gospel according to Judas* to a contemplation of how the divine, through the incarnation, can overcome the human limitations of sin and death.[106] The book is an imaginative work of pastoral theology that considers what Jesus would say to Judas if he encountered him after both of their deaths.[107] In it, Anderson concentrates on three important points. First, it is significant that Jesus does not remind Judas that he still loves him and forgives him, as that seems taken for granted. Jesus' ministry was always about how he loved and forgave, so that cannot be what is causing Judas despair. Instead, Judas is reminded by Jesus that he still loves Jesus and should forgive himself: "I felt that nothing could restore within me the belief I once had in my own capacity to love and trust. But I was wrong. . . . Then it was that I felt it possible to love again and to make promises again."[108] If Judas hated Jesus, then it was not betrayal and he shouldn't feel so bad; but since he clearly does feel remorse and feels that he has committed an unpardonable sin, then he must still love Jesus. As in Dostoyevsky, the vulnerability and fragility of any act of love is emphasized: the potential danger of betrayal that became actual in Judas's case looms over every loving relationship in this life.[109] Second, Jesus' incarnation and suffering as a human make it easier to understand and accept one's own suffering. Jesus himself experienced despair, and therefore could understand, forgive, and heal it:

> When I saw him as the innocent Son of God, it only compounded my own sense of sin and opened a chasm between us. But when he touched my pain with his own, and when he shared with me his own "loss of innocence" in becoming human under sentence of death, I felt closer to him than at any point in our three years together. I knew then that it was not the love of God from a distance that saves us; through the pain and suffering of a loving God who is with us, comes the love that heals and redeems us.[110]

One has not offended the all-powerful creator of the universe; one has marred the human creation that God himself also experienced as flawed during his incarnation and that he has repaired through his death and resurrection. Finally, in order to be forgiven, Judas must realize that neither his sin nor any of ours have caused Jesus' death:

> I was wrong when I assumed that my betrayal had caused his death. I was wrong to inflict upon myself the terrible burden of bearing my own sin and so destroy myself through guilt. And you would be wrong to feel that the cross of Jesus Christ stands over against you as a sign of his innocence and your guilt. Neither your sins nor mine *caused* him to die on the cross. In allowing himself to be put to death without resistance, he did bear the consequence of our sins. But he did this *because of God's love for us and because of his love and obedience to God, his Father.* We're mistaken when we think that it was our sin, not the love of God, that brought Jesus to the point of his own death.[111]

The crucifixion was an act of love, not punishment. God willingly chose to die in order to defeat sin, which one participates in but did not originate or cause. Judas acknowledged and repented of his own sins, but this overwhelmed him with despair and death because his sins (incorrectly) seemed to him unique and different from everyone else's. But whereas

Dostoyevsky and others have focused on the interconnectedness and universal guilt of human sin as a remedy for one's own individual sinfulness, Anderson turns instead towards the divine defeat of human sin, guilt, and death. Judas and all of us find ourselves on the losing side of God's battle against sin, but only until we see that sin is our enemy as well. Then God accepts Judas as well as the rest of us, and no amount of sin can undo this divine victory. This is essentially a more optimistic and upbeat version of what we have already seen in the other versions that depict Judas's sin as like our own, for they all emphasize that Judas is not unique in his sin, and God's love and forgiveness can overcome any human obstacle that Judas or any of us can put in its way, even despair and suicide. Although more about God than about Judas, the work is a lovely meditation on the anatomy of forgiveness and how God makes it available to us. Judas's story becomes the occasion for exploring the essence of God's nature and how we can come into a permanent relationship with him.

With a somewhat more sinister view of the divine, the second half of Moore's *Judas* also makes a profound point about God and how humans could become God's children through forgiveness.[112] Following Jesus' arrest, Judas sees himself as quite literally a pawn in God's game:

> Like chessmen on a board of inlaid chequers:
> Himself and others were moved from white to black
> But Jesus only trod the ivory squares.
> Thus evil seemed endowed with divine wit
> To play with things more worthy than itself.[113]

The inevitability and unfairness of "divine wit" occupy Judas's thoughts for the rest of the book, which is increasingly hallucinatory, as he sees first his dead family and then the repentant thief who was crucified with Jesus.[114] Judas then unsuccessfully attempts suicide by hanging but dies later anyway.[115] Amidst all this hallucinating, Judas is shown trying to understand how he is still a "child of God," despite all the terrible things he has done but also *despite all the terrible things God has done to him.*[116] As soon as Judas stops being angry with God for all the misery God has heaped on him, he also stops being angry with himself. Thus it seems that from the potentially trite phrase "We are all children of God," Moore has crafted a rather intriguing implication: God accepts us as his children, no matter what we have done, when we accept God as our parent, no matter what he has done. This seems to me a fairly subtle thinking-through of the psychological and theological dimensions of despair and hope. It is also an image that in the hands of a much more talented author could attain the level of the profound or sublime. I am thinking of the constantly alternating image in *Moby Dick* of Nature as loving, nurturing mother on the one hand and cruel, murderous stepmother on the other, and humans as victims or witnesses to this cosmic and divine duality, whether it is symbolized by the color of the whale or the image of the sea. In this life we are only orphans, an image invoked earlier in the novel—"Our souls are like those orphans whose unwedded mothers die in bearing them: the secret of our paternity lies in their grave, and we must there to learn it"[117]—and most memorably in the final, haunting line: "It was the devious-cruising Rachel, that in her retracing search after her missing children, only found another orphan."[118] We may well be, or have the potential to be, God's children, but only when we accept his unusual, ambivalent, and often very unsatisfying form of parenting.

The creative arts hardly need the approval or confirmation of theology: if anything, theology should be judged by the art, music, and literature that is produced in conjunction or dialogue with it. But it is worth noting that several modern theologians are finally reinforcing the point made nearly three hundred years ago by the sermons of Rev. Moodey and echoed in musical and fictional work since: Judas's story should not lead us to think of him as being judged but to contemplate humbly and perhaps angrily our own responsibility for his action and how we might be forgiven.[119] They have done this by emphasizing that all humanity is implicated in every evil action: every human being is responsible for Jesus' death (as they are responsible for the Crusades, for Auschwitz, or for the killing fields of Cambodia or Rwanda), an idea that we have already seen articulated in Dostoyevsky. And in a remarkable admission of the superiority of story, Gollwitzer, like Anderson, illustrates his theology by writing the story of what Jesus would say to Judas if he were to encounter him before he could hang himself:

> When I called you to be one of the Twelve I already knew you as the one who you are today. You did not destroy the hopes I had misplaced in you. Nor were you merely a pawn in a higher plan, "to fulfill Scripture" in order to now be cast away. I accepted you as the one who you have now proved to be, you are the one I love, you are the one I wanted by my side in order to be for you. For a long time it was apparent that not only you but that all of you [my disciples] would bring me death according to who you are and who I am. Why did I not protect you from your guilt by protecting myself from you? The servant is not above his Lord, so I said to you, and I am not above the One

who sent me, who wishes to be there for you through me. . . . We both, he and I, remain life for those who cast us into death—not only as long as they do not do it, but especially when they do it.[120]

As with Father Zossima, this idea is not one that crushes Judas or us with despair but one that gives us the highest and most liberating hope. By focusing on our own sins individually, we destroy ourselves with despair and by focusing on the sins of others, we destroy ourselves with pride and self-righteousness. It is only by focusing on the power of God's incarnation and redemption, as well as the connection and even the identity between the sins of others and our own, that we can be forgiven, liberated, and loved, and Judas is an important literary and conceptual figure in this process.

Judas as Agent of Salvation

Rather than focusing on the possibility of Judas's forgiveness, others have rehabilitated him by focusing on the necessity of his actions. Although this is clearly related to the idea of his fate or destiny, these authors focus not on Judas's fate—on how his actions affect him—but on the historical and theological necessity of his actions—on how his actions affect us. If Christ had to die, and Judas helped this to happen, to what extent and in what way should we not blame him for what he did but indeed thank him?[121]

Robinson Jeffers's poem "Dear Judas"[122] makes Judas into God's instrument to effect salvation. God needs for Jesus to be betrayed, and he uses Judas as his instrument to accomplish this. Jesus explains this to Judas, but in a way that does not really leave any room for Judas's agreement or cooperation.[123] God's plan for Judas will happen regardless of his attitude: Judas can only choose whether this will make him despair or ask for forgiveness. Jesus explains that Judas has been caught in God's "net"—an unchosen fate quite similar to that dropped on Oedipus (and all of us). But while we saw in the previous chapter how this idea is not incompatible with either free will or responsibility, Jeffers has taken this another step, and has made it the "roots of forgiveness." Human free will is the basis of responsibility, as we freely choose our actions. But divine will is the basis of forgiveness, because God knows that he has "duped" us, that he has put us all in situations in which we have chosen our actions based on faulty information and conflicted motivations. Who indeed could be easier to forgive than a person who doesn't know either the consequences or the causes for what she is doing? The challenge that Jesus pugnaciously leaves Judas to "suck on" is whether he will feel anger and despair at being "duped" by God, or feel "honor" at being chosen by God for such a great and terrible responsibility. This ultimately is the only decision of Judas that is totally his own, and on which his eternal fate relies: he can choose whether or not to ask for forgiveness for the things he has been "duped" into doing.

Italian author Mario Brelich (b. 1910) envisions an even more sinister and depressing scenario in *The Work of Betrayal*.[124] Brelich's reconstruction includes elements of fate and tragic heroism that we have seen previously, but the real force of his work is to place Judas in the midst of an internal divine power struggle. Like Jack Miles's *God: A Biography*,[125] Brelich views all of the events of the Old Testament as an alternation and conflict between God's loving, creative side and his selfish, destructive side. But Brelich goes on to tie this into the New Testament. His fictional narrator, Dupin, hypothesizes that Yahweh became alarmed when his chosen people began expecting some things that he had never promised them and that he had no idea how to provide—things that the Israelites began to demand when they saw their non-Israelite neighbors longing for them: immortality, redemption, and eternal reward.[126] So Yahweh hit upon a brilliant scheme to save face, satisfy the chosen people, and win over many of the heretofore unchosen at the same time. He would beget a son who would promise salvation to everyone, though the chosen people would not recognize him and would go on hoping nonetheless:

> Indeed yes, it would be an ugly about-face, but what an advantageous one, and, at the same time, a well-disguised maneuver too. The son would win for Him a large part of the world, and He would not even lose the chosen people, since they would not see through the dodge and would keep right on waiting for the 'true' Messiah. Moreover, the new covenant to be concluded with these new faithful would demand far less of Him: it would not commit him to anything, while assuring Him of everything in return.[127]

The son is essentially a way of stringing along a much larger part of the human race that involves no sacrifice or responsibility on God's part. Clearly, God's selfish side has won out, but with the added irony that he can do it under the guise of complete loving-kindness.

Whatever one may think of Brelich's theology, he is very revealing about the origin of his speculations. The idea of an immortal being who exists outside of space and time creating and then interacting with a race of beings that exists within these limitations is the problematic that fuels his reconstruction: "Such were the compromises imposed upon the Lord

for having yielded a small part of His absolute omnipotence and acknowledged the rules of the game of History!"[128] And once God decides to
intrude into human beingness and human history in this way, it is not his
relation with humanity that will be problematic, but his relation with his
newly begotten son: "Yahweh's scheme was inspired and farsighted,
enabling Him to reduce His many and complicated problems to just one,
that is, to the problem of His relations with His son."[129] And as Yahweh
feared, Jesus does indeed get out of hand, conceiving that his death is the
key and must, in effect, undo the power of the Father: "He was not always
nor perfectly in agreement with the Father, and specifically on the point
which for him mattered most."[130] Jesus enlists Judas's help to defeat the
Father:

> If you turn back, none of this will come to pass. And so no one will
> be saved. Even in the future times humankind will remain under the
> yoke of the Father's law, and man will remain a toy, played with by
> the capricious hand that giveth and taketh away. Never shall the reign
> of free will come about! It is from the Father's arbitrariness I shall
> save man. . . . I will vanquish Him with your help.[131]

Since Judas is helping Jesus fulfill his mission, there is nothing in what
Judas does for which he could or should feel remorse: "But how could you
repent a deed for which you are not guilty and hence cannot feel guilt?"[132]
There is nothing to repent, so there is nothing to forgive, and therefore
Judas falls outside of the power of Jesus: "My law makes provision for
remorse, not for tragedies. Those singled out by fate will always remain
within the Father's competence. I cannot do anything for you, Judas."[133]
Although Judas does Jesus' will in order to destroy and dethrone the arbi-
trariness and destructiveness of the Father, Jesus cannot save Judas from
the punishment that the Father will mete out for this disobedience. In a
remarkable reversal, the crucifixion does not bring about the rehabilita-
tion of humanity through the sacrifice of God: instead, it brings about a
transformation in the nature of God, accomplished by the eternal sacrifice of the one obedient disciple, Judas.

Other stories make much the same point through the language of myth
and folklore. These are the legends that identify both Jesus' cross and
Judas's gallows as coming from the same tree, either having both from the
same species[134] or both from the tree of the knowledge of good and evil.[135]
Even I, sitting in my office in front of my computer in what I am told is a
postreligious age, must pause before I connect the dots of that picture and
say that perhaps Christ and Judas are typologically identified: certainly a

medieval author or audience would have had a similar reticence.[136] But in good folklore fashion, that did not stop them from playing with the idea, of laying it before us unadorned and uninterpreted, any more than the difficulties of identifying Judas with Oedipus stopped them from making that equation. (And indeed, the suggestion now that the fatal trees of both Judas and Jesus are identical may reinforce the previous suggestion that both are typologically based on Oedipus.) And just as Oedipus functions as one of the greatest figures of both myth and psychology, the Jesus/Judas typology may be powerful because it answers a psychological need: we need Jesus as a scapegoat to remove all our bad feelings, but then we feel bad about killing him, so we then need his killer Judas to be a scapegoat we can hate and kill with a deep and satisfying feeling of fulfillment.[137] From a psychological point of view, Jesus without Judas might not be much a savior, bringing more guilt than he removes.

Of course, for Jesus and Judas to be presented as parallel does not mean they are to be seen as equivalent: one could just as easily be the antitype of the other.[138] This is exactly how Maccoby takes it: "Yet [Judas] remains, of all mankind, unexpiated, since he is chosen to be the instrument of expiation for others. . . . He is thus the symbol of unregenerate humanity, unredeemed by the sacrifice of the Cross."[139] But even Maccoby's statement comes awfully close to making the identification that these folk tales constantly, paradoxically, and playfully tease us with: calling Judas "the instrument of expiation" seems to be a short step away from saying that he is as necessary a part of the drama of salvation as Christ, and that statement is an even shorter step away from saying that he is as responsible for our salvation as Christ is. And of course, that statement might be one that a Christian theologian would hesitate making, but it is equally one that no good storyteller could resist.

This is exactly the scenario that one of the great modern storytellers, Martin Scorsese, plays with in his film version of Nikos Kazantzakis's *The Last Temptation of Christ*.[140] Often reviled for religious and aesthetic reasons, the film is powerful and challenging for its taking seriously exactly how tempted Jesus must have been (whether he was a man or God) by everything that is attractive about living a normal, human life rather than going to a humiliating death: giving up sex, love, comfort, children, and friends is a lot to ask of anyone, even (or especially?) God. And Judas's role in the film is to help Jesus overcome this temptation and his weakness in the face of it. Apparently a friend of Jesus even before the film begins, Judas is always at Jesus' side throughout the movie. Played by Harvey Keitel (with annoyingly orange hair), he is thuggish and decisive to Willem

Dafoe's neurotic and disassociated Jesus: "Two men, closer than brothers, with complementary abilities and obsessions, who must connive in each other's destiny."[141] While Keitel is almost never appealing, he is effective here as the strongest and most intelligent of the disciples, and that is why Jesus picks him as his betrayer: he knows that neither he himself nor the other disciples could go through with it, and he encourages Judas by telling him that God picked him for this task and made him stronger than Jesus.

But more surprising than his role in the betrayal is Judas's role in the final controversial dream sequence of the film. As he is dying on the cross, Jesus imagines his last temptation. The devil comes to him in the shape of a beautiful little girl, pulls the nails from his hands and feet, tenderly kisses his wounds, and leads him away. He imagines himself living a normal life of marriage (and adultery), work, and children, and dying peacefully at a ripe old age, all of this his reward for all the pain he suffered for God's cause. But as he imagines his peaceful death, Judas intrudes, being introduced by the craven and indecisive Peter with the warning "He's still angry." Judas then shames Jesus into rejecting this devilish vision of domestic tranquility and ordinariness, telling him that he doesn't belong there. He was supposed to die on the cross, and he is not only a coward if he rejects this call but a traitor to his loyal friend Judas, who had gone through the painful act of betrayal at Jesus' command. (Jesus had already been given a taste of this embarrassment by Saul, who had calmly rejected him, the uncrucified and pathetic Jesus, in favor of his own powerful, crucified Christ.) Although it is disturbing to some critics that "only through the efforts of Judas . . . is the establishment of Christianity made possible,"[142] it is a powerful culmination to this particular tradition that sees Judas's act as one of self-sacrifice and submission to the divine will. He is as much the actor and the accomplisher of God's plan as his friend Jesus.

Finally, as we have considered throughout this work the tension and the interplay between theologians and storytellers, it is appropriate to end with Protestant theologian Karl Barth (1886–1968), who saw in the story of Judas the exact paradoxes we have been considering.[143] While he was not enough of a storyteller to make them as entertaining as many of the versions we have considered, Barth was enough of a narrative critic to appreciate them and not try to reduce them to agreement or harmony. He first insists on the genuineness and permanence of Judas's apostleship: Judas was and remains an apostle, even in the act of betrayal. This is important, because it means that Judas's election cannot finally be eliminated or undone. This is paradoxical, however, because in spite of this, Judas is nonetheless rejected, a sinner and a betrayer. For Barth, he must be simultaneously elected and rejected; these cannot occur sequentially or to the exclusion of one another: "What [the New Testament] does say is that it was one of the genuine apostles, one of the genuinely elect, who was at the same time rejected as the betrayer of Jesus."[144] Second, it is crucial for Barth that Judas's act be both "paltry," insignificant, unnecessary, and at the same time monumental, completely necessary, utterly significant: "We must see both the paltriness and the tremendous consequences of this event properly to understand the Judas of the Evangelists. . . . Judas Iscariot is certainly not an accidental figure. He is an essential one in the totality of the evangelical record."[145] Barth goes on to explain that this must be so in order that once again there be a paradoxical connection between the elected and the rejected, between divine and human, between sinless and sinful: "At one point—and at the decisive point—the apostles have to share the guilt of Israel and the Gentile world towards Jesus, in order that Jesus may carry out the will of God, not only in relation to them, but also to Israel and the world."[146] The fact that one is elected does not remove one's sinfulness, and the fact of one's sinfulness does not remove one's election.

Barth now turns to what has fascinated us throughout this chapter: What is Judas's end? Has he been forgiven? Again, the answer is coy and seductive in its paradoxes. First, Barth insists on the genuineness of Judas's repentance as described in Matthew: "There is no reason not to take seriously this repentance, this confession, this attempt of Judas to make restitution. . . . all the things which were later said to constitute true repentance are there."[147] But Barth is true to the New Testament text's silence regarding the answer to that repentance: "And so, according to the New Testament account, his repentance is left an open question which is not met or heard or answered by a promise of grace."[148] Exactly like Brelich, Barth sees Judas on the pre-atonement side of an abyss that is impossible to cross: "Judas, and his penitence, stood on this side of the event—dependent on his own work, his own freedom of choice and decision."[149] Judas brought about the possibility of grace only by rejecting that grace, so Barth cannot see a way in which his repentance, though completely real and sincere, can possibly be accepted.

But exactly like Origen, Barth cannot finally let matters remain at that point. Although the fate of Judas seems settled, it cannot be, for the idea that divine grace can be defeated or foiled is abhorrent to him, and he must ask again, "What is the will of God for him [Judas]? What has God determined concerning him?"[150] Again Barth turns to the idea of Judas's election as an apostle, which he has already decided cannot be rejected or nullified. The key to the significance of the betrayal is that it be carried out by an apostle. But that means that it could have been carried out by any apostle, and the historical accident of its being carried out by this particular apostle is, therefore, fairly insignificant: "Judas and the other apostles belong together as closely as possible—with all the closeness with which Jesus chose and called them together (the others with Judas, and Judas with them). What Judas did affects them also. . . . the point is that they obviously could have done it."[151] Barth then turns to the footwashing scene, wherein the direction of his exegesis seems to turn subtly towards an affirmation of Judas's redemption. For, as with Origen, the loss of Judas would not merely be a judgment on him, but a disturbing failure of Jesus and God: "Can it be that the 'loving unto the end' of Jesus does not reach him, the very one who in his person and act simply makes manifest the fact and extent that without His death Jesus had not yet loved His own unto the end?"[152] Barth says that we will never know the answer to the question of Judas's final status before God, but it will always stand before us as an unresolved contrast between the power of Jesus' grace and the intractability of human sin:

> On the one hand, it places no limits to the grace of Jesus Christ even with regard to Judas. It sets Judas against the brightest radiance of this grace. And on the other hand, it does not use even a single word to suggest that Judas is an example of *apokatastasis* [Origen's idea that eventually everyone would be redeemed and return to God]. The situation between Jesus and Judas which is only a heightened form of the situation between Jesus and all other men—between God's election of man, and his necessary rejection—is obviously described, therefore, as the open one of proclamation. . . . It is the situation which involves the contrast between the irresistible divine grace of Jesus Christ and a hostility of man towards this grace which humanly speaking—but only humanly speaking—is absolutely immovable. . . . The church will not then preach an *apokatastasis*, nor will it preach a powerless grace of Jesus Christ or a wickedness of men which is too powerful for it. But without any weakening of the contrast, and also without any arbitrary dualism, it will preach the overwhelming power of grace and the weakness of human wickedness in face of it. For this is how the "for" of Jesus and the "against" of Judas undoubtedly confront one another.[153]

Although he speaks of contrasts and uncertainties in this life, Barth's language ultimately seems to favor a resolution of this contrast in favor of

Judas's redemption: Jesus' grace is "irresistible" and "overwhelming," while human sinfulness is "weak." In this life we can not know if Judas (or anybody else) is saved, but our faith is that with God all things are possible (Matt. 19:26), and therefore no one can be beyond the possibility of salvation.

In these stories of Judas as the agent who has made possible our salvation, we are invited again not to sit in judgment of him but to sit in humbled awe, perhaps even gratitude, for what he did.[154] He may still be damned in these versions, or he may be saved, but the conclusion persists that he was not a villain but an actor who peered deeply into the nature of God, Christ, and humanity and made an awesome choice based on what he saw there. At the same time, God peered deeply into Judas and did something to him and with him that we can neither describe nor explain but at which we can only wonder. In these depictions, Judas and our attitude towards him have become, as profoundly as the incarnation itself, the mysterious and paradoxical foundation of our possible union with God.

Epilogue

Although I began this work promising that I would not claim to tell readers what *really* happened but instead what people have said happened, I now feel as though I can offer my version of Judas's life. If this were the 1850s, I would dress this up and present it as biblical scholarship; if I were a better writer, I might elaborate it into a historical novel. But being just an interested student who thrives on the divergences of traditions, I can only offer it here as an entertaining piece that, like all the versions we have examined, says more about me than about Judas. Again, what I am claiming is not historical accuracy but a story that ends the way I would like it to.

Judas was a regular guy. He met up with Jesus and joined his group. He was as confused and alarmed by Jesus' actions and teachings as the other disciples. On the night of Jesus' arrest, Jesus had suggested that they all do some heavy drinking in the garden (let's not forget, Jesus was known to his detractors as a "drunkard"—Matt. 11:19; Luke 7:34)—not the most appropriate way to celebrate Passover, but Jesus was not known to stick to rules regarding food and drink (Matt. 12:1; Mark 2:23; Luke 6:1). Things got pretty out of hand, and the authorities showed up. Most of the other disciples were passed out by then (referred to as "sleeping" in the Gospels—Matt. 26:40–45; Mark 14:37–41; Luke 22:45–46), but Judas had the misfortune of having to watch his friend Jesus arrested, made more humiliating because Judas himself was hiding behind a bush, and Jesus was shouting ineffectually and incoherently for help, something about, "Here comes my betrayer!" (cf. Matt. 26:46; Mark 14:42). The next day, Judas was quite embarrassed at the previous night's events. He went to the authorities to beg for Jesus' release, or even to offer himself in exchange, but they were bent on Jesus' destruction, turning Judas's embarrassment into devastating guilt, worsened by the fact that he (as well as all the other disciples) had always been envious of Jesus' power and charisma and may have secretly held some desire to see him ruined and brought down. The authorities did, however, see some usefulness in Judas: they asked him to help guard Jesus' tomb (cf. Matt. 27:62–66). At first Judas was shocked that they were even talking about Jesus' death; then he was appalled that they wanted him to be a part of it. But then he remembered all the strange prophecies that Jesus had made about rising from the dead, and he thought that being near Jesus' tomb would in fact be the best place for him. They paid him more than he expected, and just before dawn, with the other guards having fallen asleep, Judas was the first to see the risen Christ. Before leaving, Christ forgave him and told him that they would not meet again until they were both in paradise, so Judas never had the problems with imminent eschatological expectation that other early Christians had. Judas went back to the authorities and told them the truth, still hoping to change their hard hearts, but all they wanted to do was to bribe him into saying that the other disciples had taken Jesus' body (cf. Matt. 28:11–15). He couldn't agree to that deception but did agree just not to say anything at all, not to tell anyone else of Jesus' resurrection. Judas had always preferred anonymity anyway and could not see himself as much of an evangelist. He took their money, asking them to circulate the rumor that he had committed suicide (cf. Matt. 27:3–10), since he didn't really want to see the other disciples again. He had never been very close to them, except to Matthew, who as a former tax collector had also been ostracized by the group. Judas had now been paid twice by the authorities, and quite a lot the second time, so he had plenty of money to buy a farm near Jerusalem (cf. Acts 1:18–19). He did always keep in touch with Matthew, and that is why Matthew's Gospel is the more sympathetic and accurate regarding Judas, though Matthew agreed to perpetuate the rumor of his friend's death. Judas later married the eminently practical Martha (cf. Luke 10:38–42), raised several children, and died peacefully shortly before the Jewish War (66–70 C.E.), God sparing him the pain of that disaster in recognition of all that he had been through.

So there's my version. It's all pretty ordinary because my experience of life is pretty ordinary: there is no high drama or low, debasing religious polemic. It's just a story of a guy who makes a mistake but still gets forgiven, and then goes on to get the money and the girl. It's an ordinary story but a happy one. After the way Judas has been treated over the centuries—being either stretched to the heights and limits of human endurance and accomplishment like Oedipus, or thrust down to the deepest abyss of hell and the lowest, most debased human drives—I really think he deserves this rather more simple version. Although it is hardly a vision for which one should strive, one could certainly do much worse.

Notes

Preface

1. On Judas Priest, see Stan Soocher, *They Fought the Law: Rock Music Goes to Court* (New York: Schirmer Books, 1999), 153–70.
2. On Bach's depiction of Judas, see also L. A. Harper, "Judas, Our Brother," *St. Luke's Journal of Theology* 29, no. 2 (1986): 96–102, esp. 101–2.
3. B. H. Throckmorton, *Jesus Christ: The Message of the Gospels, The Hope of the Church* (Louisville, Ky.: Westminster John Knox Press, 1998), 21.
4. B. Kennelly, *The Book of Judas: A Poem* (Newcastle upon Tyne: Bloodaxe Books, 1991).
5. K. Paffenroth, "The Character of Judas in Bach's *St. Matthew Passion*," *The Midwest Quarterly* 36 (1995): 125–35.
6. K. Paffenroth, "The Stories of the Fate of Judas and Differing Attitudes towards Sources," *Proceedings: Eastern Great Lakes and Midwest Biblical Societies* 12 (1992): 67–81.

Chapter 1

1. Material common to Matthew and Luke but absent from Mark is commonly referred to as Q material because of its supposed origin in a now lost "source" designated by the letter "Q," for the German word for "source" *(Quelle)*.
2. Cf. A. Loisy, *The Origins of the New Testament* (trans. L. P. Jacks; London: George Allen & Unwin, Ltd., 1950), 100: "A traitor being needed for the elaboration of the drama, imagination invented the role of Judas."
3. On Paul's use of the term, see W. Klassen, *Judas: Betrayer or Friend of Judas?* (Minneapolis: Fortress Press, 1996), 35, 51; and his more recent, "The Authenticity of Judas' Participation in the Arrest of Jesus," in *Authenticating the Activities of Jesus* (eds. B. D. Chilton and C. A. Evans; Leiden: E. J. Brill, 1999), 389–410, esp. 395.
4. On the absence of Judas from the earliest traditions as confirmation of its fabrication, see J. M. Robertson, *Jesus and Judas: A Textual and Historical Investigation* (London: Watts, 1927), 28–31.
5. For discussions of the film, see L. Baugh, *Imaging the Divine: Jesus and Christ-Figures in Film* (Kansas City: Sheed & Ward, 1997), 113–29; R. C. Stern, C. N. Jefford, and G. Debona, *Savior on the Silver Screen* (New York: Paulist Press, 1999), 298–333.
6. Dostoyevsky's vision of Judas and universal guilt will be considered in our final chapter.
7. Except, possibly, as an allegorical image on the wall of the subway at the end: see Baugh, *Imaging the Divine*, 123; Stern, *Savior on the Silver Screen*, 313.
8. Cf. Baugh, *Imaging the Divine*, 125, who defends the integrity of Daniel's death.

9. See H. Jursch, "Das Bild des Judas Ischarioth im Wandel der Zeiten," in *Akten des VII Internationalen Kongresses für Christliche Archäologie Trier 1965* (Rome: 1969), 565–73, esp. 569.

10. Cf. Baugh, *Imaging the Divine*, 277; the resulting image is remarkable, haunting, but, from a narrative point of view, fake and contrived.

11. On Mark's use of this device, see J. R. Edwards, "Markan Sandwiches: The Significance of Interpolations in Markan Narratives," *Novum Testamentum* 31 (1989): 193–216.

12. On the popularity of the name, see Samuel Pearce Carey, *Jesus and Judas* (New York: Richard R. Smith, Inc., 1931), 17–19; W. Klassen, *Judas: Betrayer or Friend of Judas?* (Minneapolis: Fortress Press, 1996), 29.

13. See Klassen, *Judas*, 30.

14. As suggested by M. S. Enslin, "How the Story Grew: Judas in Fact and Fiction," in *Festschrift to Honor F. Wilbur Gingrich* (ed. E. Barth; Leiden: E. J. Brill, 1972), 123–41, esp. 141; J. D. M. Derrett, "The Iscariot, M^{e}sira, and the Redemption," *Journal for the Study of the New Testament* 8 (1980), 2–23, esp. 8–9.

15. Klassen, *Judas*, 86.

16. Cf. below, chapter 5, and also B. Dieckmann, "Judas als Doppelgänger Jesu? Elemente und Probleme der Judastradition," in *Dramatische Erlösungslehre* (eds. J. Niewiadomski and W. Palaver; Innsbruck: Tyrolia-Verlag, 1992).

17. For discussions of these and other possible derivations, see R. B. Halas, *Judas Iscariot, a Scriptural and Theological Study of His Person, His Deeds, and His Eternal Lot* (Washington, D.C.: Catholic University of America, 1946), 10–38; R. O. McClain, "Judas Iscariot" (Diss., Southern Baptist Seminary, 1951), 54–74.

18. E.g., A. W. Alexander, "Judas Iscariot: A Study," *Methodist Quarterly Review* 58 (1909): 331–40, 359–61, esp. 334; J. G. Tasker, "Judas Iscariot," in *A Dictionary of Christ and the Gospels* (ed. J. Hastings; Edinburgh: T. & T. Clark, 1911), 907–13; more recently endorsed by J. A. Fitzmyer, *The Gospel According to Luke* (2 vols.; New York: Doubleday, 1981, 1984), 620; and L. A. Harper, "Judas, Our Brother," *St. Luke's Journal of Theology* 29, no. 2 (1986): 96–102, esp. 97. It is rejected by many, such as Robertson, *Jesus and Judas*, 50.

19. E. Nestle, "Another Peculiarity of Codex Bezae," *Expository Times* 9 (1897–98): 140.

20. Harris, "Suggested Primacy," 7.

21. H. Ingholt, "The Surname of Judas Iscariot," In *Studia orientalia Ioanni Pedersen* (Copenhagen: Einar Munksgaard, 1953), 152–62.

22. A. Ehrman, "Judas Iscariot and the Abba Saqqara," *Journal of Biblical Literature* 97 (1978): 572–73; Y. Arbeitman, "The Suffix of Iscariot," *Journal of Biblical Literature* 99 (1980): 122–24.

23. O. Cullmann, "Le douzième apôtre." *Revue d'histoire et de philosophie religieuses* 42 (1962): 133–40.

24. See W. B. Smith, "Judas Iscariot," *The Hibbert Journal* 9 (1911): 529–44, esp. 529–35; Robertson, *Jesus and Judas*, 51; J. A. Morin, "Les deux derniers des douze: Simon le Zélote et Judas Iskariôth," *Revue Biblique* 80 (1973): 332–58, esp. 353–58.

25. C. C. Torrey, "The Name 'Iscariot,'" *Harvard Theological Review* 36 (1943): 51–62; B. E. Gärtner, *Iscariot* (trans. V. I. Gruhn; Philadelphia: Fortress Press, 1971), 6–7.

26. Derrett, "The Iscariot," 9–10; cf. the critique of L. Nortjé, "Matthew's Motive for the Composition of the Story of Judas's Suicide in Matthew 27:3–10," *Neotestamentica* 28 (1994): 41–51, esp. 41–42.

27. Cf. Robertson, *Jesus and Judas*, 51: "If the very interesting thesis that *Skariot* was but an epithet signifying 'surrenderer' should be established, the problem is substantially solved in terms of the myth theory. Judas is once for all not merely not a historical person but a traditional *functionary*, the person who in the mystery-drama played the part of 'deliverer-up' of the divine victim" (emphasis in original).

28. Cf. the discussions of H.-J. Klauck, *Judas—ein Jünger des Herrn* (Freiburg: Herder, 1987), 40–44; G. Schwarz, G. *Jesus und Judas: aramaistische Untersuchungen zur Jesus-Judas-Überlieferung der Evangelien und Apostelgeschichte* (Stuttgart: Kohlhammer, 1988), 6–12; Klassen, *Judas*, 32–34.

29. Cf. Robertson, *Jesus and Judas*, 50–51: "Iskariot was already unintelligible to the evangelist."

30. For a discussion of this, see A. Wright, "Was Judas Iscariot 'the First of the Twelve'?" *Journal of Theological Studies* 18 (1916): 32–34; A. T. Robertson, "The Primacy of Judas Iscariot," *Expositor* 8, no. 13 (1917): 278–86; A. Wright, "Was Judas Iscariot the First of the Twelve?" *Interpreter* 13 (1917): 18–25; J. R. Harris, "The Suggested Primacy of Judas Iscariot." *Expositor* 8, no. 14 (1917): 1–16.

31. Cf. Klassen, *Judas*, 38: "His name always appears last in the lists of the Twelve, and, according to Jewish custom, this does not detract from his importance."

32. See Klassen, *Judas*, 47–58; cf. Klauck, *Judas*, 45–48; G. Schwarz, *Jesus und Judas*, 24–26. The suggestion goes back at least to Robertson, *Jesus and Judas*, 31.

33. On the disciples' role and especially their failure, see W. H. Kelber, *Mark's Story of Jesus* (Philadelphia: Fortress Press, 1979), 30–42; R. C. Tannehill, "The Disciples in Mark: the Function of a Narrative Role," in *The Interpretation of Mark* (ed. W. Telford; Philadelphia: Fortress Press/London: SPCK, 1985), 134–57.

34. On Markan irony, see D. Rhoads and D. Michie, *Mark as Story: An Introduction to the Narrative of a Gospel* (Philadelphia: Fortress Press, 1982), 59–62.

35. Cf. V. K. Robbins, "Last Meal: Preparation, Betrayal, and Absence (Mark 14:12–25)," in *The Passion in Mark: Studies on Mark 14–16* (ed. W. H. Kelber; Philadelphia: Fortress Press, 1976), 21–40, esp. 32: "In other words, it is necessary to separate the action (which is judged as wrong) from the result of the action (which fulfills the plan of God). This is expressed by introducing two subjects in the oracle rather than one—'that man' (who does the evil deed) and 'the Son of man' (who fulfills the sovereign will of God)." Cf. Klassen, *Judas*, 81–84, who tries to make something positive of the "woe."

36. On the kiss as possibly showing repentance in Mark, see F. W. Belcher, "A Comment on Mark 14:45," *Expository Times* 64 (1952–53): 240.

37. On the historical question, see also Klauck, *Judas*, 53–55.

38. Cf. Klassen, *Judas*, 35.

39. K. Lüthi (*Judas Iskarioth in der Geschichte der Auslegung von der Reformation bis zur Gegenwart* [Zürich: Zwingli-Verlag, 1955], 126–27) defends the historicity of the story, based on its scandalous nature; also in favor of its historicity is H. L. Stein-Schneider, "À la recherche du Judas historique: Une enquête exégétique à la lumière des textes de l'ancien testament et des LOGIA," *Études Théologiques et Religieuses* 60 (1985): 403–23. On the other hand, cf. Robertson, *Jesus and Judas*, 49, who sees the story as "a Gentile invention to discredit the Judaic Christians and the Twelve."

40. Origen, *Against Celsus* (trans. F. Crombie; New York: Charles Scribner's Sons, 1899), bk. 2, chap. 12. Cf. Robertson, *Jesus and Judas*, 13.

41. For discussions of this problem, see Halas, *Judas Iscariot,* 52–57; McClain, "Judas Iscariot," 153–55.

42. Thus L. G. Lévy, "Que Judas Iscariote n'a jamais existé," *Grande Revue* 55 (1909): 533–39; Loisy, *Origins of the New Testament,* 100; J. S. Spong, "Did Christians Invent Judas?" *The Fourth R* (March-April 1994): 3–11, 16; and with a slightly different reconstruction (that Judas was a disciple, but not the betrayer), H. Maccoby, *Judas Iscariot and the Myth of Jewish Evil* (New York: Free Press, 1992). On the other hand, S. Krauss, "Judas Iscariot," *Jewish Review* 4 (1913): 199–207, defends the story as not anti-Jewish.

43. Cf. J. F. Moore, "A New Christian Midrash: On the Frontier of Theology after the Shoah," in *What Have We Learned? Telling the Story and Teaching the Lessons of the Holocaust* (ed. F. Littell, et al.; Lewiston, N.Y.: Edwin Mellen, 1993), 271–313, esp. 291: "Mark apparently saw Judas' actions as only a vehicle for the story." On Judas's narrative role in Mark, cf. also Klauck, *Judas,* 48–49.

44. See the analyses of the film by Baugh, *Imaging the Divine,* 24–32; Stern, *Savior on the Silver Screen,* 127–60.

45. Stern, *Savior on the Silver Screen,* 130; cf. Baugh, *Imaging the Divine,* 29–30.

46. Cf. Stern, *Savior on the Silver Screen,* 139–40.

47. Cf. Baugh, *Imaging the Divine,* 31.

48. I have never visited the Holy Land, but the Field of Blood is listed on the itinerary of a walking tour of Jerusalem by Frommer's: see http://www.frommers.com/destinations/jerusalem/0088010008.html.

49. Cf. D. Senior, "The Fate of the Betrayer: A Redactional Study of Matthew 27:3–10," *Ephemerides Theologicae Lovaniensis* 48 (1972): 372–426, esp. 416: "It [the field] does not arise immediately from the context of Judas' betrayal: i.e., there is no *intrinsic* reason why Matthew would redactionally choose to associate the purchase of a field with the death of Judas."

50. Cf. Senior, "Fate of the Betrayer," 417: "It [the field] is not clearly found in the quotation mixture. . . . This suggests that there may have been some vague tradition available to Matthew which popularly associated either the name of a field or the fact of the purchase of a field with Judas' betrayal or death. . . . which may have prompted Matthew's construction of the pericope and the application of the Old Testament quotation." Cf. his similar conclusion in D. Senior, "A Case Study in Matthean Creativity (Matthew 27:3–10)," *Biblical Review* 19 (1974): 23–36: 34, "It is highly unlikely that the story of the death of Judas and the return of his wages would be connected with the purchase of a field and its name simply as an elaboration of an Old Testament text."

51. On Matthew's possible literary dependence on Luke here, see R. H. Gundry, *Matthew: A Commentary on His Literary and Theological Art* (Grand Rapids: Wm. B. Eerdmans Publishing Co., 1982), 552–58. In support of their independence, see G. D. Kilpatrick, *The Origins of the Gospel according to St. Matthew* (London: Oxford University Press, 1946), 46; P. Benoit, "The Death of Judas," in *Jesus and the Gospel,* vol. 1 (London: Darton, Longman, & Todd, 1973), 189–207, esp. 189; W. C. van Unnik, "The Death of Judas in Saint Matthew's Gospel," *Anglican Theological Review Supplementary Series* 3 (1974): 44–57.

52. On the pre-Matthean traditions about the field, see Kilpatrick, *Origins,* 46; P. Bonnard, *L'Évangile selon Saint Matthieu* (Paris: Delachaux et Niestlé, 1963), 394; R. H. Gundry, *The Use of the Old Testament in St. Matthew's Gospel* (Leiden: E. J. Brill, 1967),

202; K. Stendahl, *The School of St. Matthew and Its Use of the Old Testament* (Philadelphia: Fortress Press, 1968), 197; R. McConnell, *Law and Prophecy in Matthew's Gospel* (Basel: Friedrich Reinhardt, 1969), 132; Benoit, "The Death of Judas," 190–92; J. D. M. Derrett, "Akeldama (Acts 1:19)," *Bijdragen, Tijdschrift voor Filosofie en Theologie* 56 (1995): 122–32.

53. On the field's location, see C. Kopp, *The Holy Places of the Gospels* (trans. R. Walls; New York: Herder & Herder, 1963), 361–65; J. Jeremias, *Jerusalem in the Time of Jesus* (trans. F. H. and C. H. Cave; Philadelphia: Fortress Press, 1969), 138–40; and Benoit, "The Death of Judas," 200–7.

54. We will consider the full impact of Matthew's story only in the last chapter.

55. See M. Wilcox, "The Judas Tradition in Acts 1:15–26," *New Testament Studies* 19 (1973): 438–52, esp. 442: "Now v. 19 clearly goes with v. 18 and, as we noted at the outset, seems to disturb the flow of Peter's speech: it has thus sometimes been regarded as an insertion into the speech."

56. Cf. Wilcox, "Judas Tradition," 442–44.

57. Wilcox, "Judas Tradition," 444, following R. Bultmann, *History of the Synoptic Tradition* (trans. J. Marsh; rev. ed.; Peabody, Mass.: Hendrickson, 1963), 272.

58. On the possible literary dependence of Luke's version on Matthew's, see M. S. Enslin, "How the Story Grew: Judas in Fact and Fiction," in *Festschrift to Honor F. Wilbur Gingrich* (ed. E. Barth; Leiden: E. J. Brill, 1972), 123–41, esp. 128.

59. My translation; for the Greek text, see K. Bihlmeyer, *Die apostolischen Väter* (Tübingen: J. C. B. Mohr, 1924), 136–37; J. Kürzinger, *Papias von Hierapolis und Evangelien des Neuen Testaments* (Regensburg: Friedrich Pustet, 1983), 104–5.

60. On the possible literary dependence of Papias on a version similar to Luke's, see J. R. Harris, "Did Judas Really Commit Suicide?" *American Journal of Theology* 4 (1900): 490–513, esp. 502.

61. Cf. Benoit's description of Papias, "The Death of Judas," 194: "Compared to Papias' story and its numerous parallels, our two canonical descriptions have a refreshing soberness; they flow from purer sources."

62. On the likelihood that the tradition was oral, see Benoit, "The Death of Judas," 191. For a general discussion of orality, see W. J. Ong, *Orality and Literacy: The Technologizing of the Word* (London and New York: Methuen, 1982).

Chapter 2

1. "Daimonic" refers to any nonearthly being, whether hellish or heavenly. I have avoided the simpler term "supernatural," since, until recently, angels, demons, and gods were considered integral parts of "nature" and not at all "supernatural."

2. See S. R. Garrett, *The Demise of the Devil: Magic and the Demonic in Luke's Writings* (Minneapolis: Fortress Press, 1989).

3. With his subsequent resurrection, the similarities between Osiris and Jesus have often been noted, but there also seem to be specific similarities between Judas and Seth, including the common belief that they both had red hair: see Dickey, *Judas Iscariot*, 85–92; on the hair color, see P. F. Baum, "Judas's Red Hair," *Journal of English and Germanic Philology* 21 (1922): 520–29, esp. 525; R. Mellinkoff, "Judas's Red Hair and the Jews," *Journal of Jewish Art* 9 (1982): 31–46, esp. 31–32.

4. Though John Milton in *Paradise Lost* would seem to appreciate this exact dynamic, making the Son essentially Satan's annoying, preferred, younger brother and filling Satan with exactly the kind of sibling rivalry one would expect.

5. Cf. J. B. Green, *The Gospel of Luke* (Grand Rapids: Wm. B. Eerdmans Publishing Co., 1997), 260.

6. Cf. Klassen, *Judas*, 116–17.

7. See Fitzmyer, *Gospel according to Luke*, 253–57.

8. On Luke's redactional habit of omitting doublets, see ibid., 81–82.

9. Besides the location, time, and the part of Jesus anointed (head in Mark and Matthew, feet in Luke and John), there is the overall point of the story: forgiveness in Luke, a Christophany in the others; see Fitzmyer, *Gospel according to Luke*, 683–94; Green, *Gospel of Luke*, 305–15.

10. Cf. Fitzmyer, *Gospel according to Luke*, 1030: "One must recall that for Luke Christianity in the long run is a logical sequel to Pharisaic Judaism."

11. Ibid., 518.

12. See Luke 4:2, 3, 6, 13; 8:12; 10:18; 11:18; 13:16; 22:31; Acts 5:3; 10:38; 13:10; 26:18; cf. Garrett, *Demise of the Devil*; Klassen, *Judas*, 120–21; Green, *Gospel of Luke*, 753–54.

13. Green, *Gospel of Luke*, 754.

14. Cf. J. M. Ford, *My Enemy Is My Guest: Jesus and Violence in Luke* (Maryknoll, N.Y.: Orbis Books, 1984), 115–16; Klassen, *Judas*, 123; Green, *Gospel of Luke*, 764–65.

15. Even if the saying is suspect (against its inclusion, see Fitzmyer, *Gospel according to Luke*, 1503–4; in favor of its authenticity, Green, *Gospel of Luke*, 817), it clearly represents Lukan theology: see Ford, *My Enemy Is My Guest*, 131; Klassen, *Judas*, 124–27; Green, *Gospel of Luke*, 819–20.

16. Cf. Ford, *My Enemy Is My Guest*, 120.

17. See H. J. Cadbury, *The Style and Literary Method of Luke* (HTS 6; Cambridge, Mass.: Harvard University Press, 1920), 91–92; Fitzmyer, *Gospel according to Luke*, 94–95.

18. Cf. Ford, *My Enemy Is My Guest*, 121: "These words are peculiar to Luke and imply that armed resistance belongs to the realm of supernatural evil."

19. For a full discussion of the scriptural fulfillment here, see J. Dupont, "La destinée de Judas prophetisée par David (Actes 1,16–20)," *Catholic Biblical Quarterly* 23 (1961): 41–51.

20. For a very different view of the justice of this end, see J. D. M. Derrett, "Miscellanea: a Pauline Pun and Judas' Punishment," *Zeitschrift für die neutestamentliche Wissenschaft* 72 (1981): 131–33, who believes that his horrible death in Acts was in order that he might be spared further punishment in the afterlife.

21. However, harmonizations have constantly been attempted; see J. I. Munro, "The Death of Judas (Matt xxvii.3–8; Acts i.18–19)," *Expository Times* 24 (1912–13): 235–36; Carey, *Jesus and Judas*, 222–24, 231; A. B. Gordon, "The Fate of Judas according to Acts 1:18," *Evangelical Quarterly* 43 (1971): 97–100. See also the list of harmonizations in Foakes-Jackson & Lake, *Beginnings of Christianity*, 5:22–30.

22. For a comparison of Matthew's more sympathetic version with the more consistently villainous version of Luke, see L. Desautels, "La mort de Judas (Mt 27,3–10; Ac 1,15–26)," *Science et Esprit* 38 (1986): 221–39.

23. Cf. T. W. Berkley, "OT Exegesis and the Death of Judas," *Proceedings: Eastern Great Lakes and Midwest Biblical Societies* 14 (1994): 29–45, esp. 32: "All of these stories emphasize the power of God to deal with troublemakers, though each serves a specific purpose in its context."

24. On the influence of the Wisdom passage on Luke's version, see Foakes-Jackson & Lake, *Beginnings of Christianity*, 5:29; Benoit, "Death of Judas," 194; Klassen, *Judas*, 169; contra Berkley, "OT Exegesis and the Death of Judas," 34, though he admits

the passage is "consistent with one of Luke's underlying concerns." (I also discounted the influence earlier: Paffenroth, "Stories of the Fate of Judas," 80.)

25. The stereotyped stories often had things bursting from the victim's body, especially bowels or worms, as here and at Acts 12:23. See E. Jacquier, *Les Actes des Apotres* (Paris: Gabalda, 1926), 374; Desautels, "La mort de Judas," 236. See below on Papias for the full list of ghastly details.

26. Cited by D. Daube, "Judas," *California Law Review* 82 (1994): 95–108.

27. Or, "which caused pain when bodily necessities were fulfilled"; cf. the translation of P. W. van der Horst, "A Note on the Judas Curse in Early Christian Inscriptions," in *Hellenism-Judaism-Christianity* (ed. P. W. van der Horst; Kampen, Holland: Kok Pharos, 1994), 146–50, esp. 147–48.

28. My translation; for the Greek text, see K. Bihlmeyer, *Die apostolischen Väter* (Tübingen: J. C. B. Mohr, 1924), 136–37; J. Kürzinger, *Papias von Hierapolis und Evangelien des Neuen Testaments* (Regensburg: Friedrich Pustet, 1983), 104–5. For text and discussion, see E. Locard, "La mort de Judas Iscariote, étude critique d'exégèse et de médecine légale sur un cas de pendaison célèbre," *Archives d'anthropologie criminelle, de criminologie et psychologie normale et pathologique* 19 (1904): 421–54, esp. 446–47.

29. On their possible literary dependence, see Harris, "Did Judas Really Commit Suicide?" 502.

30. On the Papias fragment, see K. Paffenroth, "The Stories of the Fate of Judas," 73–75.

31. For lists of these, see Jacquier, *Actes des Apotres*, 374; Benoit, "Death of Judas," 194; Klauck, *Judas*, 116–21. For examples from other cultures, see J. Herber, "La mort de Judas," *Revue de l'histoire des religions* 129 (1945): 47–56.

32. See Numbers 5:27; *Babylonian Talmud, Ned.* 50b; *The Legend of Ahikar* 8:38–41, in *The Apocrypha and Pseudepigrapha of the Old Testament* (ed. R. H. Charles; Oxford: Clarendon Press, 1913), 776. On Ahikar, see also J. R. Harris, "St. Luke's Version of the Death of Judas," *American Journal of Theology* 18 (1914): 127–31.

33. See *The Legend of Ahikar* 8:38–41; Josephus, *Jewish War*, 7.11.4.453.

34. See 2 Macc. 9:7–12; Acts 12:23; Herodotus, *Persian Wars*, 4.205; Plutarch, *Lives*, Sulla, 36.

35. See Lucian, *Pseudomantis*, 59; Josephus, *Jewish Antiquities*, 27.6.5.169.

36. See 2 Macc. 9:7–12; Josephus, *Jewish Antiquities*, 27.6.5.169.

37. This connection is from Maccoby, *Judas Iscariot and the Myth of Jewish Evil*, 112.

38. On Abraham a Sancta Clara, see below, "Dante and the Middle Ages."

39. For dating, summary, and discussion, see J. K. Elliott, *The Apocryphal New Testament: A Collection of Apocryphal Christian Literature in an English Translation* (Rev. ed.; Oxford: Clarendon Press, 1993), 100–7. Cf. the discussion of it in Maccoby, *Judas Iscariot and the Myth of Jewish Evil*, 89–91.

40. Arabic Infancy Gospel, chapter 35; see A. Walker, trans., *Apocryphal Gospels, Acts, and Revelations* (Ante-Nicene Christian Library, vol. 16; Edinburgh: T. & T. Clark, 1873), 116–17.

41. For descriptions of the depiction of evil in some of these films, see P. Malone, *Movie Christs and Antichrists* (New York: Crossroad, 1990), 120–31.

42. For the last three years, the theme of my spring semester Core Humanities Seminar at Villanova University has been "Evil." My ruminations here come directly out of my class discussions with my students: as usual, I have learned more from them than they have from me.

43. Rufus in "The Lame Shall Enter First" is the most destructive, but the sadistic children in "The River" and "The Turkey" seem like less developed versions of the same, all pervasive evil; the annoying children in "A Good Man is Hard to Find" don't evoke much sympathy either. See F. O'Connor, *The Complete Stories* (New York: Farrar, Straus & Giroux, 1971).

44. See the excellent study by E. Kuryluk, *Salome and Judas in the Cave of Sex. The Grotesque: Origins, Iconography, Techniques* (Evanston, Ill.: Northwestern University Press, 1987), 259–98, 344–47.

45. The discussion of Judas and fate will be postponed until chapter 4.

46. My translation, from the French in J. Kahn, "Judas Iscariot: A Vehicle of Medieval Didacticism" (Ph.D. diss., University of Utah, 1976), 96.

47. See the discussion in O. Goetz, "Hie hencktt Judas," in *Form und Inhalt. Festschrift O. Schmitt* (Stuttgart: 1950), 105–37, esp. 112–13.

48. See Kahn, "Judas Iscariot," 96.

49. On Dante's version, especially its non–anti-Semitic character, see Maccoby, *Judas Iscariot and the Myth of Jewish Evil*, 117–18.

50. Dante, *Inferno* (trans. M. Musa; New York: Penguin Books, 1971), canto 34, lines 55–63.

51. See Dante, *Inferno*, canto 4, line 123; *Purgatory*, canto 18, 76–78; on Trajan, see Dante, *Paradise*, canto 20, lines 44–48, 103–14.

52. Cf. Maccoby, *Judas Iscariot and the Myth of Jewish Evil*, 117: "The other two mouths gnaw Brutus and Cassius, whom Dante regards as the sinners who destroyed the possibility of a universal Christian state when they murdered Julius Caesar."

53. Besides the exhortations considered here, Abraham also included the Oedipal legends that will be considered in chapter 4. He was also vehemently anti-Semitic, like the traditions considered in the next chapter. Abraham is of interest to historians precisely because he was so typical of his age, and yet emerged as more of a leader and spokesperson than anyone else of his time: "Nobody in the intervening period between the early eighteenth and the late nineteenth centuries in German-Austrian history handled the complex instrument of mass appeal with the mastery of Abraham a Sancta Clara. . . . nobody in the intervening period came even remotely as close . . . to the position of spokesman of the feelings of an urban lower middle class" (R. A. Kann, *A Study in Austrian Intellectual History: From Late Baroque to Romanticism* [New York: Frederick A. Praeger, 1960], 114; also quoted in Klassen, *Judas*, 18).

54. On Abraham, see W. Creizenach, "Judas Ischarioth in Legende und Sage des Mittelalters," *Beiträge zur Geschichte der Deutschen Sprache und Literatur* 2 (1875): 177–207, esp. 179–81; Baum, "Medieval Legend of Judas Iscariot," 569–71; Lüthi, *Judas Iskarioth*, 192–94; Kann, *A Study in Austrian Intellectual History*, 50–115; Klassen, *Judas*, 18–20.

55. See Baum, "Medieval Legend of Judas Iscariot," 570.

56. See P. F. Baum, "Judas's Red Hair," *Journal of English and Germanic Philology* 21 (1922): 520–29, esp. 520–21.

57. See Baum, "Medieval Legend of Judas Iscariot," 570.

58. Kann, *A Study in Austrian Intellectual History*, 84–88.

59. Baum, "Medieval Legend of Judas Iscariot," 570. On this point and the next, Abraham's misogyny is overt; see Kann, *A Study in Austrian Intellectual History*, 80–82.

60. Klassen, *Judas*, 19.

61. Baum, "Medieval Legend of Judas Iscariot," 571.

62. As we will see in the next chapter, this is very close to some anti-Semites' use of Judas as epitomizing every evil of which Jews have ever been accused. On Abraham's anti-Semitism, see Kann, *A Study in Austrian Intellectual History*, 76–79.

63. On these, see the studies by H. Martin, "The Judas Iscariot Curse," *The American Journal of Philology* 37 (1916): 434–51; A. Taylor, "Judas Iscariot in Charms and Incantations," *Washington University Studies* 8 (1920): 3–17; W. D. Hand, *A Dictionary of Words and Idioms Associated with Judas Iscariot: A Compilation Based Mainly on Material Found in the Germanic Languages* (Berkeley and Los Angeles: University of California Press, 1942), 323–24; B. McClean, "A Christian Epitaph: The Curse of Judas Iscariot," *Orientalia Christiana Periodica* 58 (1992): 241–44; P. W. van der Horst, "A Note on the Judas Curse in Early Christian Inscriptions," 146–50.

64. See Creizenach, "Judas Ischarioth in Legende und Sage des Mittelalters," 184–86; A. Taylor, "The Burning of Judas," *Washington University Studies* 11 (1923): 159–86; J. G. Frazer, *The Golden Bough*, vol. 10 (New York: Macmillan Co., 1935), 121.

65. See Martin, "The Judas Iscariot Curse," 442.

66. See the examples in Martin, "The Judas Iscariot Curse," 441–42; and Taylor, "Judas Iscariot in Charms," 13–14.

67. Text and translation from McLean, "Christian Epitaph," 241.

68. See van der Horst, "A Note on the Judas Curse," 147–49.

69. See Taylor, "Judas Iscariot in Charms," 3–17.

70. All the known examples are in French, and therefore involve a wordplay between "heat" *(chaleur)* and "color" *(couleur)*, which probably were originally both "heat": "O fever, lose your heat, as Judas lost his heat (fervor) when he betrayed our Lord"; see Taylor, "Judas Iscariot in Charms," 9.

71. Cf. S. Tarachow, "Judas the Beloved Executioner," *Psychoanalytical Quarterly* 29 (1960): 528–54, who notes the "curious ambivalence" in these traditions that use Judas "not only in curses but also in beneficent roles" (Tarachow, "Judas the Beloved Executioner," 547).

72. Fatou Sisé (class presentation, Calvin College, July 17, 2000) verified that this celebration was still practiced in Gambia.

73. See Taylor, "The Burning of Judas," 159–60. There is an interesting display about the Latin American celebrations at The Smithsonian Institute, Washington, D.C.

74. Taylor, "The Burning of Judas," 164.

75. Ibid., 172.

76. See the next chapter for more examples of hatred and violence towards "Judah" turning into real hatred and violence against the people of "Judah."

77. E.g., in Cyprus it was made to look like an Englishman, while in Portugal the practice was forbidden because the effigy resembled a local official; see Taylor, "The Burning of Judas," 164, 166.

78. E.g., among Indians in New Mexico; see Taylor, "The Burning of Judas," 184.

Chapter 3

1. Klassen, *Judas*, 143.

2. Cf. J. V. Brownson, "Neutralizing the Intimate Enemy: The Portrayal of Judas in the Fourth Gospel," *Society of Biblical Literature Seminar Papers* (1992): 49–60, esp. 58–59: "Yet in this gospel where demons are effectively absent, it is striking that the devil should play such a significant role in the characterization of Judas. This mode of symbolizing evil suggests that evil is regarded not as random and chaotic but as

malevolent and purposive. The transcendent evil which operates in the world of the fourth gospel intends not the random destruction and oppression of human life which we find in the synoptic exorcism stories, but rather a conscious and deliberate resistance to God's revelation in Jesus."

3. Cf. Brownson, "Neutralizing the Intimate Enemy," 57: "Thus it is clear that the fourth gospel takes the major motifs of the characterization of Judas (defection of an insider, association with the devil, and objections to Johannine christology) and uses the same motifs to characterize a whole group of people within the narrative."

4. Cf. Brownson, "Neutralizing the Intimate Enemy," 49–51.

5. On the gesture as one of contempt and hatred, see E. F. F. Bishop, "'He that eateth bread with me. . . .'" *Expository Times* 70 (1959–60): 331–33; Klassen, *Judas*, 149.

6. Cf. Klassen, *Judas*, 149: "But for John, light and darkness are essential parts of moral reality. When Judas departs, he takes leave of the light and goes out into the darkness."

7. Cf. Brownson, "Neutralizing the Intimate Enemy," 50: "Indeed, it may well be that John's omission of the synoptics' 'deal with the chief priests' is part of a larger effort to reconfigure the portrayal of Judas' motivation for betraying Jesus."

8. Klassen, *Judas*, 153.

9. Brownson, "Neutralizing the Intimate Enemy," 53.

10. On this passage, see W. E. Sproston, "The Scripture in John 17:12," in *Scripture: Meaning and Method. Essays Presented to Anthony Tyrrell Hanson on His Seventieth Birthday* (ed. B. Thompson; Hull: Hull University Press, 1987), 24–36.

11. Klassen, *Judas*, 154.

12. E.g., C. S. Griffin, *Judas Iscariot, the Author of the Fourth Gospel* (Boston: Scott-Parkin, 1892).

13. Thus John E. Hueter, *Matthew, Mark, Luke, John—Now Judas and His Redemption (In Search of the Real Judas)* (Brookline Village, Mass.: Branden Press, 1983), 150–77; on 178–91 he goes on to make Judas the author of Q as well. Other than his suggestion about Q, he is following the suggestion of Ludwig Noack (1819–85), *Die Geschichte Jesu auf Grund freier geschichtlicher Untersuchungen über das Evangelium und die Evangelien* (1876), summarized in Albert Schweitzer, *The Quest of the Historical Jesus: A Critical Study of Its Progress from Reimarus to Wrede*, 2d ed. (trans. W. Montgomery; London: A. & C. Black, 1936), 172–79.

14. Cf. Maccoby, *Judas Iscariot and the Myth of Jewish Evil*, 6: "In the ancient world, even the most virulent of Hellenistic anti-semites, such as Apion and Manetho, never accused the Jews of being money-hungry. On the contrary, they dismissed them as uncouth agriculturists who were unversed in trade, a charge from which Josephus, the Jewish historian, tried to defend them."

15. Quoted in L. Dinnerstein, *Antisemitism in America* (New York and Oxford: Oxford University Press, 1994), 57.

16. John Chrysostom, *Homilies on Matthew* (trans. G. Prevost; Edinburgh: T. & T. Clark; Grand Rapids: Wm. B. Eerdmans Publishing Co.; first published 1851; available online at http://www.ccel.org/fathers2/NPNF1-10/TOC.htm) homily 85.2; cf. Gärtner, *Iscariot*, 3.

17. John Chrysostom, *Discourses against Judaizing Christians* (trans. P. W. Harkins; Washington, DC: Catholic University Press, 1979), 1.7.1, 1.7.5. Despite the apologetic new title of this translation (instead of *Homilies against the Jews*), passages such as this are clearly directed against Jews, not Christians.

18. John Chrysostom, *Homilies on the Acts of the Apostles* (trans. J. Walker, et. al.; Edinburgh: T. & T. Clark; Grand Rapids: Wm. B. Eerdmans Publishing Co.; first published 1889; available online at http://www.ccel.org/fathers2/NPNF1-11/npnf1-11-10.htm#P272_117779) Homily 3. Cf. the discussion in Maccoby, *Judas Iscariot and the Myth of Jewish Evil*, 194–95.

19. My translation, from the French in Kahn, "Judas Iscariot," 43. For some reason, Kahn never considers the anti-Semitic overtones of the story.

20. On the increased brutality of the crucifixion scene in these plays, see G. Frank, *The Medieval French Drama* (Oxford: Clarendon Press, 1954), 178; F. G. Cohen, "Jewish Images in Late Medieval German Popular Plays," *Midstream* (Aug./Sept. 1989), 21–26; Maccoby, *Judas Iscariot and the Myth of Jewish Evil*, 107–8. For a general discussion of depictions of Jews in medieval drama, see H. Pflaum, "Les Scènes de Juifs dans la littérature dramatique du Moyen-âge," *Revue des études Juives* 89 (1930): 111–34.

21. Cf. Cohen, "Jewish Images in Late Medieval German Popular Plays," 22–23, 25: "Thus, when the distance in time between the staged events and the image of the contemporary Jew are telescoped into something like simultaneity, the times when Passions were given could be—and often were—perilous for the local Jews.... While no documented evidence exists that performances were followed by assaults on Jews, there are in city archives ordinances restricting Jews to their quarters under guard while such plays were given. The rationale was the need for their protection from violence"; Maccoby, *Judas Iscariot and the Myth of Jewish Evil*, 108: "Thus the Christian populace indulged in an orgy of dramatic sadism, performed by imaginary Jews, for whose imaginary cruelty the real Jews were punished with real cruelty"; J. Shapiro, *Oberammergau: The Troubling Story of the World's Most Famous Passion Play* (New York: Pantheon Books, 2000), 57–58.

22. On the haggling and attempted cheating, see Frank, *Medieval French Drama*, 127; Kahn, "Judas Iscariot," 42; Maccoby, *Judas Iscariot and the Myth of Jewish Evil*, 108.

23. Cohen, "Jewish Images in Late Medieval German Popular Plays," 25.

24. Cf. Cohen, "Jewish Images in Late Medieval German Popular Plays," 25: "While no doubt amusing by contemporary standards, its intent was to reinforce the contemporary notion of the Jew as swindler. As moneylenders and pawnbrokers they were easy targets for accusations of avarice, cupidity, and hard-heartedness."

25. My translation, keeping the rhyme to accentuate the comic villainy of the scene, from the French in Kahn, "Judas Iscariot," 43–44.

26. See the next chapter for a consideration of how a similar comic villainy functions differently in Jewish tales of Jesus and Judas. Cf. Maccoby, *Judas Iscariot and the Myth of Jewish Evil*, 182: "It should be noted that there is a certain savage humour about the portrayal of Jews (including Judas and Herod) in the Passion Plays. It should not be thought, however, that this humour mitigates the hatred and contempt expressed."

27. Shapiro, *Oberammergau*, 59.

28. On the Oberammergau passion play, see Shapiro, *Oberammergau*, esp. 58–100. Cf. how different is the glowing, sentimental praise and the complete ignoring of anything negative from the Nazi years in an earlier account by E. H. C. Corathiel, *Oberammergau and Its Passion Play* (Westminster, Md.: Newman Press, 1960). On the 2000 production of the passion, see T. Dashuber, *Ecce Homo: The Making of the Passion Play* (Munich: Prestel, 2000).

29. Shapiro, *Oberammergau*, 58.

30. Ibid., 12.
31. Ibid., 105–7.
32. Ibid., 59–61.
33. Ibid., 61.
34. Ibid., 65–68.
35. Ibid., 70.
36. Ibid., 70.
37. Ibid., 72.
38. W. T. Stead, *The Passion Play at Ober Ammergau 1910* (London: Stead's Publishing, 1910), act 2, tableau 3, 99. Cf. the German edition of 1930, J. A. Daisenberger, *Das Passions-Spiel in Oberammergau* (Munich: Joseph Hubers, 1930), 22. This violent call to arms is accentuated in the 1934 version, which excises the call to mercy that follows these lines: "Nay!—not to destroy—whate'er our merit— / Came He from His Father's place, / Sinners through His mercy shall inherit / Mercy, blessedness, and grace"; see Shapiro, *Oberammergau*, 159–60.
39. See Shapiro, *Oberammergau*, 165–70.
40. Ibid., 149–50.
41. On the history of the protest, see ibid., 73–87.
42. For discussion of the 2000 production, see ibid., 187–223.
43. Daisenberger, *Das Passions-Spiel*, act 4, scene 4, 141–43.
44. Ibid., act 6, scene 2, 173–75.
45. Ibid., act 10, scene 7, 249–51.
46. Edouard Drumont, quoted in Maccoby, *Judas Iscariot and the Myth of Jewish Evil*, 121.
47. Maccoby, *Judas Iscariot and the Myth of Jewish Evil*, ix.
48. T. T. Timayenis, *Judas Iscariot: An Old Type in a New Form* (New York: Minerva, 1889).
49. The biographical details are from L. A. Greenberg and H. J. Jonas, "An American Anti-Semite in the Nineteenth Century," in *Essays on Jewish Life and Thought* (eds. J. L. Blau, et al.; New York: Columbia University Press, 1959), 265–83.
50. The other two are *The Original Mr. Jacobs: A Startling Exposé* (New York: Minerva, 1888) and *The American Jew: An Exposé of His Career* (New York: Minerva, 1888).
51. This is the hypothesis of Greenberg and Jonas, "An American Anti-Semite," 279.
52. See ibid., 276–77.
53. Timayenis, *Judas Iscariot*, 6.
54. Ibid., 8–15, 113.
55. Ibid., 117–30.
56. Not even I had heard of this one before: ibid., 13.
57. Ibid., 16–18, 140–41. Of course, the biological principle behind how this offers any solution to their supposed sterility is left unstated.
58. Ibid., 19–26, 200–21.
59. Another new accusation to me, and one he seems to relish especially: ibid., 36–43.
60. Ibid., 61–64.
61. Ibid., 91–92, 281–84.
62. Ibid., 181–82.
63. Ibid., 221–40, 267–84.
64. Ibid., 241–67.
65. Ibid., 56.

66. Ibid., 218.
67. Cf. the discussion of Luther in Cohen, "Jewish Images in Late Medieval German Popular Plays," 26.
68. Timayenis, *Judas Iscariot*, 292; on the Nazis' Madagascar plan, see L. S. Dawidowicz, *The War against the Jews 1933–1945* (New York: Bantam Books, 1986), 118–19.
69. Greenberg and Jonas, "An American Anti-Semite," 279.
70. Dinnerstein, *Antisemitism in America*, 35.
71. Timayenis, *Judas Iscariot*, 130–37, 273.
72. Ibid., 120, 185–91.
73. This connection comes from Maccoby, *Judas Iscariot and the Myth of Jewish Evil*, 112–13.
74. Sermon by Sidney Dean, quoted in D. B. Chesebrough, *"No Sorrow like Our Sorrow": Northern Protestant Ministers and the Assassination of Lincoln* (Kent, Ohio, and London: Kent State University Press, 1994), 41.
75. It was still used in the section title, "American Judas," in a popular book on Lincoln seventy-six years after his death: L. Lewis, *Myths after Lincoln* (New York: Press of the Readers Club, 1941).
76. Lewis, *Myths after Lincoln*, 169–71.
77. Ibid., 144.
78. Ibid., 232–41.
79. Ibid., 203–4, 243.
80. J. W. T. Hart, *The Autobiography of Judas Iscariot: A Character Study* (London: Kegan Paul, Trench, & Co., 1884), vii.
81. Ibid., 3; emphasis in original.
82. Ibid., 28–29.
83. Ibid., 36.
84. Ibid., 146.
85. H. Monro, *Judas* (London: Sampson Low, Marston, & Co., 1911).
86. Ibid., 5.
87. Ibid., 5–8.
88. Dante, *Inferno*, canto 17, lines 55–75. Significantly, Dante's usurers are not depicted as typically or exclusively Jewish: cf. Maccoby, *Judas Iscariot and the Myth of Jewish Evil*, 117–18.
89. Monro, *Judas*, 18.
90. Ibid., 20.
91. Ibid., 26–27.
92. E. Linklater, *Judas* (London: Jonathan Cape, 1939).
93. Ibid., 12.
94. Ibid., 23.
95. Ibid., 60–67.
96. Ibid., 112–14.
97. Ibid., 21.
98. Ibid., 145.
99. Ibid., 216–17.
100. See Flannery O'Connor, *The Complete Stories* (New York: Farrar, Straus & Giroux, 1971). There are many such characters in her work: I am thinking of Sheppard in

"The Lame Shall Enter First," Mrs. May in "Greenleaf," and Mrs. Turpin in "Revelation," whose epiphany is the only one among these that is not fatal.

101. See Baum, "Judas's Red Hair," 520–29; Hand, *Words and Idioms Associated with Judas Iscariot*, 322–23; R. Mellinkoff, "Judas's Red Hair and the Jews," *Journal of Jewish Art* 9 (1982): 31–46. The providential coincidences continue to pile up, as the present author (partly) shares this characteristic with Judas.

102. On the caricaturing of Judas and Jews in art, see Maccoby, *Judas Iscariot and the Myth of Jewish Evil*, 112–15.

103. Cf. Mellinkoff, "Judas's Red Hair," 44: "The portrayals of Judas with red hair (both with and without Jewish caricatures) discussed in this article, as well as others I have collected, are in fact scanty evidence of this red hair (or skin) theme. Judas was depicted with caricatured Jewish features and dark hair, perhaps more often then [sic] with red hair. It is the prolonged rumors of faulty scholarship that have generated the belief that Judas was always, or almost always, depicted with red hair."

104. As in Cecil B. DeMille's *The King of Kings*, in which Judas's features are very Roman, and he is beardless, as opposed to Jesus and the other disciples, all of whom look very Semitic and are bearded. See the next chapter for a discussion of the film.

105. Heretics were also made to wear yellow robes *(sanbenitos)* in the Inquisition; see H. Kamen, *The Spanish Inquisition* (New Haven and London: Yale University Press, 1997), 209–10. In *Jesus Christ Superstar*, Judas and several other disciples are played by African Americans, and Judas is dressed in a striking red pantsuit to further set him apart: see the next chapter for a discussion of the film.

106. See the list in Mellinkoff, "Judas's Red Hair," 31. Cf. the fuller analyses of visual depictions in H. Jursch, "Judas Iskarioth in der Kunst," in *Wissenschaftliche Zeitschrift der Friedrich Schiller Universität* (Jena: 1952), 101–5, who does an excellent job tracing the development of these depictions of Judas from a deservedly punished villain to an enigma *(rätsel)* of good and evil. See also G. Schiller, *Iconography of Christian Art. Volume 2: The Passion of Jesus Christ* (trans. J. Seligman; London: Lund Humphries, 1972), 28–41, 51–56.

107. See Baum, "Judas's Red Hair," 526–27; Mellinkoff, "Judas's Red Hair," 46.

108. Mellinkoff, "Judas's Red Hair," 46. The aversion to left-handedness as "sinister" would seem exactly the same.

109. Baum, "Judas's Red Hair," 524.

110. Ibid., 523.

111. See the critique of this position in Shapiro, *Oberammergau*, 160–62.

112. E. Wiesel, *Trial of God* (New York: Random House, 1979).

113. Smith, "Judas Iscariot," 539; emphasis in original. Cf. the critique of this by Krauss, "Judas Iscariot," 199–207. Cf. the similar conclusion of Loisy, *Origins of the New Testament*, 100, that Judas was "a symbol of Judaism as the villain of the piece," and the summary of Loisy in P. E. Lapide, "Verräter oder verraten? Judas in evangelischer und jüdischer Sicht," *Lutherisches Monatsheft* 16 (1977): 75–79: 78.

114. D. Bonhoeffer, "Predigt am Sonntag Judika über Judas," in *Gesammelte Schriften*, vol. 4 (ed. E. Bethge; Munich: Chr. Kaiser Verlag, 1961), 406–13: 412; cited and translated in Klassen, *Judas*, 31.

115. K. Barth, *Church Dogmatics*, vol. 2.2 (trans. G. W. Bromiley, et al.; Edinburgh: T. & T. Clark, 1957), 464–65; cf. the discussion of Barth's anti-Semitism in Klassen, *Judas*, 190–91.

116. T. S. Moore, *Judas* (London: G. Richards, 1923). The biographical details are from

Great Writers of the English Language: Poets (ed. J. Vinson; London: Macmillan Publishers, 1979), 713.

117. Ibid., 9, 29, 31, 57.
118. Ibid., 44–45.
119. Ibid., 10, 20–21, 48.
120. Ibid., 40.
121. Ibid., 16.
122. Ibid., 35.
123. Ibid., 58–59.
124. Ibid., 41, 51.
125. Ibid., 50.
126. Cf. the similarly anti-Semitic contrast in W. W. Story, *A Roman Lawyer in Jerusalem* (Boston: Loring, 1870), reprinted as *In Defense of Judas* (Wausau, Wisc.: Philosopher Press, 1902). Jesus and his followers were nascent socialists, fighting against the evil, wealthy Jews: "What most aroused the wealthy Rabbis' rage was that he set the poor against the rich" (10).
127. Moore, *Judas*, 26–27.
128. Moore, *Judas*, 30; for the roots of this theory, see Frazer, *The Golden Bough*, vol. 9, 392–407, who believed Purim is reminiscent of an ancient festival in which a man in the character of a god was sacrificed. For the same theory, see also A. Drews, *The Christ Myth* (repr. ed. Amherst, N.Y.: Prometheus Books, 1998; originally published: Chicago: Open Court, 1910), 75.
129. A. Nicole, *Judas the Betrayer* (Grand Rapids: Baker Book House, 1957). The book first appeared in French in 1924. Biographical details are from J. W. Flight, "Judas the Betrayer [review]," *Journal of Bible and Religion* 26 (1958): 274–75, and from personal correspondence with Audrey Leach and Amy Nemecek of Baker Book House (March 13 and 16, 2000).
130. Nicole, *Judas the Betrayer*, 13.
131. Ibid., 76–77.
132. Ibid., 9–10.
133. Ibid., 23–24.

Chapter 4

1. Irenaeus, *Against the Heresies* (trans. D. J. Unger; New York: Paulist Press, 1992), 102–3; Epiphanius, *The Panarion* (trans. P. R. Amidon; New York and Oxford: Oxford University Press, 1990), 133–35. For discussion of the Gnostics, see Locard, "La mort de Judas," 428–30; Gärtner, *Iscariot*, 3; Maccoby, *Judas Iscariot and the Myth of Jewish Evil*, 92–96.
2. Epiphanius, *Panarion*, 38.1.3–38.1.5; 38.3.3–38.3.5.
3. Ibid., section 2.1.1, on the possible connection between Judas's death and that of Korah.
4. Ibid., 38.3.1.
5. Irenaeus, *Against the Heresies*, 31.1.
6. Cf. K. Beyschlag, "Franz von Assisi und Judas Iskariot," *Theologische Literaturzeitung* 85 (1960): 849–52.
7. H. Kemp, *Judas* (New York: Mitchell Kennerley, 1913). On Kemp, see W. Brevda, *Harry Kemp, the Last Bohemian* (London and Toronto: Associated University Presses, 1986).

8. Kemp, *Judas*, 181–82.
9. Ibid., 177, 207, 223.
10. See "Judas the Disillusioned and Vengeful Patriot," p. 83, and "Judas the Instigating Revolutionary," p. 86.
11. Kemp, *Judas*, 245.
12. Ibid., 245.
13. E. S. Bates, *The Gospel according to Judas Iscariot* (London: William Heinemann, 1929).
14. Ibid., 9–83.
15. Ibid., 98.
16. Ibid., 151.
17. Ibid., 181.
18. Ibid., 203.
19. Ibid., 226.
20. Albert Lévitt, *Judas Iscariot: An Imaginative Autobiography* (Hancock, N.H.: Flagstone Publications, 1961). Biographical information on Lévitt is from the Washington and Lee University website: http://www.law.wlu.edu/faculty/history/levitt.htm. On Lévitt, cf. the introduction in Gärtner, *Iscariot*, x. Cf. the similar reconstruction of W. Jens, *Der Fall Judas* (Stuttgart: Kreuz-Verlag, 1975), summarized in Lapide, "Verräter oder verraten?" 79.
21. Lévitt, *Judas Iscariot*, 13.
22. Ibid., 15–16.
23. Ibid., 21–22.
24. Ibid., 52.
25. Ibid., 65.
26. On the movie, see Baugh, *Imaging the Divine*, 42–47.
27. Judas is equated with John the Baptist in *Godspell*, an identity that is also hinted at in *Jesus of Montreal*; see Baugh, *Imaging the Divine*, 123.
28. Baugh, *Imaging the Divine*, 44.
29. Ibid., 45.
30. Klassen, *Judas*, 202–3; cf. the earlier reconstruction of Griffin, *Judas Iscariot, the Author of the Fourth Gospel*, 3: "That Judas was not a traitor will be shown further on, although he went to the enemy in the guise of a betrayer, but he only did as Jesus told him privately to do."
31. Klassen, *Judas*, 47–61.
32. Ibid., 77–95.
33. Ibid., 96–159.
34. Ibid., 203.
35. Kim Paffenroth, "Review of *Judas: Friend or Betrayer of Jesus?*" *Journal of Religion* 78 (1998): 104–5: 104.
36. Paffenroth, "Review," 105.
37. M. Callaghan, *A Time for Judas* (Toronto: Macmillan of Canada, 1983).
38. Cf. Klauck (*Judas, ein Jünger des Herrn*, 26–28, 30–32) considers that Judas may be a product of the story (*Sagenbildung*) or a function of the story structure (*Erzählstruktur*).
39. Callaghan, *A Time for Judas*, 125.
40. Ibid., 245.
41. This balance is part of what made the story fascinating and troubling for Origen. See S. Laeuchli, "Origen's Interpretation of Judas Iscariot," *Church History* 22 (1953):

253–68, esp. 266: "Here is Judas, and to omit any active part on his side means to land in a monistic neoplatonism; there is God, and to leave him out would make the world an immanent realm and the death of Christ a result of merely historical constellations. . . . [Origen] is not willing to sacrifice either the human responsibility nor the devil's participation nor the presence of God in the life of Christ." Cf. Gärtner, *Iscariot*, 4.

42. Thus C. C. Cary, "The Case of Judas Iscariot," *Methodist Quarterly Review* 59 (1910): 825–29; L. D. Weatherhead, *Personalities in the Passion: A Devotional Study of Some of the Characters Who Played a Part in the Drama of Christ's Passion and Resurrection* (Nashville: Abingdon-Cokesbury Press, 1943), 26–39.

43. H. Wagner, "Judas: Das Geheimnis der Sünde, menschliche Freiheit und Gottes Heilsplan," in *Judas Iskariot: Menschliches oder heilsgeschichtliches Drama?* (H. Wagner, ed.; Frankfurt: Knecht, 1985), 11–38.

44. See "Judas the Misunderstood Revolutionary and Patriot" and "Judas the Lover," pp. 82 and 101. See also the strange amalgamation in G. D'Arci (pseudonym for F. Tavani), *The Tragedy of Judas Iscariot* (Amersham, U.K.: Mascot Press, 1926), in which Judas stops courting his mother as soon as he finds out who she is, but still feels totally bound by fate for some reason:

The flower from its own beauty is not free;
The hand of God to it its path assigns:
Free is not man for other destiny
Than that which God within man's will designs. (D'Arci, *Tragedy of Judas*, 14)

45. See the excellent history in P. F. Baum, "The Medieval Legend of Judas Iscariot," *Publications of the Modern Language Association* 31 (1916): 481–632.

46. Cf. J. Kahn, "Judas Iscariot: A Vehicle of Medieval Didacticism" (Ph.D. diss., University of Utah, 1976), 107. For a fuller discussion of literate and oral influences on the stories, see L. Edmunds, *Oedipus: The Ancient Legend and Its Later Analogues* (Baltimore and London: Johns Hopkins University Press, 1985), 17–19. Also cf. Baum, "Medieval Legend of Judas Iscariot," 607–20, who presents both the case that the stories are completely folkloristic and have no reliance on the literary tradition of Oedipus, as well as the case that the stories could have been derived from the literary tradition of Oedipus, concluding that both are equally probable.

47. Origen, *Contra Celsum* (trans. H. Chadwick; Cambridge, U.K.: Cambridge University Press, 1965), 2.20.85.

48. On the history and development of the versions before *The Golden Legend*, see E. K. Rand, "Medieval Lives of Judas Iscariot," in *Anniversary Papers by Colleagues and Pupils of George Lyman Kittredge* (Boston: Ginn & Co., 1913), 305–16; P. F. Baum, "The Medieval Legend of Judas Iscariot," 481–632; Kahn, "Judas Iscariot," 104–8.

49. Jacobus de Voragine, *The Golden Legend* (trans. G. Ryan and H. Ripperger; New York: Arno Press, 1969), 172–74; cf. the summary in Baum, "Medieval Legend of Judas," 482–83. See also the discussions in Creizenach, "Judas Ischarioth in Legende und Sage des Mittelalters," 193–202; P. Lehmann, "Judas Ischarioth in der lateinischen Legendenüberlieferung des Mittelalters," *Studi medievali* 2 (1929): 289–346; Maccoby, *Judas Iscariot and the Myth of Jewish Evil*, 102–7. An incomplete version (ca. fifteenth century) is found in *The Wakefield Mystery Plays* (ed. M. Rose; New York and London: W. W. Norton, 1969), 390–92.

50. See Baum, "Medieval Legend of Judas Iscariot," 532, 542–44; T. Hahn, "The Medieval Oedipus," *Comparative Literature* 32 (1980): 225–37.
51. My translation, from the French in Kahn, "Judas Iscariot," 159–60.
52. The first time I encountered this story was in an eighteenth-century version: Anonymous, *The Life, Character, and Death of Judas Iscariot, that Traytor, Who Betray'd Our Blessed Lord and Saviour Jesus Christ* (London: Edward Midwinter, 1711). The story is given similarly in other eighteenth- and nineteenth-century versions: Anonymous, *The Life of Judas Iscariot, Who Betrayed his Lord and Master* (Philadelphia, 1794); J. Thompson, *The Lost and Undone Son of Perdition: Or the Birth, Life, and Character of Judas Iscariot* (Catskill: Samuel Peck, 1808). On these late versions, see Baum, "Medieval Legend of Judas," 571–81.
53. Cf. Baum, "Medieval Legend of Judas," 483; Kahn, "Judas Iscariot," 102–3, and esp. 171: "Before Judas becomes a deicide, we see him guilty of murder, parricide, and incest, already an object of horror and disgust."
54. Cf. the similar analysis of R. Axton, "Interpretations of Judas in Middle English Literature," in *Religion in the Poetry and Drama of the Late Middle Ages in England* (eds. P. Boitani and A. Torti; Cambridge, U.K.: D. S. Brewer, 1990), 179–97, esp. 182.
55. Kahn's criticism of the passion plays' depiction of Judas: Kahn, "Judas Iscariot," 160–61.
56. Cf. Baum, "Medieval Legend of Judas," 484: ". . . but the truth is rather that the Middle Ages were not too particular about finical consistency. If the story were a good one and the moral a good one, why, what more could be desired? From the early Fathers and homilists down, there was ample precedent for finding instructive illustrations where they did not exist, as well as for appending morals that did not fit with extreme accuracy."
57. Cf. Axton, "Interpretations of Judas in Middle English Literature," 197: ". . . yet the medieval authors do not usually point to the *contrast* between the two cycles of sin; rather, they seem fascinated by the way in which his deeds fulfil a divine prophecy, and by the small space which that seems to allow for the operation of freewill" (emphasis in original).
58. See Creizenach, "Judas Ischarioth in Legende und Sage des Mittelalters," 202–3; D. Schendler, "Judas, Oedipus, and Various Saints," *Psychoanalysis* 2–3 (1954): 41–46; Edmunds, *Oedipus*, 17–22; Axton, "Interpretations of Judas," 197.
59. Schendler, "Judas," 46: ". . . if Christ was indeed God, as the Christians say, then his story is as incestuous a tale as has ever been told. For having as God taken to wife his own mother, he becomes his own father and dies atoning for the sins of the world." Even the imagery of lameness and blindness may have been used to equate Jesus and Oedipus: see N. Reider, "Medieval Oedipal Legends about Judas," *Psychoanalytic Quarterly* 29 (1960): 515–27, esp. 523. See also Mela, "Oedipe, Judas, Osiris," 205–8.
60. See V. Diederichs, "Russische Verwandte der legende von Gregor auf dem stein und der sage von Judas Ischariot," *Russische Revue* 17 (1880): 119–46; Baum, "Medieval Legend of Judas Iscariot," 595–97; Schendler, "Judas, Oedipus and Various Saints," 43–44; Edmunds, *Oedipus*, 17–22, 79–88; Axton, "Interpretations of Judas in Middle English Literature," 197; C. Mela, "Oedipe, Judas, Osiris," in *Histoire et Société: Mélanges offerts à Georges Duby* (C. La Ronciére, ed.; Aix-en-Provence: Université de Provence, 1992), 201–20, esp. 210–11.

61. See Baum, "Medieval Legend of Judas Iscariot," 597–98; Edmunds, *Oedipus*, 186–87, 188–92, 195–97.
62. See Baum, "Medieval Legend of Judas Iscariot," 598–99; Schendler, "Judas, Oedipus and Various Saints," 44.
63. See Schendler, "Judas," 42–43; Edmunds, *Oedipus*, 36–38.
64. Cf. Schendler, "Judas," 42–43: ". . . mother-son incest . . . elicits a purgation of the spirit in a fury of repentance, and a subsequent spiritual rarefaction that is sometimes quite saintly. The incestuous act is something in the nature of a revelation which uncovers dark unconscious motives." For a modern meditation on how the stories of Oedipus and Judas function in similar ways to contemplate the mystery of fate and evil, see also D. Stalter-Fouilloy, "Les maudits," *Revue d'Histoire et de Philosophie Religieuses* 66 (1986): 451–58.
65. Hahn, "The Medieval Oedipus," 237.
66. Ibid., 237, cf. his discussion on 228–29.
67. Ibid., 227.
68. For text and discussion, see P. F. Baum, "The English Ballad of Judas Iscariot," *Publications of the Modern Language Association* 31 (1916): 181–89; D. G. Schueler, "The Middle English *Judas:* An Interpretation," *Publications of the Modern Language Association* 91 (1976): 840–45; Hahn, "The Medieval Oedipus," 227–28; M. Stouck, "A Reading of the Middle English *Judas,*" *Journal of English and Germanic Philology* 80 (1981): 188–98; R. Axton, "Interpretations of Judas in Middle English Literature," in *Religion in the Poetry and Drama of the Late Middle Ages in England* (P. Boitani and A. Torti, eds.; Cambridge, U.K.: D. S. Brewer, 1990), 179–97.
69. Trans. Schueler, "The Middle English *Judas,*" 840.
70. J. J. Niles, *The Ballad Book of John Jacob Niles* (New York: Dover Publications, 1960), 93.
71. See "Judas the Lover," p. 101. Cf. Baum, "The English Ballad of Judas Iscariot," 183, 188, who discounts the Oedipal theme and accentuates the woman-blaming theme. See also Hand, *Dictionary of Words and Idioms*, 346, on the *Judas-schwester.* See Taylor, "The Gallows of Judas Iscariot," 149, for a similar folk tale in which Judas loses the money and betrays Jesus to replace it, but which does not include his sister.
72. See Axton, "Judas in Middle English Literature," 194.
73. See Stouck, "A Reading of the Middle English *Judas,*" 189; Axton, "Judas in Middle English Literature," 195.
74. Contra Stouck, "A Reading of the Middle English *Judas,*" 198: "The Judas of the poem is the same villain as the Judas traditionally despised throughout Christendom; only here he is fully and imaginatively revealed."
75. Cf. Axton, "Judas in Middle English Literature," 196: "As a result Judas seems robbed of active power, to be merely the object of commands thrust upon him by others—Christ, the woman, Pilate. It is notable that his most decisive action is against himself—a proleptic image of suicide."
76. See W. D. Hand, "The Birthday of Judas Iscariot: A Study in Folklore," *Modern Language Forum* 25 (1940): 1–8, who reckons that the speculations go back at least to the sixteenth century, but probably not before the fourteenth: Hand, "The Birthday of Judas," 2–3. The examples he gives are from Austria, Germany, Hungary, Ireland, Scotland, and Portugal. Cf. also Hand, *Words and Idioms Associated with Judas Iscariot,* 348–49.

77. Hand, "The Birthday of Judas," 8. Perhaps not insignificantly, I was born on March 7.
78. Ibid., 5.
79. Ibid., 7.
80. See "Judas the Lover," p. 101, on the many versions that depict Judas as a great and ill-fated lover.
81. Hand, "The Birthday of Judas," 5, 8.
82. Cf. Hand, "The Birthday of Judas," 1: "In the broadest sense the fixing of Judas' birthday represents an attempt, I suppose, to view the dire deed of Judas in terms of a predetermined fate, of which the birthday itself becomes, consciously or unconsciously, the outward symbol."
83. See G. F. Hill, "The Thirty Pieces of Silver," *Archaeologia* 59 (1905): 235–54, repr. in G. F. Hill, *The Medallic Portraits of Christ. The False Shekels. The Thirty Pieces of Silver* (Oxford: Clarendon Press, 1920), 91–116; his analysis greatly expands on that of F. de Mély, "Les deniers de Judas dans la tradition du moyen age," *Revue numismatique* 4, no. 3 (1899): 500–9. See also Lehmann, "Judas Ischarioth," 295–301; and B. Dieckmann, *Judas als Sündenbock: eine verhängnisvolle Geschichte von Angst und Vergeltung* (Munich: Kösel, 1991), 107–121.
84. See P. Cherchi, "A Legend from St. Bartholomew's Gospel in the Twelfth-Century," *Revue Biblique* 91 (1984): 212–18. Coptic fragments have been assigned to various known or hypothetical works, and they date from the fifth or sixth century; see J. K. Elliott, *The Apocryphal New Testament: A Collection of Apocryphal Christian Literature in an English Translation* (rev. ed.; Oxford: Clarendon Press, 1993), 161–63, 652–53.
85. None of these relics are of a kind that was in circulation in first-century Judea: Hill, "Thirty Pieces," 245. Most of them are from Rhodes, possibly because the word *RODION* was taken to be a reference to Herod; see Mély, "Les deniers," 509; *contra* Hill, "Thirty Pieces," 250–51.
86. Hill, "Thirty Pieces," 240.
87. Ibid., 249.
88. This question is taken up ably by J. Shapiro, *Shakespeare and the Jews* (New York: Columbia University Press, 1996).
89. On Shakespeare's interest in Judas, see P. Milward, *Shakespeare's Religious Background* (Bloomington & London: Indiana University Press, 1973): 99–100. Thanks to Robert McCutchen for this reference.
90. Shakespeare, *As You Like It* 3.4.8–9; *Love's Labours Lost* 5.2.595–630.
91. Nine archetypal great men in medieval legend; see A. S. Mercante, *The Facts on File Encyclopedia of World Mythology and Legend* (New York and Oxford: Facts on File, 1988), 482.
92. *The Winter's Tale*, 1.2.412–19:

> POLIXENES: O then my best blood turn
> To an infected jelly, and my name
> Be yoked with his that did betray the best!
> Turn then my freshest reputation to
> A savour that may strike the dullest nostril
> Where I arrive, and my approach be shunned,
> Nay, hated too, worse than the great'st infection
> That e'er was heard or read.

93. *Timon of Athens* 1.2.40; 3.2.68.
94. *Othello* 5.2.347–48.
95. Put forth by N. Cervo, "Shakespeare's 'Othello,'" *The Explicator* 53 (1995): 189–91.
96. Although he discredits the reference to Judas, cf. Cervo, 191: "One of the play's themes, I believe, is not only that Desdemona is wholly innocent but also, as contemplated within a valuable metaphor, a Holy Innocent." I think this is correct, but then the clearest reference would be to Christ, the undisputedly holy innocent in Christian tradition, rather than Cervo's suggestion that this refers to Herod's killing of Mariamne (never mentioned in the New Testament) and of the "Holy Innocents" (the infants of Matt. 2:16, never called "Holy Innocents").
97. *King John* 5.6.23–30; see the discussion of J. H. Morey, "The Death of King John in Shakespeare and Bale," *Shakespeare Quarterly* 45 (1994): 327–31.
98. On Shakespeare's use of his predecessors, see Morey, "The Death of King John," 330. Again, the swelling may show knowledge of Papias's version of Judas's death.
99. Morey, "Death of King John," 331, who draws the parallel in *King John*, but hesitates to do it for *Richard II*.
100. *Richard II* 3.2.132 and 4.1.170.
101. Ibid., 5.6.38–44.
102. See M. Hattaway, ed., *The Third Part of King Henry VI* (Cambridge, U.K.: Cambridge University Press, 1993), 14–15.
103. Ibid., 5.7.33.
104. *Richard III* 1.4.107–10.
105. For recent scholarly discussions of Judas as Zealot, see S. G. F. Brandon, *Jesus and the Zealots: A Study of the Political Factor in Primitive Christianity* (New York: Charles Scribner's Sons, 1967), 204; Lapide, "Verräter oder verraten?" 75–76. For the most popular argument for there being a Zealot temptation (not necessarily from Judas) that Jesus rejected, see J. H. Yoder, *The Politics of Jesus*, 2d ed. (Grand Rapids: Wm. B. Eerdmans Publishing Co., 1994), 56–59.
106. See Stephen Happel, "The Postmodernity of Judas: Religious Narrative and the Deconstruction of Time," in *Postmodernism, Literature, and the Future of Theology* (ed. D. Jasper; London: Macmillan/New York: St. Martin's Press, 1993), 91–119, on the psychologizing trend in these versions.
107. Though the accusation of greed still has its defenders; see above, chapter 3, on Albert Nicole, and also R. Stade, "Der Verrat des Judas vom kriminalistischen Gesichtspunkt aus," *Zeitschrift für Religionspsychologie* 3 (1909): 273–82, 311–23.
108. Cf. R. Goetz, "Judas as Patron Saint," *The Christian Century* 104 (March 18, 1987): 262–63, esp. 262: "And if the impoverished Jesus *were* God's answer to Israel's desperate cry, this seemed like a cruel joke."
109. For a Freudian analysis of such a disaffection, see D. Roquefort, "Judas: une figure de la perversion," *Études Théologiques et Religieuses* 58 (1983): 501–13.
110. J. Bonar, *Observations on the Conduct and Character of Judas Iscariot, in a Letter to the Reverend Mr. J. P.*, 2d ed. (Edinburgh: W. Miller, 1751). Biographical information on Bonar is from *The Dictionary of National Biography*, vol. 5 (ed. L. Stephen; London: Smith, Elder, & Co., 1886), 336; and Hew Scott, *Fasti Ecclesiae Scoticanae: The Succession of Ministers in the Church of Scotland from the Reformation*, vol. 4 (Edinburgh: Oliver & Boyd, 1923), 235. Thanks to Jim Fieser of the University of Tennessee at Martin for his help with this.
111. Bonar, *Observations on the Conduct and Character of Judas Iscariot*, 29.

112. Ibid., 19–20, 33.
113. Almost the same scenario appears in Carey, *Jesus and Judas*, see esp. 83–84.
114. F. Kendon, *A Life and Death of Judas Iscariot* (London: John Lane, 1926).
115. Ibid., 10.
116. Ibid., 10–22. Here Kendon also speculates that Judas was a potter (10–33), which is also part of Carey's depiction (Carey, *Jesus and Judas*, 27).
117. Kendon, *Life and Death of Judas Iscariot*, 39–42, 71–73.
118. Ibid., 95–96.
119. Ibid., 97.
120. Ibid., 106.
121. C. W. Topping, *Jewish Flower Child: An Historical Novel* (Toronto: McClelland & Stewart, 1970).
122. Biographical details are from the book's dust jacket, from the University of British Columbia's website (http://www.library.ubc.ca/spcoll/ubc_arch/u_arch/topping.html), and from personal correspondence with Erwin Wodarczak of the University of British Columbia and Kelly Duncan of the Vancouver School of Theology.
123. Topping, *Jewish Flower Child*, 161. Caiaphas makes the same promise in H. D. C. Pepler, *Judas, or, The Betrayal: A Play in One Act with Prologue and Epilogue* (Ditchling, U.K.: St. Dominic's Press, 1956), 9–10, and in G. D'Arci, *The Tragedy of Judas Iscariot, A Modern Drama in a Prologue and Five Acts* (Amersham, U.K.: Mascot Press, 1926), 43.
124. Topping, *Jewish Flower Child*, 187.
125. Ibid., 191.
126. For a recent and perhaps overly psychologized biography, see G. Lindop, *The Opium Eater: A Life of Thomas De Quincey* (New York: Taplinger Publishing Co., 1981).
127. T. DeQuincey, "Judas Iscariot," in *Theological Essays and Other Papers* (Boston: J. R. Osgood, 1873), 115–53.
128. Ibid., 115.
129. Ibid., 118; emphasis in original.
130. Ibid., 121.
131. Ibid., 120; emphasis in original.
132. Ibid., 115, 126.
133. Ibid., 136.
134. Ibid., 115; cf. Lüthi, *Judas Iskarioth in der Geschichte*, 87–89; Dieckmann, *Judas als Sündenbock*, 149–57; Klassen, *Judas*, 5–6, 20.
135. R. H. Horne, *Judas Iscariot: A Mystery* (London: C. Mitchell, 1848); repr. in *Bible Tragedies* (London: Newman & Co., 1881), 109–91. References are to the 1881 edition. Biographical information on Horne is from *The Dictionary of National Biography*, vol. 27 (ed. S. Lee; London: Smith, Elder, & Co., 1891), 358–59.
136. Horne, *Judas Iscariot*, 111.
137. Ibid., 125–26.
138. Ibid., 189.
139. Ibid., 154; emphasis in original.
140. Ibid., 189.
141. Ibid., 189.
142. On the film, see Baugh, *Imaging the Divine*, 18–24; Stern, *Savior on the Silver Screen*, 59–91.

143. On *Rebel*, see the excellent Web site at http://allmovie.com/cg/avg.dll.
144. Biographical information on Story is from the Web site of the Los Angeles County Museum of Art, which includes an image of his sculpture *Cleopatra*: http://www.lacma.org/art/perm_col/american/amer.htm.
145. W. W. Story, *A Roman Lawyer in Jerusalem* (Boston: Loring, 1870). Repr. as *In Defense of Judas* (Wausau, Wisc.: Philosopher Press, 1902). Several of Story's works, including *Roman Lawyer*, are available on-line as scanned images: http://moa.umdl.umich.edu/cgi/sgml/moa-idx?notisid=AAN7467.
146. Story, *Roman Lawyer*, 10.
147. Ibid., 30.
148. Ibid., 33.
149. Ibid., 20.
150. G. A. Page, *The Diary of Judas Iscariot or The Gospel according to Judas* (London: Charles H. Kelly, 1912).
151. Ibid., 54, 62, 71, 88–89, 96–97, 100–101.
152. Ibid., 132–35, 150–53, 160–63.
153. Ibid., 181–87.
154. Ibid., 189–91.
155. Ibid., 196–97.
156. Ibid., 208–9.
157. Ibid., 215–16.
158. Ibid., 223; such a suggestion is rejected by Cary, "The Case of Judas Iscariot," 828–29.
159. Bob Hartman, "Judas' Kiss" (Nashville: Dawn Treader Music, 1982).
160. T. Caldwell and J. Stearn, *I, Judas* (New York: Atheneum, 1977). See the criticism of it by D. R. Phillips, "We Don't Want to Own the Likeness: Contemporary literature and films have recast Judas as a tragic and therefore noble figure," *Christianity Today* 24 (April 4, 1980): 30–31.
161. Caldwell, *I, Judas*, 137.
162. Ibid., 322.
163. Ibid., 345.
164. Ibid., 270.
165. Ibid., 340, 344.
166. Ibid., 349.
167. For text and discussion, see H. J. Schonfield, *According to the Hebrews* (London: Duckworth, 1937), 35–61; cf. the discussions by J. Klausner, *Jesus of Nazareth: His Life, Times, and Teaching* (trans. H. Danby; New York: Macmillan & Co., 1925), 47–54; B. Heller, "Über Judas Ischariotes in der jüdischen Legende." *Monatsschrift für die Geschichte und Wissenschaft des Judentums* 76 (1932): 33–42; idem., "Über das Alter der jüdischen Judas-Sage und des Toldot Jeschu," *Monatsschrift für die Geschichte und Wissenschaft des Judentums* 77 (1933): 198–210; J. Jocz, *The Jewish People and Jesus Christ: A Study in the Controversy between Church and Synagogue* (London: SPCK, 1962), 60–64; Maccoby, *Judas Iscariot and the Myth of Jewish Evil*, 96–100.
168. On the date, see Klausner, *Jesus*, 51–53; Schonfield (who dates it all the way back to the fourth century), *According to the Hebrews*, 214–27; Jocz, *Jewish People and Jesus Christ*, 62–63; Maccoby, *Judas Iscariot and the Myth of Jewish Evil*, 96 (sixth or seventh century).
169. On the confusing variability and interchangeability of the characters in the tradition,

see E. Bammel, "Judas in der jüdischen Überlieferung," in E. Bammel, *Judaica et Paulina* (Tübingen: J. C. B. Mohr, 1997), 23–33.

170. *Toledoth* 3:24–32; see Schonfield, *According to the Hebrews,* 44–45.
171. *Toledoth* 4:5–11; see Schonfield, *According to the Hebrews,* 48–49.
172. *Toledoth* 5:19; see Schonfield, *According to the Hebrews,* 53.
173. Cf. Jocz, *Jewish People and Jesus Christ,* 60–62, who describes it as "parody" and "satirical."
174. Cf. Klausner, *Jesus,* 53: "The Jews, unable to exact physical vengeance from their strong enemies, retaliated in speech and writing. The inventions and legends, compact of hatred and sometimes of penetrating and stinging ridicule against Christianity and its Founder, went on increasing"; Maccoby, *Judas Iscariot and the Myth of Jewish Evil,* 98: "But it is plainly a pathetic attempt of a beleaguered people to sustain their morale in the face of denigration."
175. It is prominent in two of the most famous accounts: V. Frankl, *Man's Search for Meaning* (New York: Washington Square Press, 1959); E. Wiesel, *Night* (New York: Bantam, 1960).
176. R. Jeffers, "Dear Judas," in *The Collected Poetry of Robinson Jeffers,* vol. 2 (ed. T. Hunt; Stanford, Calif.: Stanford University Press, 1989), 5–45; excerpted in *Epiphany* 4, no. 3 (1984): 44–46.
177. On Jeffers, see A. B. Coffin, *Robinson Jeffers: Poet of Inhumanism* (Madison, Wisc.: University of Wisconsin Press, 1971); W. Everson, *The Excesses of God: Robinson Jeffers as a Religious Figure* (Stanford, Calif.: Stanford University Press, 1988).
178. Jeffers, "Dear Judas," 28–29.
179. Ibid., 25–26.
180. Ibid., 21, 23.
181. See chap. 5, "Judas as Agent of Salvation," p. 135.
182. A. and E. van Heurn, *Judas* (Philadelphia: Muhlenberg Press, 1958). Thanks to George Taylor of Lang Syne Books and Babette Polzer of Squirrel's Nest Books for their help with this. On the van Heurns, cf. the introduction to Gärtner, *Iscariot,* x.
183. van Heurn, *Judas,* 260.
184. Ibid., 305.
185. Ibid., 293.
186. R. Graves, *King Jesus* (New York: Creative Age Press, 1946).
187. Ibid., 344.
188. Ibid., 356.
189. Ibid., 367.
190. Ibid., 363, 367.
191. Ibid., 368.
192. Ibid., 401.
193. Ibid., 402.
194. On *Superstar,* see the excellent discussions by Baugh, *Imaging the Divine,* 35–41; Stern, *Savior on the Silver Screen,* 161–93, esp. the discussion of Judas, 169–71; Mark Goodacre, "Do You Think You're What They Say You Are? Reflections on *Jesus Christ Superstar,*" *Journal of Religion and Film* 3 (1999) [http://www.unomaha.edu/~wwwjrf/jesuscss2.htm].
195. Cf. the waggish comment of Michael Singer, recorded in Baugh, *Imaging the Divine,* 249: "Ted Neeley-Jesus' 'irritating falsetto' is the reason 'why Yvonne Ellimann's Mary Magdalene didn't know how to love him.'"

196. On the casting, see Baugh, *Imaging the Divine*, 37; Stern, *Savior on the Silver Screen*, 192–93.

197. Stern, *Savior on the Silver Screen*, 192–93.

198. D. L. Sayers, *The Man Born to Be King: A Play-Cycle on our Lord and Saviour Jesus Christ* (New York: Harper & Brothers, 1943). Sayers makes the comparison with Othello explicit on p. 175. See "Necessity and Free Will Again," p. 79, on Judas and Othello.

199. Ibid., 131–35, 166–68.

200. Ibid., 133, 134.

201. Ibid., 189; emphasis in original.

202. Ibid., 207.

203. Ibid., 262.

204. Ibid., 221; emphasis in original.

205. See chap. 5, "Judas the Ultimate Penitent and Universal Guilt," p. 118.

206. E. T. Thurston, *Judas Iscariot: A Play in Four Acts* (London and New York: G. P. Putnam's Sons, 1923).

207. Ibid., 20–21.

208. Ibid., 56–60; cf. Luke 7:11–17.

209. Thurston, *Judas Iscariot*, 73.

210. Ibid., 87; emphasis in original.

211. Ibid., 95; emphasis in original.

212. From a Coptic fragment assigned to various known or hypothetical books, dating from the fifth or sixth centuries; see Elliott, *Apocryphal New Testament*, 161–63, 652–53. Cf. the discussions of it in Baum, "The English Ballad of Judas Iscariot," 185–86; and Maccoby, *Judas Iscariot and the Myth of Jewish Evil*, 91.

213. *Gospel of Nicodemus* (=*Acts of Pilate*) 1.1, in *Apocryphal Gospels, Acts, and Revelations* (trans. A. Walker; Edinburgh: T. & T. Clark, 1873), 151.

214. Maccoby, *Judas Iscariot and the Myth of Jewish Evil*, 92.

215. S. Morley, *Judas, A Poem in 1932 Lines, One for Each Year of Our Lord* (Oxford: Basil Blackwell, 1932).

216. J. L. Milligan, *Judas Iscariot, A Poetical Play*. Toronto: Ryerson Press, 1929. Biographical information on Milligan is from Omnigraphics, *Who Was Who Among North American Authors* (Detroit: Gale Research Co., 1976), 1013.

217. Milligan, *Judas Iscariot*, 7.

218. Ibid., 9; cf. 16.

219. G. C. Alborn, *Ish Kerioth. The Story of a Traitor* (Boston: Morning Publishing, 1904). Biographical information is from the Web site of the Fairwater Historical Society: http://www.wlhn.org/fond_du_lac/communities/fairwater/writings/alborn_rhythms/rhythms_cover.htm.

220. Alborn, *Ish Kerioth*, 65.

221. Ibid., 133.

222. Ibid., 46.

223. Ibid., 126.

224. Ibid., 187.

225. Ibid., 263.

226. Urban Nagle, *Barter* (London, New York, and Toronto: Longmans, Green & Co., 1935). Biographical information on Nagle comes from M. Powell, *God Off-Broadway: The Blackfriars Theatre of New York* (Lanham, Md., and London: Scarecrow Press, 1998), 14–17, 73–74.

227. A total of twenty-two other chapters of it were founded, and the one in Rochester, N.Y., is still active (see their Web site: http://www.blackfriars.org).
228. On the film, see Baugh, *Imaging the Divine*, 12–13; Stern, *Savior on the Silver Screen*, 27–57.
229. Cf. Stern, *Savior on the Silver Screen*, 31, 40–41.
230. P. R. Dillon, *Judas of Kerioth: A Romance of Old Judea* (New York: Exposition Press, 1953).
231. Ibid., 18–25.
232. Ibid., 57.
233. N. Richard Nash, *Behold the Man* (Garden City, N.Y.: Doubleday, 1986).
234. Ibid., 25–31.
235. Dante, *Paradise*, canto 19, lines 103–11.
236. William Rayner, *The Knifeman* (New York: William Morrow & Co., 1969). My biographical information on the author comes from *Contemporary Authors Online* [http://www.galenet.com].
237. Rayner, *The Knifeman*, 151.
238. *King Lear*, act 4, scene 1, lines 36–37.
239. Kent's description of Lear: *King Lear*, act 1, scene 1, line 151.

Chapter 5

1. See D. Senior, "The Passion Narrative in the Gospel of Matthew," in *L'Évangile selon Matthieu* (ed. M. Didier; Gembloux: Duculot, 1972), 343–57.
2. D. Senior, *The Passion according to Matthew: A Redactional Study* (Leuven: Leuven University Press, 1982), 1.
3. On Matthew's special interest in Judas, see Nortjé, "Matthew's Motive," 45.
4. Matthew would normally soften the reproach of the disciples; cf. D. Senior, *The Passion of Jesus in the Gospel of Matthew* (Wilmington, Del.: Michael Glazier, 1985), 53–54.
5. As has often been noted, e.g., McClain, "Judas Iscariot," 139–44.
6. On the link that the money provides, see Klassen, *Judas*, 98–99.
7. Thus R. H. Gundry, *The Use of the Old Testament in St. Matthew's Gospel* (Leiden: E. J. Brill, 1967), 143–44.
8. Thus the allusion is rejected by Klassen, *Judas*, 98.
9. Cf. P. Benoit, "The Death of Judas," in *Jesus and the Gospel*, vol. 1 (London: Darton, Longman, & Todd, 1973), 189–207, esp. 197; Senior, *Passion of Jesus in the Gospel of Matthew*, 56–57.
10. Thus Senior, *Passion of Jesus in the Gospel of Matthew*, 63–64.
11. Thus R. H. Gundry, *Matthew: A Commentary on His Literary and Theological Art* (Grand Rapids: Wm. B. Eerdmans Publishing Co., 1982), 527.
12. Contra Klassen, *Judas*, 100–2, who has to argue for this "fragment" being composed in ignorance of Matt. 26:14–16. In the present plan of Matthew, I cannot see how one can maintain this, or what difference it would make.
13. Cf. Senior, *Passion of Jesus in the Gospel of Matthew*, 64.
14. Klassen, *Judas*, 103, simply asserts the meaning is different here than in the previous two Matthean occurrences. On the connection between Matt. 22:12 and 26:50, see K. R. J. Cripps, "A Note on Matthew 22:12," *Expository Times* 69 (1957): 30. Pascal also saw a connection between the two: Pascal, *Pensées* (trans. A. J. Krailsheimer; New York: Penguin Books, 1966), *pensée* # 549 (780).

15. For discussions of the translation problems, see A. Deissmann, "Friend, Wherefore Art Thou Come?" *Expository Times* 33 (1922): 491–93; F. Rehkopf, "Mt 26:50: Ἑταῖρε, ἐφ᾽ ὃ πάρει," *Zeitschrift für die neutestamentliche Wissenschaft* 52 (1961): 109–15; R. Brown, *The Death of the Messiah* (2 vols.; Garden City, N.Y.: Doubleday, 1994), 2:1385–88; Klassen, *Judas*, 103–4.

16. Cf. the conclusion of W. Eltester, "Freund, wozu du gekommen bist (Mt 26:50)," in *Neotestamentica et Patristica: O. Cullman* (ed. A. N. Wilder; Leiden: E. J. Brill, 1962), 70–91.

17. Senior, *Passion Narrative*, 344.

18. On Matthew's close similarity to Mark even in this story that is unparalleled in Mark, see D. Senior, "The Fate of the Betrayer: A Redactional Study of Matthew 27:3–10," *Ephemerides Theologicae Lovaniensis* 48 (1972): 372–426, esp. 375–76.

19. Thus G. D. Kilpatrick, *The Origins of the Gospel according to St. Matthew* (London: Oxford University Press, 1946), 45; Senior, "Fate of the Betrayer," 375–81; Gundry, *Matthew*, 552–53; Senior, *Passion Narrative*, 347–49. This is taken as partial confirmation of Markan priority by R. M. Fowler, "Thoughts on the History of Reading Mark's Gospel," *Proceedings: Eastern Great Lakes and Midwest Biblical Societies* 4 (1984): 120–30, esp. 128–29.

20. The consensus would still seem to be that Matthew intends here an allusion to 2 Sam. 17:23: thus D. Haugg, *Judas Iskarioth in den neutestamentlichen Berichten* (Freiburg: Herder, 1930), 167; K. Lake, "The Death of Judas," in *The Beginnings of Christianity* (eds. F. J. Foakes-Jackson and K. Lake; London: Macmillan, 1933), 5:22–30, esp. 29; P. Bonnard, *L'Évangile selon Saint Matthieu* (Paris: Delachaux et Niestlé, 1963), 394; Gärtner, *Iscariot*, 36–38; Benoit, "Death of Judas," 194–95; T. E. Glasson, "Davidic Links with the Betrayal of Jesus," *Expository Times* 85 (1973–74): 118–19; Gundry, *Matthew*, 555.

21. Cf. Paffenroth, "Stories of the Fate of Judas," 78.

22. I am now following the minority opinion of W. C. van Unnik, "The Death of Judas in Saint Matthew's Gospel," *Anglican Theological Review Supplementary Series* 3 (1974): 44–57, esp. 50–51; J. A. Upton, "The Potter's Field and the Death of Judas," *Concordia Journal* 8 (1982): 213–19; Klassen, *Judas*, 170.

23. Thus F. V. Filson, *A Commentary on the Gospel according to Saint Matthew* (London: Adam & Charles Black, 1960), 287; W. Thomas, *Outline Studies in the Gospel of Matthew* (Grand Rapids: Wm. B. Eerdmans Publishing Co., 1961), 419; Bonnard, *Matthieu*, 393; Senior, "Fate of the Betrayer," 404; idem., *Passion of Jesus in the Gospel of Matthew*, 105.

24. Nowhere else in the Gospels, elsewhere in the New Testament only at 2 Cor. 7:8; Heb. 7:21.

25. Cf. Paffenroth, "Stories of the Fate of Judas," 69.

26. Cf. L. Desautels, "La mort de Judas (Mt 27,3–10; Ac 1,15–26)," *Science et Esprit* 38 (1986): 221–39, esp. 224–25. Daube, "Judas," 95–97, is emphatic in his rejection of what he calls a "tendentious treatment" of the word.

27. On Judas's suicide as expiatory, see van Unnik, "Death of Judas," 56–57; Derrett, "The Iscariot," 14; Nortjé, 48; on all Judas's actions here as showing the reality of his repentance, see W. Schwarz, "Die Doppelbedeutung des Judastodes," *Bibel und Liturgie* 57 (1984): 227–33.

28. Cf. Harper, "Judas," 97: "What is the tragedy of Judas?. . . . Believing himself forever condemned, Judas committed suicide."

29. On the money as unifying the story, see A. Vanhoye, "Les récits de la Passion chez les Synoptiques," *Nouvelle Revue Théologique* 89 (1967): 135–63, esp. 144–45; A. Descamps, "Redaction et christologie dans le récit matthéen de la Passion," in *L'Évangile selon Matthieu* (ed. M. Didier; Gembloux: Duculot, 1972), 359–415, esp. 389; Desautels, "La mort de Judas," 222; Klauck, *Judas*, 93; Klassen, *Judas*, 165.

30. On the guilt of the chief priests here, see K. Stendahl, *The School of St. Matthew and Its Use of the Old Testament* (Philadelphia: Fortress Press, 1968), 126; S. van Tilborg, *The Jewish Leaders in Matthew* (Leiden: E. J. Brill, 1972) 89; Gundry, *Matthew*, 557; Upton, "Death of Judas," 218; Desautels, "La mort de Judas," 230; S. van Tilborg, "Matthew 27.3–10: An Intertextual Reading," in *Intertextuality in Biblical Writings: Essays in Honor of Bas van Iersel* (ed. S. Draisma; Kampen: J. H. Kok, 1989), 159–74, esp. 165–67; T. W. Berkley, "OT Exegesis and the Death of Judas," *Proceedings: Eastern Great Lakes and Midwest Biblical Societies* 14 (1994): 29–45, esp. 35.

31. Thus Nortjé, "Matthew's Motive," 50.

32. On the preexistence of this tradition, see Kilpatrick, *Origins*, 46; Stendahl, *School of St. Matthew*, 197; Bonnard, *Matthieu*, 394; Senior, "Fate of the Betrayer," 416–17; Benoit, "Death of Judas," 190–92; Gundry, *Use of the Old Testament*, 202.

33. The latter at Matt. 1:22; 2:15, 23; 4:14; 8:17; 12:17; 13:35; 21:4; the former only here and at Matt. 2:17.

34. Cf. Senior, "Fate of the Betrayer," 393–94; Gundry, *Matthew*, 557; Desautels, "La mort de Judas," 223–24; Brown, *Death*, 1:648.

35. Brown, *Death*, 1:648 (emphasis in original); for full discussions of this fulfillment text, see Stendahl, *School of St. Matthew*, 120–26; G. Strecker, *Der Weg der Gerechtigkeit: Untersuchung zur Theologie des Matthäus* (Göttingen: Vandenhoeck & Ruprecht, 1966), 76–82; Gundry, *Use of the Old Testament*, 122–27; Senior, "Fate of the Betrayer," 381–98; Brown, *Death*, 1:648–52.

36. On the word play, see Berkley, "Death of Judas," 36; Nortjé, "Matthew's Motives," 49. This is further complicated by the reading "treasury" in the Peshitta: Stendahl, *School of St. Matthew*, 124–25. For another interpretation of the "treasury," cf. also C. C. Torrey, "The Foundry of the Second Temple at Jerusalem," *Journal of Biblical Literature* 60 (1936): 247–60.

37. Stendahl, *School of St. Matthew*, 123.

38. Cf. the critique of this hypothesis in Brown, *Death*, 1:650–51.

39. Thus Bonnard, *Matthieu*, 394; Stendahl, *School of St. Matthew*, 122–23; Brown, *Death*, 1:652.

40. Cf. Gundry, *Use of the Old Testament*, 124: "We cannot assume that Mt connected two such unrelated passages in Jer with each other and then with Zech 11." See also Senior, *Passion Narrative*, 358–59, for reasons against Jeremiah 32 and 18 as sources for Matt. 27:3–10.

41. Gundry, *Use of the Old Testament*, 124–25; idem., *Matthew*, 557–58. He is followed in the main by Senior, *Passion Narrative*, 359–61; Berkley, "Death of Judas," 36–38; and A. Conrad, "The Fate of Judas: Matthew 27:3–10," *Toronto Journal of Theology* 7 (1991): 158–68.

42. On "potter" as the connection, see Upton, "Death of Judas," 216; Berkley, "Death of Judas," 36.

43. Cf. Gundry, *Use of the Old Testament*, 125: "Mt . . . makes the ascription to Jer because the manifestness of the quotation from Zech and the lack of verbal resemblance to Jer would cause the Jer-side of the prophecies to be lost."

44. The destruction may therefore refer to the impending (from Matthew's perspective, accomplished) destruction of Jerusalem: thus Berkley, "Death of Judas," 39.
45. Upton, "Death of Judas," 218.
46. This observation comes from Nortjé, "Matthew's Motives," 45.
47. Cf. Conrad, "The Fate of Judas," 165: ". . . the figure of Judas seems to emerge more humanly in Matthew's gospel than it does in Mark or Luke. This is partly due to Matthew's insistence on the guilt of the chief priests and elders."
48. On the nobility of the suicide, see W. Wrede, "Judas Iscarioth in der urchristlichen Überlieferung," In *Vortäge und Studien* (Tübingen: J. C. B. Mohr, 1907), 127–46, cited by Klassen, *Judas,* 175; more recently, C. F. Whelan, "Suicide in the Ancient World: A Re-examination of Matt 27:3–10," *Laval Théologique et Philosophique* 49 (1993): 505–22; and Daube, "Judas," 100–101.
49. Origen, *Against Celsus,* 2.11.
50. On Judas's avarice, cf. Origen, *Commentary on the Gospel of Matthew* (trans. J. Patrick; Edinburgh: T. & T. Clark; Grand Rapids: Wm. B. Eerdmans Publishing Co., 1951; available on-line at http://www.ccel.org/fathers2/ANF-10/TOC.htm), 11.9: "And perhaps, when the Apostle says, 'The love of money is a root of all evils,' he says it because of Judas' love of money, which was a root of all the evils that were committed against Jesus."
51. See Origen, *Commentary on the Gospel of John,* 10.30; *Commentary on the Gospel of Matthew,* 11.9; 13.8–9; Laeuchli, "Orgien's Interpretation of Judas Iscariot," 262–64.
52. On Origen's possible endorsement of this idea, see Laeuchli, "Origen's Interpretation of Judas Iscariot," 259; Daube, "Judas," 103.
53. Laeuchli, "Origen's Interpretation of Judas Iscariot," 260.
54. Which Theophylactus is meant has been a source of confusion: most modern authors do not bother to specify whether it is the seventh-century historian or the eleventh-century archbishop. Klassen, *Judas,* 173, incorrectly identifies him as the former; van der Horst, "Note on the Judas Curse," 148, correctly identifies him as the latter.
55. Translation by J. R. Harris, "Did Judas Really Commit Suicide?" *American Journal of Theology* 4 (1900): 490–513: 494–95; cf. the translations and discussions of Locard, "La mort de Judas," 445; K. Lake, "The Death of Judas," in *The Beginnings of Christianity* (6 vols.; eds. F. J. Foakes-Jackson and K. Lake; London: Macmillan, 1933; repr. ed., Grand Rapids: Baker Book House, 1979), 5:22–30, esp. 25; M. S. Enslin, "How the Story Grew: Judas in Fact and Fiction," in *Festschrift to Honor F. Wilbur Gingrich* (ed. E. Barth; Leiden: E. J. Brill, 1972), 123–41: 130.
56. On this aspect, see K. Paffenroth, "The Stories of the Fate of Judas and Differing Attitudes towards Sources," *Proceedings: Eastern Great Lakes and Midwest Biblical Societies* 12 (1992): 67–81.
57. E.g., L. D. Weatherhead, "Judas," in *Personalities in the Passion: A Devotional Study of Some of the Characters Who Played a Part in the Drama of Christ's Passion and Resurrection* (Nashville: Abingdon-Cokesbury Press, 1943), 26–39, esp. 38.
58. Translation from Klassen, *Judas,* 7; cf. Dieckmann, *Judas als Sündenbock,* 139–40.
59. My translation, from the French given in Kahn, "Judas Iscariot," 44.
60. My translation, from the French given in Kahn, "Judas Iscariot," 93.
61. See the discussions of Baum, "Medieval Legend of Judas Iscariot," 552–59; and Axton, "Judas in Middle English Literature," 188–90, of the Provençal version that combines both the Oedipal legend and the 10 percent allowance for Judas's family.

62. My translation, from the French given in Kahn, "Judas Iscariot," 47; cf. his discussions of the depiction of Judas's repentance in the French passion plays: Kahn, "Judas Iscariot," 93–95, 165–68.

63. My translation, from the French given in Kahn, "Judas Iscariot," 168.

64. My discussion of these is based on A. Taylor, "The Gallows of Judas Iscariot," *Washington University Studies* 9 (1922): 135–56; cf. Creizenach, "Judas Ischarioth in Legende und Sage des Mittelalters," 183–84.

65. Shakespeare's identification: *Love's Labours Lost* 5.2.605; on the elder in French passion plays, see Kahn, "Judas Iscariot," 65.

66. On the redbud, see Hand, *Dictionary of Words and Idioms Associated with Judas*, 349–50; Topping, *Jewish Flower Child*, 191; and A. J. Cronin (1896–1981), *The Judas Tree* (Boston: Little, Brown & Co., 1961).

67. Taylor, "The Gallows of Judas Iscariot," 136.

68. Ibid., 147, 149–50; cf. 140.

69. Ibid., 149.

70. W. Doroschewitch, "Judas Iscariot," in *Judas Iscariot and Other Stories* (ed. G. Bruno; New York: 1919), 5–12. I have been unable to find any biographical information on the author.

71. Ibid., 6.

72. Ibid., 11.

73. Ibid., 12.

74. Michel de Montaigne, "On Repentance," in *Essays and Selected Writings* (trans. and ed. D. M. Frame; New York: St. Martin's Press, 1963), 341.

75. See P. F. Baum, "Judas' Sunday Rest," *Modern Language Review* 18 (1923): 168–82; Lehmann, "Judas Ischarioth," 308–9; L. Kretzenbacher, "Sankt Brandan, Judas und die Ewigkeit," in *Bilder und Legenden Erwandertes und erlebtes Bilder-Denken und Bild-Erzählen zwischen Byanz und dem Abendland* (Klagenfurt: 1971), 150–76.

76. Text from Baum, "Judas' Sunday Rest," 173; cf. Kretzenbacher, "Sankt Brandan," 161.

77. Cf. Baum, "Judas' Sunday Rest," 176: "Not merely is it one of the very few incidents to be borrowed from the *Navigatio* during the Middle Ages; it is also the only incident that has survived into modern literature, when all the other events of the voyage have been forgotten."

78. See Baum, "Judas' Sunday Rest," 176; Kretzenbacher, "Sankt Brandan," 161.

79. Augustine, *Enchiridion on Faith, Hope, and Love* (trans. B. Harbert; Hyde Park, NY: New City Press, 1999), 29.112. See the discussions in Baum, "Judas' Sunday Rest," 178–80; and Kretzenbacher, "Sankt Brandan," 165.

80. Baum, "Judas' Sunday Rest," 181.

81. Samuel Moodey, *Judas the Traitor Hung up in Chains: To Give Warning to Professors, that They Beware of Worldlymindedness and Hypocrisy* (New Haven, Conn.: S. Diodate, 1761). The latter part of this was published separately as *Dialogue: Containing Questions and Answers, Tending to Awaken the Secure, and Direct the Seeking Soul* (New London: T. Green, 1768).

82. Biographical information on Moodey is from F. G. Halpenny, ed., *The Dictionary of Canadian Biography* (Toronto: University of Toronto Press, 1966), 470–71. Thanks to Cliff Wunderlich of Andover-Harvard Theological Library for his help on this.

83. Moodey, *Dialogue*, 14.

84. Carey, *Jesus and Judas*, 228.

85. See the image and discussion in Jursch, "Judas Ischarioth in der Kunst," 104–5.
86. For a fuller analysis of this, see Kim Paffenroth, "The Character of Judas in Bach's *St. Matthew Passion*," *Midwest Quarterly* 36 (1995): 125–35.
87. D. B. Lutyens, *Judas Iscariot* (London: Eyre & Spottiswoode, 1951). There is also a New Age version of this idea in Dickey, *Judas Iscariot*, 78–81.
88. Lutyens, *Judas Iscariot*, 15–16.
89. Ibid., 77.
90. Cf. Goetz, "Judas as Patron Saint," 263: "We, of all people, should find it difficult to condemn Judas. . . . In many ways, we are as guilty as Judas in the death of God."
91. Dostoyevsky, *The Brothers Karamazov* (trans. C. Garnett; New York, et al.: Penguin Books, 1980), 698.
92. Ibid., 278.
93. Ibid., 310.
94. Cf. Dieckmann's treatment of Dostoyevsky: *Judas als Sündenbock*, 311–14, 324–26.
95. C. E. Lawrence, *Spikenard: A Play in One Act* (London: Gowan & Gray/Boston: Baker International Play Bureau, 1929).
96. On the Wandering Jew, see G. K. Anderson, *The Legend of the Wandering Jew* (Providence, R.I.: Brown University Press, 1970).
97. The names of the thieves crucified with Jesus are given (with various spellings) in versions of the *Gospel of Nicodemus* (=*The Acts of Pilate*); see M. R. James, *The Apocryphal New Testament* (Oxford: Clarendon Press, 1924), 104; J. K. Elliott, *The Apocryphal New Testament: A Collection of Apocryphal Christian Literature in an English Translation* (rev. ed.; Oxford: Clarendon Press, 1993), 177.
98. Lawrence, *Spikenard*, 22.
99. D. S. Williams, "Rub Poor Lil' Judas's Head," *Christian Century* 107 (October 24, 1990): 963.
100. Dostoyevsky, *Brothers Karamazov*, 279.
101. The criticism of Phillips, "We Don't Want to Own the Likeness," 30–31.
102. Schueler, "The Middle English *Judas*," 842.
103. On Sayers, see chap. 4, "Judas the Anti-Revolutionary," p. 92.
104. Sayers, *Man Born to Be King*, 267; emphasis in original.
105. Dostoyevsky, *Notes from Underground* (trans. M. Ginsburg; New York: Bantam Books, 1974), 145–46.
106. Ray S. Anderson, *The Gospel according to Judas* (Colorado Springs, Colo.: Helmers & Howard, 1991).
107. Cf. Klassen, *Judas*, 193.
108. Anderson, *Gospel according to Judas*, 148, 150; cf. 7–18.
109. Ibid., 18–23.
110. Ibid., 150; cf. 71–89, 145–46.
111. Ibid., 152–53, emphasis in original; cf. 91–99.
112. On Moore, see chap. 3, "Judas and Theological Anti-Semitism," p. 51.
113. Moore, *Judas*, 50.
114. Ibid., 84–85, 90–91, 98–100.
115. Ibid., 100–101, 107.
116. Ibid., 60–64, 74–76, 92, 103–7.
117. Herman Melville, *Moby Dick* (Norton Critical Edition; New York and London: W. W. Norton & Co., 1967), 406.
118. Ibid., 470.

119. See H. Gollwitzer, "Gute Botschaft für Judas Ischarioth," in *Krummes Holz-aufrechter Gang: Zur Frage nach dem Sinn des Lebens* (2d ed.; Munich: Chr. Kaiser Verlag, 1970), 271–96; Wagner, "Judas," 11–38; Dieckmann, *Judas als Sündenbock*, 237–326; and the discussion of their theologies in Klassen, *Judas*, 178–82.

120. Gollwitzer, *Judas als Sündenbock*, 278–79, cited and translated by Klassen, *Judas*, 180.

121. Cf. Klauck, *Judas*, 24–26. For a critique of this point of view, see J. Brun, "Témoignage et trahison: les adorateurs de Judas," in *Le Témoignage* (ed. E. Castelli; Aubier: Éditions Montaigne, 1972), 493–503. Similar also is the conclusion of Stalter-Fouilloy, "Les maudits," 457: "Changing evil into good is done only from the divine point of view, not the human" (my translation).

122. See chap. 4, "Judas the Anti-Revolutionary," p. 92.

123. Jeffers, "Dear Judas," 30–31.

124. M. Brelich, *The Work of Betrayal* (trans. R. Rosenthal; Marlboro, Vt.: Marlboro Press, 1988).

125. J. Miles, *God: A Biography* (New York: Alfred A. Knopf, 1995).

126. Brelich, *Work of Betrayal*, 99–102.

127. Ibid., 105.

128. Ibid., 98.

129. Ibid., 105.

130. Ibid., 125.

131. Ibid., 234, 236.

132. Ibid., 235.

133. Ibid., 235.

134. Taylor, "The Gallows of Judas Iscariot," 142.

135. Ibid., 138; on the legend of the wood of the cross being from the tree of knowledge of good and evil, see L. de Combes, *The Finding of the Cross* (trans. L. Cappadelta; London: Kegan Paul, 1907), 267–78.

136. On Judas's identification with Jesus and his role in salvation, see B. Dieckmann, "Judas als Doppelgänger Jesu?" esp. 233–36.

137. See Tarachow, "Judas the Beloved Executioner," 547, 551: "Christian mythology solves its ambivalence by having two scapegoats, Christ and Judas. One is for love and one is for aggression, one for killing and the other for being killed, one for eating and the other for being eaten.... Jesus and Judas are pictured as the pair of scapegoats necessary to solve by projection the ambivalent problems of the Christian: Jesus for passive love, Judas for active. The relationship between the two, however, is one of identification and love, expressed in the theme of the killer and the slain." For a psychoanalytic analysis of Judas, see also T. Reik, T. "Das Evangelium des Judas Iskariot," and "Die psychoanalytische Deutung des Judas-problems," in *Der eigene und der fremde Gott: Zur Psychoanalyse der religiösen Entwicklung* (Frankfurt am Main: A. Mitscherlich, 1972), 75–97, 98–129. On scapegoating in general, see the classic works by R. Girard, *Violence and the Sacred* (trans. P. Gregory; Baltimore: Johns Hopkins University Press, 1977), and *The Scapegoat* (trans. Yvonne Freccero; Baltimore: Johns Hopkins University Press, 1986).

138. For a lengthy discussion of Jesus and Judas as similar but opposite, see T. Reik, "Das Evangelium des Judas Iskariot" and "Die psychoanalytische Deutung des Judas-problems," in *Der eigene und der fremde Gott: Zur Psychoanalyse der religiösen Entwicklung* (Frankfurt am Main: A. Mitscherlich, 1972), 75–97, 98–129.

139. H. Maccoby, *Judas Iscariot and the Myth of Jewish Evil*, 106.

140. For analysis of the film, see Baugh, *Imaging the Divine*, 51–71; Stern, *Savior on the Silver Screen*, 265–95.

141. Richard Corliss, quoted in Baugh, *Imaging the Divine*, 56.

142. Pam Cook, quoted in Baugh, *Imaging the Divine*, 69.

143. See Barth, *Church Dogmatics*, vol. 2.2, 458–506. My analysis is much indebted to P. McGlasson, *Jesus and Judas: Biblical Exegesis in Barth* (Atlanta: Scholars Press, 1991), 135–47; see also Klassen, *Judas*, 182–92. Cf. the similar conclusions of R. P. Scharlemann, "Why Christianity Needs Other Religions," in *Christianity and the Wider Ecumenism* (ed. P. Phan; New York: Paragon House, 1990), 35–46, who meditates on the necessity of rejection in order for there to be confession; cf. also Klauck, *Judas*, 21–23.

144. Barth, *Church Dogmatics*, vol. 2.2, 459.

145. Ibid., vol. 2.2, 460–61.

146. Ibid., vol. 2.2, 461.

147. Ibid., vol. 2.2, 466.

148. Ibid.

149. Ibid., vol. 2.2, 467.

150. Ibid., vol. 2.2, 471.

151. Ibid.

152. Ibid., vol. 2.2, 475–76.

153. Ibid., vol. 2.2, 476–77.

154. Cf. Goetz, "Judas as Patron Saint," 263: "We, of all people, should find it difficult to condemn Judas. He never did anything to *us*, except to be the agent whose dark work was a necessary part of our salvation."

Bibliography

Abraham a Sancta Clara. *Judas der Ertzschelm*. Berlin and Stuttgart: W. Spemann, 1884.

Aitken, B. "The Burning of the 'May' at Belorado." *Folk-Lore* 37 (1926): 289–96.

Akylas, M. 'Οί τελευταῖς μέρες τοῦ 'Ιούδα. Athens: 1934.

Alborn, G. C. *Ish Kerioth. The Story of a Traitor*. Boston: Morning Publishing, 1904.

Alexander, A. W. "Judas Iscariot: A Study." *Methodist Quarterly Review* 58 (1909): 331–40; 359–61.

Allen, J. W. "Judas Iscariot Not Lost." *Methodist Quarterly Review* 66 (1917): 488–90.

Anderson, R. S. *The Gospel according to Judas*. Colorado Springs, Colo.: Helmers & Howard, 1991.

Anonymous. *The Life, Character, and Death of Judas Iscariot, that Traytor, Who Betray'd Our Blessed Lord and Saviour Jesus Christ*. London: Edward Midwinter, 1711.

Arbeitman, Y. "The Suffix of Iscariot." *Journal of Biblical Literature* 99 (1980): 122–24.

Augspurger, A. *Der Verzweiflende Verräther Judas*. Dresden: 1642.

Axton, R. "Interpretations of Judas in Middle English Literature." In *Religion in the Poetry and Drama of the Late Middle Ages in England*, 179–97. Eds. P. Boitani and A. Torti. Cambridge, U.K.: D. S. Brewer, 1990.

Ayad, B. A. "The So-Called Gospel of Barnabas Denies Christ's Death on the Cross and His Resurrection." *Coptic Church Review* 8 (fall 1987): 84–88.

Bacon, B. W. "What Did Judas Betray?" *Hibbert Journal* 19 (1920–21): 476–93.

Bagge, D. "Le mythe des Judas dans la littérature française contemporaine." *Critique* 10 (1956): 423–37.

Baldwin, A. D. *The Gospel of Judas Iscariot*. Chicago: Jamieson-Higgins, 1902.

Bammel, E. "Judas in der jüdischen Überlieferung." In E. Bammel, *Judaica et Paulina*, 23–33. Tübingen: J. C. B. Mohr, 1997.

Barth, K. *Church Dogmatics*. Trans. G. W. Bromiley, et al. Edinburgh: T. & T. Clark, 1957.

Bartlett, D. L. "John 13:21–30." *Interpretation* 43 (1989): 393–97.

Bartnik, C. "Judas l'Iscariote, histoire et théologie." *Collectanea Theologica* 58 (1988): 57–69.

Bassewitz, G. von. *Judas, eine Tragödie von Gerdt von Bassewitz*. Leipzig: E. Rowohlt, 1911.

Bates, E.S. *The Friend of Jesus*. New York: Simon & Schuster, 1928.

———. *The Gospel according to Judas Iscariot*. London: William Heinemann, 1929.

Baugh, L. *Imaging the Divine: Jesus and Christ-Figures in Film*. Kansas City, Mo.: Sheed & Ward, 1997.

Baum, P. F. "The English Ballad of Judas Iscariot." *Publications of the Modern Language Association* 31 (1916): 181–89.

———. "Judas's Red Hair." *Journal of English and Germanic Philology* 21 (1922): 520–29.

————. "Judas's Sunday Rest." *Modern Language Review* 18 (1923): 168–82.
————. "The Medieval Legend of Judas Iscariot." *Publications of the Modern Language Association* 31 (1916): 481–632.
————. "Roland 3220, 3220a." *The Romanic Review* 7 (1916): 211–20.
Baumbach, G. "Judas-Jünger und Verräter Jesu." *Zeichen der Zeit* 17 (1963): 91–98.
Becker, I. C. "Satan und Judas: Der lukanische Bericht." *Entschluss* 44 (1989): 20–22.
Belcher, F. W. "A Comment on Mark 14:45." *Expository Times* 64 (1952–53): 240.
Benoit, P. "The Death of Judas." In *Jesus and the Gospel*, vol. 1, 189–207. London: Darton, Longman, & Todd, 1973.
Bergmann, R. "Mittelalterliche geistliche Spiele." In *Reallexikon der deutschen Literaturgeschichte*, vol. 4, 64–100. Eds. W. Kohlschmidt and W. Mohr. Berlin: DeGruyter, 1979.
Berkley, T. W. "OT Exegesis and the Death of Judas." *Proceedings: Eastern Great Lakes and Midwest Biblical Societies* 14 (1994): 29–45.
Besnard, A. M. "Judas bouc émissaire des apôtres? Un compagnon dangereusement semblable." *BTS* 158 (1974): 8f.
Betz, O. "The Dichotomized Servant and the End of Judas Iscariot." *Revue de Qumran* 5 (1964): 43–58.
Beyschlag, K. "Franz von Assisi und Judas Iskariot." *Theologische Literaturzeitung* 85 (1960): 849–52.
Bihlmeyer, K. *Die apostolischen Väter.* Tübingen: J. C. B. Mohr, 1924.
Billings, J. S. "Judas Iscariot in the Fourth Gospel." *Expository Times* 51 (1939–40): 156–57.
Birbaumer, V. *Studien zur Judasdarstellung in der italienischen Malerei des Tre- und Quattrocento.* Diss. University of Munich, 1980.
Bishop, E. F. F. "Guide to Those Who Arrested Jesus." *Evangelical Quarterly* 40 (1968): 41–42.
————. "'He that eateth bread with me. . . .'" *Expository Times* 70 (1959–60): 331–33.
————. "With Jesus on the Road from Galilee to Calvary. . . ." *Catholic Biblical Quarterly* 11 (1949): 428–44.
Bjerg, S. "Judas als Stellvertreter des Satans." *Evangelische Theologie* 52 (1992): 42–55.
Blair, E. P. "Judas Iscariot." In *The Interpreter's Dictionary of the Bible*, vol. 2, 1006–8. New York and Nashville: Abingdon Press, 1962.
Blinzler, J. "Judas Iskarioth." In *Lexikon für Theologie und Kirche* 2 (1960) 5:1152–54.
Blöcker, G. "Der notwendige Mensch: Die literarischen Deutungen der Judasfigur." *Neue Deutsche Hefte* 1 (1954–55): 64–69.
Bonar, J. *Observations on the Conduct and Character of Judas Iscariot, in a Letter to the Reverend Mr. J. P.,* 2d ed. Edinburgh: W. Miller, 1751.
Bonhoeffer, D. "Predigt am Sonntag Judika über Judas." In *Gesammelte Schriften*, vol. 4, 406–13. Ed. E. Bethge. Munich: Chr. Kaiser Verlag, 1961.
Bonnard, P. *L'Évangile selon Saint Matthieu.* Paris: Delachaux et Niestlé, 1963.
Borg, M. *Jesus: A New Vision.* San Francisco: HarperSanFrancisco, 1987.
Borges, J. L. *Labyrinths.* New York: New Directions, 1964.
Bosch, J. *Judas Iscariote, el calumniado.* Santiago, Chile: Editorial Prensa Latinoamerica, 1955.
Bousset, W. *The Antichrist Legend.* Trans. A. H. Keane. London: Hutchinson & Co., 1896.
Brandon, S. G. F. *Jesus and the Zealots: A Study of the Political Factor in Primitive Christianity.* New York: Charles Scribner's Sons, 1967.
Braswell, M. F. "Chaucer's Palimpsest: Judas Iscariot and the 'Pardoner's Tale.'" *The Chaucer Review* 29 (1995): 303–10.

Breitenbucher, J. R. *Die Judasgestalt in den Passionspielen*. Ph.D. diss. Ohio State University, 1935.

Brelich, M. *The Work of Betrayal*. Trans. R. Rosenthal. Marlboro, Vt.: Marlboro Press, 1988.

Brevda, W. *Harry Kemp, the Last Bohemian*. London and Toronto: Associated University Presses, 1986.

Broderick, R. *Rock Opera: The Creation of Jesus Christ Superstar.* New York: Hawthorn Books, 1973.

Bronikowski, R. J. "Judas Iscariot: The Apostle Who Couldn't Love." *Cross and Crown* 27 (1975): 269–79.

Brown, R. *The Gospel according to John*. 2 vols. Garden City, NY: Doubleday, 1966, 1970.

————. *The Death of the Messiah*. 2 vols. Garden City, N.Y.: Doubleday, 1994.

Brownson, J. V. "Neutralizing the Intimate Enemy: The Portrayal of Judas in the Fourth Gospel." *Society of Biblical Literature Seminar Papers* (1992): 49–60.

Brun, J. "Témoignage et trahison: les adorateurs de Judas." In *Le Témoignage*, 493–503. Ed. E. Castelli. Aubier: Éditions Montaigne, 1972.

Buchheit, G. *Judas Iskarioth: Legende, Geschichte, Deutung*. Gütersloh: Rufer Verlag, 1954.

Büchner, A. *Judas Ischarioth in der deutschen Dichtung: Ein Versuch*. Freiburg: E. Guenther, 1920.

————. "Das Judasproblem." *Zeitschrift für den deutschen Unterricht* 27 (1913): 693–98.

Bulgakov, S. "Judas Ischarioth, der Verräter-Apostel." In *Orient und Occident*, heft 11, 8–24. Leipzig: 1932.

Bull, J. *Judas Iscariot! John Burns's Verdict on Himself.* London: Twentieth Century Press, 1907.

Bultmann, R. *History of the Synoptic Tradition*, rev. ed. Trans. J. Marsh. Peabody, Mass.: Hendrickson, 1963.

Cabassut, A. "La mitigation des peines de l'Enfer d'après les livres liturgiques." *Revue d'histoire ecclésiastique* 23 (1927): 65–70.

Cadbury, H. J. *The Style and Literary Method of Luke*. HTS 6. Cambridge, Mass.: Harvard University Press, 1920.

Caldwell, T., and J. Stearn. *I, Judas*. New York: Atheneum Publishers, 1977.

Callaghan, M. *A Time for Judas*. Toronto: Macmillan of Canada, 1983.

Carey, S. P. *Jesus and Judas*. New York: R. R. Smith, 1931.

Cary, C. C. "The Case of Judas Iscariot." *Methodist Quarterly Review* 59 (1910): 825–29.

Cebulj, C. "Die Nachtseite Gottes: Zum Judasbild im Johannesevangelium." *Entschluss* 44 (1989): 16.

Celada, B. "El nombre de 'Iscariote.'" *Cultura Biblica* 23 (1967): 41.

Cervo, N. "Shakespeare's 'Othello.'" *The Explicator* 53 (1995): 189–91.

Charles, R. H., ed. *The Apocrypha and Pseudepigrapha of the Old Testament*. Oxford: Clarendon Press, 1913.

Cherchi, P. "A Legend from St. Bartolomew's Gospel in the Twelfth Century." *Revue Biblique* 91 (1984): 212–18.

Chesebrough, D. B. *"No Sorrow like Our Sorrow": Northern Protestant Ministers and the Assassination of Lincoln*. Kent, Ohio, and London: Kent State University Press, 1994.

Cheyne, T. K. "Judas Iscariot." *Echter Bibel* 2:2623–28.

Chrysostom, John. *Discourses against Judaizing Christians*. Trans. P. W. Harkins. Washington, D.C.: Catholic University Press, 1979.

————. *Homilies on Matthew*. Trans. G. Prevost. Edinburgh: T. & T. Clark; Grand Rapids: Wm. B. Eerdmans Publishing Co., first published 1851; available on-line at http://www.ccel.org/fathers2/NPNF1-10/TOC.htm#TopOfPage.

———. *Homilies on the Acts of the Apostles.* Trans. J. Walker, et al. Edinburgh: T. & T. Clark; Grand Rapids: Wm. B. Eerdmans Publishing Co., first published 1889; available online at http://www.ccel.org/fathers2/NPNF1-11/npnf1-11-05.htm#P153_5953.

Coffin, A. B. *Robinson Jeffers: Poet of Inhumanism.* Madison, Wisc.: University of Wisconsin Press, 1971.

Cohen, F. G. "Jewish Images in Late Medieval German Popular Plays." *Midstream* (Aug./Sept. 1989): 21–26.

Combes, L. de. *The Finding of the Cross.* Trans. L. Cappadelta. London: Routledge & Kegan Paul, 1907.

Conrad, A. "The Fate of Judas: Matthew 27:3–10." *Toronto Journal of Theology* 7 (1991): 158–68.

Constans, L. *La légende d'Oedipe.* Paris: Maisonnevve, 1881.

Conzelmann, H. *Acts of the Apostles.* Trans. J. Limburg, et al. Philadephia: Fortress Press, 1987.

———. *The Theology of St. Luke.* Trans. G. Buswell. New York: Harper & Row, 1961.

Corathiel, E. H. C. *Oberammergau and Its Passion Play.* Westminster, Md.: Newman Press, 1960.

Cortes, N. A. "Sermon de Judas." *Revue hispanique* 60 (1924): 280–91.

Cox, W. A. "Judas Iscariot." *Interpreter* 3 (1907): 414–22; 4 (1908): 218 ff.

Creizenach, W. "Judas Ischarioth in Legende und Sage des Mittelalters." *Beiträge zur Geschichte der Deutschen Sprache und Literatur* 2 (1875): 177–207.

Cripps, K. R. J. "A Note on Matthew 22:12." *Expository Times* 69 (1957): 30.

Cronin, A. J. *The Judas Tree.* Boston: Little, Brown & Co., 1961.

Crossan, J. D. *Who Killed Jesus? Exposing the Roots of Anti-Semitism in the Gospel Story of the Death of Jesus.* San Francisco: HarperCollins, 1995.

Cullmann, O. "Le douzième apôtre." *Revue d'histoire et de philosophie religieuses* 42 (1962): 133–40.

Czarnecki, J. "The Significance of Judas in Giotto's Arena Chapel Frescoes." In *The Early Renaissance,* 35–47. Ed. A. Bernardo. Binghamton, N.Y.: Center for Medieval and Early Renaissance Studies, 1979.

Daisenberger, J. A. *Das Passions-Spiel in Oberammergau.* Munich: Joseph Hubers, 1930.

Daniélou, J. "Le fils de perdition." In *Mélanges d'histoire des religions, offerts à Henri-Charles Puech,* 187–89. Ed. A. Bareau, et al. Paris: Presse Universitaires de France, 1974.

Dante Alighieri. *Inferno.* Trans. M. Musa. New York: Penguin Books, 1971.

———. *Paradise.* Trans. M. Musa. New York: Penguin Books, 1986.

D'Arci, G. *The Tragedy of Judas Iscariot, A Modern Drama in a Prologue and Five Acts.* Amersham, U.K.: Mascot Press, 1926.

Dashuber, T. *Ecce Homo: The Making of the Passion Play.* Munich: Prestel, 2000.

Daub, C. *Judas Ischariot oder das Böse in Verhältnis zum Guten.* Heidelberg: Mohr & Winter, 1816–18.

Daube, D. "Judas." *California Law Review* 82 (1994): 95–108.

Davies, W. W. "Judas Iscariot." *Methodist Review* 103 (1920): 466–73.

Dawidowicz, L. S. *The War against the Jews 1933–1945.* New York: Bantam Books, 1986.

Deissmann, A. "Friend, Wherefore Art Thou Come?" *Expository Times* 33 (1922): 491–93.

De Quincey, T. "Judas Iscariot." In *Theological Essays, and Other Papers,* 115–53. Boston: James R. Osgood & Co., 1873.

Derrett, J. D. M. "Akeldama (Acts 1:19)." *Bijdragen, Tijdschrift voor Filosofie en Theologie* 56 (1995): 122–32.

———. "The Footwashing in John 13 and the Alienation of Judas Iscariot." *Revue Internationale des Droits de L'Antiquité* 24 (1977): 3–19.

———. "The Iscariot, Mᵉsira, and the Redemption." *Journal for the Study of the New Testament* 8 (1980): 2–23.

———. "Miscellanea: a Pauline Pun and Judas' Punishment." *Zeitschrift für die neutestamentliche Wissenschaft* 72 (1981): 131–33.

Desautels, L. "La mort de Judas (Mt 27,3–10; Ac 1,15–26)." *Science et Esprit* 38 (1986): 221–39.

Descamps, A. "Redaction et christologie dans le récit matthéen de la Passion." In *L'Évangile selon Matthieu*, 359–415. Ed. M. Didier. Gembloux: Duculot, 1972.

Dibelius, M. "Judas und der Judaskuss." In *Botschaft und Geschichte. Gesammelte Aufsätze I: Zur Evangelienforschung*, 272–77. Tübingen: J. C. B. Mohr, 1953.

Dickey, H. B. *Judas Iscariot*. Jericho, N.Y.: Exposition Press, 1970.

Dickinson, M. *The Lost Testament of Judas Iscariot*. Kerry, Ireland: Brandon, 1994.

Dieckmann, B. "Judas als Doppelgänger Jesu? Elemente und Probleme der Judastradition." In *Dramatische Erlösungslehre*. Eds. J. Niewiadomski and W. Palaver. Innsbruck: Tyrolia-Verlag, 1992.

———. *Judas als Sündenbock: eine verhängnisvolle Geschichte von Angst und Vergeltung*. Munich: Kösel, 1991.

Diederichs, V. "Russische Verwandte der Legende von Gregor auf dem Stein und der Sage von Judas Ischariot." *Russische Revue* 17 (1880): 119–46.

Dillon, P. R. *Judas of Kerioth, A Romance of Old Judea*. New York: Exposition Press, 1953.

Dinnerstein, L. *Antisemitism in America*. New York and Oxford: Oxford University Press, 1994.

Dinzelbacher, P. *Judastraditionen*. Wien: Selßstverlag des Osterreichischen Museums für Volkskunde, 1977.

Dorn, K. "Judas Iskariot, einer der Zwölf: Der Judas der Evangelien unter der Perspektive der Rede von den zwölf Zeugen der Auferstehung in 1 Kor 15, 3b–5." In *Judas Iskariot: Menschliches oder heilsgeschichtliches Drama?* 39–89. Ed. H. Wagner. Frankfurt: Knecht, 1985.

Doroschewitch, W. "Judas Iscariot," in *Judas Iscariot and Other Stories*, 5–12. Ed. G. Bruno. New York: 1919.

D'Orsi, E. *Il Momento di Giuda*. Rome: Trevi Editore, 1971.

Dostoyevsky, F. *The Brothers Karamazov*. Trans. C. Garnett. New York: Penguin Books, 1980.

———. *Notes from Underground*. Trans. M. Ginsburg. New York: Bantam Books, 1974.

Drews, A. *The Christ Myth*, repr. ed. Amherst, N.Y.: Prometheus Books, 1998. Originally published: Chicago: Open Court, 1910.

Duden, A. *Das Judasschaf*. Berlin: Rotbuch, 1985.

Duncan, R. F. H. *Judas*. London: Anthony Blond, 1960.

Dupont, J. "La destinée de Judas prophetisée par David (Actes 1,16–20)." *Catholic Biblical Quarterly* 23 (1961): 41–51.

Edmunds, L. *Oedipus: The Ancient Legend and Its Later Analogues*. Baltimore and London: Johns Hopkins University Press, 1985.

Edwards, J. R. "Markan Sandwiches: The Significance of Interpolations in Markan Narratives." *Novum Testamentum* 31 (1989): 193–216.

Ehrman, A. "Judas Iscariot and the Abba Saqqara." *Journal of Biblical Literature* 97 (1978): 572–73.

Elliott, J. K. *The Apocryphal New Testament: A Collection of Apocryphal Christian Literature in an English Translation*, rev. ed. Oxford: Clarendon Press, 1993.

Eltester, W. "Freund, wozu du gekommen bist (Mt 26:50)." In *Neotestamentica et Patristica: O. Cullman*, 70–91. Ed. A. N. Wilder. Leiden: E. J. Brill, 1962.

Enslin, M. S. "How the Story Grew: Judas in Fact and Fiction." In *Festschrift to Honor F. Wilbur Gingrich*, 123–41. Ed. E. Barth. Leiden: E. J. Brill, 1972.

Epiphanius. *The Panarion*. Trans. P. R. Amidon. New York and Oxford: Oxford University Press, 1990.

Everson, W. *The Excesses of God: Robinson Jeffers as a Religious Figure*. Stanford, Calif.: Stanford University Press, 1988.

Fascher, E. "Judas Iskarioth." In *Die Religion in Geschichte und Gegenwart*, 3d ed., vol. 3, cols. 965–66. Tübingen: J. C. B. Mohr, 1959.

Felsenstein, F. *Anti-Semitic Stereotypes: A Paradigm of Otherness in English Popular Culture, 1660–1830*. Baltimore and London: Johns Hopkins University Press, 1995.

Fensham, F. C. "Judas' Hand in the Bowl and Qumran." *Revue de Qumran* 5 (1965): 259–61.

Ficarra, A. *Giuda non tradì Gesù*. Milan: Sugar, 1971.

Filson, F. V. *A Commentary on the Gospel according to Saint Matthew*. London: Adam & Charles Black, 1960.

Fitzmyer, J. A. *The Gospel according to Luke*. 2 vols. New York: Doubleday, 1981, 1984.

Flight, J. W. "Judas the Betrayer [review]." *Journal of Bible and Religion* 26 (1958): 274–75.

Foakes-Jackson, F. J., and K. Lake, eds. *The Beginnings of Christianity*, vol. 5. London: Macmillan & Co., 1933.

Folz, H. "Judas der Ketzapostel." In *Die Reimpaarsprüche*, 164–73. Ed. H. Fischer. Munich: Beck, 1961.

Ford, J. *My Enemy Is My Guest: Jesus and Violence in Luke*. Maryknoll, N.Y.: Orbis Books, 1984.

Forsyth, N. *The Old Enemy: Satan and the Combat Myth*. Princeton, N.J.: Princeton University Press, 1987.

Foulcke-Deboc, R. "La légende de Judas Iscarioth." *Revue hispanique* 36 (1916): 135–49.

Fowler, R. M. "Thoughts on the History of Reading Mark's Gospel." *Proceedings: Eastern Great Lakes and Midwest Biblical Societies* 4 (1984): 120–30.

Frankl, V. *Man's Search for Meaning*. New York: Washington Square Press, 1959.

Frazer, J. G. *The Golden Bough*. New York: Macmillan Co., 1935.

Freytag, H. "Judas Ischariot in der deutschen Wissenschaft, Predigt, Dichtung, und bildenden Kunst unsers Jahrhunderts." *Protestanische Kirchenzeitung für das evangelische Deutschland* 43 (1886): 769–77, 792–99, 813–18, 841–45.

Friedell, E. *Die Judastragödie*. Wien: Bastei-Verlag, 1963.

Friedman, S. S. *The Oberammergau Passion Play: A Lance against Civilization*. Carbondale, Ill.: Southern Illinois University Press, 1984.

Fuzeira, J. *Judas Iscariotes e a sua reencarnação como Joana d'Arc*. Rio de Janeiro: Editora Eco, 1968.

Garland, J. M. "The Priest, the Prophet, and the Puritan." *Expository Times* 105 (1994): 340–41.

Garrett, S. *The Demise of the Devil: Magic and the Demonic in Luke's Writings*. Philadelphia: Fortress Press, 1989.

Gärtner, B. E. *Iscariot*. Trans. V. I. Gruhn. Philadelphia: Fortress Press, 1971.

Gillabert, E. *Judas—traître ou initié*. Paris: 1989.

Gillet, J. E. "Traces of the Judas-Legend in Spain." *Revue hispanique* 65 (1925): 316–41.

Girard, R. *The Scapegoat.* Trans. Yvonne Freccero. Baltimore: Johns Hopkins University Press, 1986.

———. *Violence and the Sacred.* Trans. P. Gregory. Baltimore: Johns Hopkins University Press, 1977.

Glasson, T. E. "Davidic Links with the Betrayal of Jesus." *Expository Times* 85 (1973–74): 118–19.

Goetz, O. "Hie hencktt Judas." In *Form und Inhalt. Festschrift O. Schmitt*, 105–37. Stuttgart: W. Kohlhammer, 1950.

Goetz, R. "Judas as Patron Saint." *The Christian Century* 104 (March 18, 1987): 262–63.

Goldschmidt, H. L. "Das Judasbild im Neuen Testament aus jüdischer Sicht." In *Heilvoller Verrat? Judas im Neuen Testament.* Eds. H. L. Goldschmidt and M. Limbeck. Stuttgart: Katholisches Bibelwerk, 1976.

———. "Judas Iscariot 2. Eine jüdische Stellungnahme." *Theologische Realenzyklopädie* 17 ( ): 305–7.

Gollwitzer, H. "Gute Botschaft für Judas Ischarioth." In *Krummes Holz-aufrechter Gang: Zur Frage nach dem Sinn des Lebens.* 2d ed., 271–96. Munich: Chr. Kaiser Verlag, 1970.

Goodacre, M. "Do You Think You're What They Say You Are? Reflections on *Jesus Christ Superstar.*" *Journal of Religion and Film* 3 (1999) [http://www.unomaha.edu/~wwwjrf/jesuscss2.htm].

Gordon, A. B. "The Fate of Judas according to Acts 1:18." *Evangelical Quarterly* 43 (1971): 97–100.

Götze, H. G. *De parallelismo Judae proditoris et romanae ecclesiae.* 1706.

———. *De cultu Judae proditoris.* Lübeck: 1716.

Graves, R. *King Jesus.* New York: Creative Age Press, 1946.

Grayzel, S. "Christian-Jewish Relations in the First Millennium." In *Essays in Antisemitism*, rev. ed., 79–92. Ed. K. S. Pinson. New York: Conference on Jewish Relations, 1946.

Green, J. B. *The Gospel of Luke.* Grand Rapids: Wm. B. Eerdmans Publishing Co., 1997.

Greenberg, L. A., and H. J. Jonas, "An American Anti-Semite in the Nineteenth Century," 265–83. In *Essays on Jewish Life and Thought.* Eds. J. L. Blau, et al. New York: Columbia University Press, 1959.

Griffin, C. S. *Judas Iscariot, the Author of the Fourth Gospel.* Boston: Scott-Parkin, 1892.

Grosheide, F. W. *Judas Ischkarioth.* Kampen: J. H. Kok, 1909.

Grossouw, W. K. "A Note on John xiii 1–3." *Novum Testamentum* 8 (1966): 124–31.

Gundry, R. H. *Matthew: A Commentary on His Literary and Theological Art.* Grand Rapids: Wm. B. Eerdmans Publishing Co., 1982.

———. *The Use of the Old Testament in St. Matthew's Gospel.* Leiden: E. J. Brill, 1967.

Gunther, H. *The Footprints of Jesus' Twelve in Early Christian Tradition.* Frankfurt: Peter Lang, 1985.

Gurk, P. *Judas.* Berlin: Holle, 1931.

Gutiérrez y Gonzalez, L. *Apóstol sombrío.* Mexico: Editoria Cuauhtémoc, 1967.

Guttmann, J. "Judas." *Encyclopaedia Judaica* 9:526–28. New York: MacMillan, 1972.

Haak, B. "Nieuw licht op Judas en de Zilverlingen van Rembrandt." In *Album Amicorum J. G. vam Gelder*, 155–58. Eds. J. Bruyn, J. Emmens, et al. The Hague: Martinus Nijhoff, 1973.

Haenchen, E. *The Acts of the Apostles: A Commentary.* Trans. B. Blackwell. Philadelphia: Westminster Press, 1971.

Haes, J. de. *Judas de Verrader, begrepen in drie boeken.* Rotterdam: J. Hofhout, 1714.

Hahn, T. "The Medieval Oedipus." *Comparative Literature* 32 (1980): 225–37.

Halas, R. B. *Judas Iscariot, a Scriptural and Theological Study of His Person, His Deeds, and His Eternal Lot.* Washington, D.C.: Catholic University of America, 1946.

Hand, W. D. "The Birthday of Judas Iscariot: A Study in Folklore." *Modern Language Forum* 25 (1940): 1–8.

———. *A Dictionary of Words and Idioms Associated with Judas Iscariot: A Compilation Based Mainly on Material Found in the Germanic Languages.* Berkeley and Los Angeles: University of California Press, 1942.

Happel, S. "The Postmodernity of Judas: Religious Narrative and the Deconstruction of Time." In *Postmodernism, Literature, and the Future of Theology*, 91–119. Ed. D. Jasper. London: Macmillan/New York: St. Martin's Press, 1993.

Harden, M. "Judas Ischariot." *Die Zukunft* 13 (1905): 153–60.

Harper, L. A. "Judas, Our Brother." *St. Luke's Journal of Theology* 29:2 (1986): 96–102.

Harris, J. R. "Did Judas Really Commit Suicide?" *American Journal of Theology* 4 (1900): 490–513.

———. "St. Luke's Version of the Death of Judas." *American Journal of Theology* 18 (1914): 127–31.

———. "The Suggested Primacy of Judas Iscariot." *Expositor* 8/14 (1917): 1–16.

Harrison, E. F. "Jesus and Judas." *Bibliotheca Sacra* 105 (1948): 170–81.

Hart, J. W. T. *The Autobiography of Judas Iscariot: A Character Study.* London: Kegan Paul, Trench, 1884.

Hartman, R. "Judas' Kiss." Nashville: Dawn Treader Music, 1982.

Haugg, D. *Judas Iskarioth in den neutestamentlichen Berichten.* Freiburg: Herder, 1930.

Hein, K. C. "Judas Iscariot: Key to the Last Supper Narratives." *New Testament Studies* 17 (1971): 227–32.

Heller, B. "Über das Alter der jüdischen Judas-Sage und des Toldot Jeschu." *Monatsschrift für die Geschichte und Wissenschaft des Judentums* 77 (1933): 198–210.

———. "Über Judas Ischariotes in der jüdischen Legende." *Monatsschrift für die Geschichte und Wissenschaft des Judentums* 76 (1932): 33–42.

Hengel, M. *The Zealots.* Trans. D. Smith. Edinburgh: T. & T. Clark, 1989.

Herber, J. "La mort de Judas." *Revue de l'histoire des religions* 129 (1945): 47–56.

Heurn, A. and E. van. *Judas.* Philadelphia: Muhlenberg Press, 1958.

Heyraud, J. "Judas et la nouvelle Alliance dans la cène selon Saint Jean." *Bible et Vie Chrétienne* 44 (1962): 39–48.

Hill, G. F. *The Medallic Portraits of Christ. The False Shekels. The Thirty Pieces of Silver.* London: Oxford University Press, 1920.

———. "The Thirty Pieces of Silver." *Archaeologia* 59 (1905): 235–54.

Hoberman, B. "How Did the Gospel of Thomas Get Its Name?" *Biblical Archaeologist* 46 (winter 1983): 10–11.

Hofbauer, J. "Judas, der Verräter." *Theologische-Praktische Quartalschrift* 110 (1962): 36–42.

Horne, R. H. "Judas Iscariot: A Mystery." In *Bible Tragedies*, 109–91. London: Newman & Co., 1881.

Horsley, R. *Bandits, Prophets, Messiahs: Popular Movements in the Time of Jesus.* San Francisco: Harper & Row, 1988.

Horst, P. W., van der. "A Note on the Judas Curse in Early Christian Inscriptions." In *Hellenism-Judaism-Christianity*, 146–50. Ed. P. W. van der Horst. Kampen, Holland: Kok Pharos, 1994.

Housh, G. S. *Judas Speaks.* New York: William-Frederick Press, 1953.

Hueter, J. E. *Matthew, Mark, Luke, John—Now Judas and His Redemption (In Search of the Real Judas).* Brookline Village, Mass.: Branden Press, 1983.

Hughes, K. T. "Framing Judas." *Semeia* 54 (1991): 223–38.

Imbach, J. "'Judas hat tausend Gesichter': Zum Judasbild in der Gegenwartsliteratur." In *Judas Iskariot: Menschliches oder heilsgeschichtliches Drama?* 91–142. Ed. H. Wagner. Frankfurt: Knecht, 1985.

Ingholt, H. "The Surname of Judas Iscariot." In *Studia orientalia Ioanni Pedersen,* 152–62. Copenhagen: Einar Munksgaard, 1953.

Irenaeus. *Against the Heresies.* Trans. D. J. Unger. New York: Paulist Press, 1992.

Iseley, N. "De passione Judas." In *Studies in the Romance Languages and Literatures* 2, 31–40. Chapel Hill, N.C.: University of North Carolina, 1941.

Istrin, V. "Die griechische Version der Judas-Legende." *Archiv für slavische Philologie* 20 (1898): 605–19.

Jacobus de Voragine. *The Golden Legend.* Trans. G. Ryan and H. Ripperger. New York: Arno Press, 1969.

Jacquier, E. *Les Actes des Apotres.* Paris: Gabalda, 1926.

Jeffers, R. "Dear Judas." In *The Collected Poetry of Robinson Jeffers,* vol. 2, 5–45. Ed. T. Hunt. 2 vols. Stanford, Calif.: Stanford University Press, 1989.

———. "Dear Judas." *Epiphany* 4:3 (spring 1984): 44–46.

Jeffrey, D. L., ed. *A Dictionary of Biblical Tradition in English Literature.* Grand Rapids: Wm. B. Eerdmans Publishing Co., 1992.

Jens, W. *Der Fall Judas.* Stuttgart: Kreuz-Verlag, 1975.

Jeremias, J. *Jerusalem in the Time of Jesus.* Trans. F. H. and C. H. Cave. Philadelphia: Fortress Press, 1969.

Jervell, J. "Jesu blods aker. Matt. 27, 3–10." *Norsk Teologisk Tidsskrift* 69 (1968): 158–62.

Jocz, J. *The Jewish People and Jesus Christ: A Study in the Controversy between Church and Synagogue.* London: SPCK, 1962.

Jordan, C. *Judas: The Man from Gadera.* Americus, Ga.: Koinonia Records, 1970.

Jursch, H. "Das Bild des Judas Ischarioth im Wandel der Zeiten." In *Akten des VII. Internationalen Kongresses für Christliche Archäologie Trier 1965,* 565–73. Rome: Pontificio Instituto Di Archeologia Christiana, 1969.

———. "Judas Iskarioth in der Kunst." *Wissenschaftliche Zeitschrift der Friedrich Schiller Universität,* 1 (1952): 101–5.

———. "Die Rolle des Judas Ischariot in der Bildtradition der Fusswaschung Jesu." In *Inter Confessiones: Beiträge zur interkonfessionellen und interreligiösen Gesprächs,* 25–33. Ed. A. M. Heiler. Marburg: N. G. Elwert, 1972.

———. "Traditionsort und Aussagekraft moderner Judasbilder." In *Wort und Welt: Festgabe E. Hertzsch,* 151–64. Ed. M. Weise et al. Berlin: Evangelischer Verlagsanstalt, 1968.

Kahn, J. "Judas Iscariot: A Vehicle of Medieval Didacticism." Ph.D. diss., University of Utah, 1976.

Kallas, J. *Jesus and the Power of Satan.* Philadelphia: Westminster Press, 1968.

Kamen, H. *The Spanish Inquisition.* New Haven and London: Yale University Press, 1997.

Kann, R. A. *A Study in Austrian Intellectual History: From Late Baroque to Romanticism.* New York: Praeger Publishers, 1960.

Kazantzakis, N. *The Last Temptation of Christ.* Trans. P. A. Bien. New York: Simon & Schuster, 1960.

Kelber, W. H. *Mark's Story of Jesus.* Philadelphia: Fortress Press, 1979.

Kemner, H. *Judas Ischariot: Zwischen Nachfolge und Verrat.* Stuttgart: Neuhausen, 1988.

Kemp, H. *Judas.* New York: Mitchell Kennerley, 1913.

Kempe, M. von. *Dissertatio historico-philologica gemina.* Leipzig: L. S. Cörnerum, 1665.

Kendon, F. *A Life and Death of Judas Iscariot.* London: John Lane/Bodley Head, 1926.

Kennelly, B. *The Book of Judas: A Poem.* Newcastle upon Tyne: Bloodaxe Books, 1991.

Kermode, F. *The Genesis of Secrecy: On the Interpretation of Narrative.* Cambridge, Mass.: Harvard University Press, 1979.

Kilpatrick, G. D. *The Origins of the Gospel according to St. Matthew.* London: Oxford University Press, 1946.

Klassen, W. "The Authenticity of Judas' Participation in the Arrest of Jesus." In *Authenticating the Activities of Jesus,* 389–410. Eds. B. D. Chilton and C. A. Evans. Leiden: E. J. Brill, 1999.

———. *Judas: Betrayer or Friend of Judas?* Minneapolis: Fortress Press, 1996.

———. "Judas Iscariot." *Anchor Bible Dictionary* 3 (1992): 1091–96.

———. "Kiss (NT)." *Anchor Bible Dictionary* 4 (1992): 89–92.

Klauck, H.-J. "Judas der 'Verräter'? Eine exegetische und wirkungsgeschichtliche Studie." *Aufstieg und Niedergang der römischen Welt,* II.26.1 (1992): 717–40.

———. *Judas—ein Jünger des Herrn.* Freiburg: Herder, 1987.

Klausner, J. *Jesus of Nazareth: His Life, Times, and Teaching.* Trans. H. Danby. New York: Macmillan Co., 1925.

Knox, A. D. "The Death of Judas." *Journal of Theological Studies* 25 (1923–24): 289–95.

Komroff, M. *Jesus through the Centuries.* New York: William Sloane Associates, 1953.

Kopp, C. *The Holy Places of the Gospels.* Trans. R. Walls. New York: Herder & Herder, 1963.

Kornetter, J. "Das Judasproblem in der neuesten Literatur." *Das Neue Reich* 8 (1926): 553f.

Krauss, S. "Judas Iscariot." *Jewish Review* 4 (1913): 199–207.

Kremer, H. "Hoffnung für Judas?" *Orientierung* 40 (1976): 30.9, 189.

Kretzenbacher, L. "Sankt Brandan, Judas und die Ewigkeit." In *Bilder und Legenden. Erwandertes und erlebtes Bilder-Denken und Bild-Erzählen zwischen Byanz und dem Abendland,* 150–76. Klagenfurt: Geschichtsverein für Karnten, 1971.

Krieger, N. "Der Knecht des Hohenpriesters." *Novum Testamentum* 2 (1957): 73–74.

Kuryluk, E. *Salome and Judas in the Cave of Sex. The Grotesque: Origins, Iconography, Techniques.* Evanston, Ill.: Northwestern University Press, 1987.

Kürzinger, J. *Papias von Hieropolis und die Evangelien des Neuen Testaments.* Regensburg: Friedrich Pustet, 1983.

Laeuchli, S. "Origen's Interpretation of Judas Iscariot." *Church History* 22 (1953): 253–68.

Lake, K. "The Death of Judas." In *The Beginnings of Christianity.* 6 vols., vol. 5, 22–30. Eds. F. J. Foakes-Jackson and K. Lake. London: Macmillan Co., 1933. Repr. ed., Grand Rapids: Baker Book House, 1979.

Lange, H. C. *Jesus und Judas in ihrem Verhältniss su einander.* Altona: 1857.

Lapide, P. E. "An Judas Iskariot: Ein Brief." In *Judas, wer bist du?* Ed. R. Niemann. Gütersloh: G. Mohn, 1991.

———. "Verräter oder verraten? Judas in evangelischer und jüdischer Sicht." *Lutherisches Monatsheft* 16 (1977): 75–79.

Lapide, P. E. *Wer war Schuld an Jesu Tod?* Gütersloh: G. Mohn, 1987.

Laros, M. "Judas Iskariot." *Hochland* 8 (1910–11): 657–67.

Lawrence, C. E. *Spikenard: A Play in One Act.* London: Gowans & Gray/Boston: Baker International Play Bureau, 1929.

Leclerq, H. "Judas Iscariote." *Dictionnaire d'Archéologie Chrétienne et de Liturgie*. Paris: Letouzey et Ane, 8, no. 1 (1907): 255–79.

Lehmann, P. "Judas Ischarioth in der lateinischen Legendenüberlieferung des Mittelalters." *Studi medievali* 2 (1929): 289–346.

Léon-Dufour, X. "Situation de Jean 13." In *Die Mitte des Neuen Testaments: Einheit und Vielfalt neutestamentlicher Theologie. Festschrift für Eduard Schweizer zum siebzigsten Geburtstag*, 131–41. Eds. U. Luz and H. Weder. Göttingen: Vandenhoeck & Ruprecht, 1983.

Lévitt, A. *Judas Iscariot: An Imaginative Autobiography*. Hancock, N.H.: Flagstone Publications, 1961.

Lévy, L. G. "Que Judas Iscariote n'a jamais existé." *Grande Revue* 55 (1909): 533–39.

Lewis, L. *Myths after Lincoln*. New York: Press of the Readers Club, 1941.

Limbeck, M. "Das Judasbild im Neuen Testament aus christlicher Sicht." In *Heilvoller Verrat? Judas im Neuen Testament*, 37–101. Eds. H. L. Goldschmidt and M. Limbeck. Stuttgart: Katholisches Bibelwerk, 1976.

Lindars, B. *New Testament Apologetic*. London: SCM Press, 1961.

Lindop, G. *The Opium Eater: A Life of Thomas De Quincey*. New York: Taplinger Publishing Co., 1981.

Linklater, E. *Judas: A Novel*. London: J. Cape, 1939.

Locard, E. "La mort de Judas Iscariote, étude critique d'exégèse et de médecine légale sur un cas de pendaison célèbre." *Archives d'anthropologie criminelle, de criminologie et psychologie normale et pathologique* 19 (1904): 421–54.

Loewenstein, A. F. *Loathsome Jews and Engulfing Women: Metaphors of Projection in the Works of Wyndham Lewis, Charles Williams, and Graham Greene*. New York and London: New York University Press, 1993.

Loisy, A. *The Origins of the New Testament*. Trans. L. P. Jacks. London: George Allen & Unwin, Ltd., 1950.

Lüthi, K. "Judas Iscariot." *Theologische Realenzyklopädie* 17: 296–304.

———. *Judas Iskarioth in der Geschichte der Auslegung von der Reformation bis zur Gegenwart*. Zürich: Zwingli-Verlag, 1955.

———. "Das Problem des Judas Iskariot—neu untersucht." *Evangelische Theologie* 16 (1956): 98–114.

Lutyens, D. B. *Judas Iscariot, A Play*. London: Eyre & Spottiswoode, 1951.

Maccoby, H. "Jesus and Barabbas." *New Testament Studies* 16 (1968): 55–60.

———. *Judas Iscariot and the Myth of Jewish Evil*. New York: Free Press, 1992.

———. *The Sacred Executioner*. London: Thames & Hudson, 1982.

———. "Who Was Judas Iscariot?" *Jewish Quarterly* (summer 1991): 8–13.

Malbon, E. S. and A. Berlin, eds. *Characterization in Biblical Literature. Semeia* 63. Atlanta: Society of Biblical Literature, 1993.

Malone, P. *Movie Christs and Antichrists*. New York: Crossroad, 1990.

Manning, R. J. S. "Kierkegaard and Post-Modernity: Judas as Kierkegaard's Only Disciple." *Philosophy Today* 37 (1993): 133–52.

Manns, F. "Un midrash chrétien: Le récit de la mort de Judas." *Revue des Sciences Religieuses* 54 (1980): 197–203.

Marcus, R. "Antisemitism in the Hellenistic-Roman World." In *Essays in Antisemitism*, rev. ed., 61–78. Ed. K. S. Pinson. New York: Conference on Jewish Relations, 1946.

Marin, L. *The Semiotics of the Passion Narrative: Types and Figures*. Trans. A. M. Johnson Jr. Pittsburgh: Pickwick Press, 1980.

Martin, H. "The Judas Iscariot Curse." *American Journal of Philology* 37 (1916): 434–51.

McClain, R. O. "Judas Iscariot." Diss., Southern Baptist Seminary, 1951.

McClean, B. "A Christian Epitaph: The Curse of Judas Iscariot." *Orientalia Christiana Periodica* 58 (1992): 241–44.

McConnell, R. *Law and Prophecy in Matthew's Gospel.* Basel: Friedrich Reinhardt, 1969.

McGlasson, P. *Jesus and Judas: Biblical Exegesis in Barth.* Atlanta: Scholars Press, 1991.

Medisch, R. "Der historische Judas—und was aus ihm gemacht wurde." *Theologie und Gegenwart* 31 (1988): 50–54.

Meinertz, M. "Zur Frage nach der Anwesenheit des Verräters Judas bei der Einsetzung der Eucharistie." *Biblische Zeitschrift* 10 (1912): 372–90.

Mela, C. "Oedipe, Judas, Osiris." In *Histoire et Société: Mélanges offerts à Georges Duby,* vol. 4, 201–20. Ed. C. La Ronciére. Aix-en-Provence: Université de Provence, 1992.

Mellinkoff, R. "Judas's Red Hair and the Jews." *Journal of Jewish Art* 9 (1982): 31–46.

Melville, H. *Moby Dick.* Norton Critical Edition. New York and London: W. W. Norton & Co., 1967.

Mély, F. de. "Les deniers de Judas dans la tradition du moyen age." *Revue Numismatique* 4, no. 3 (1899): 500–9.

Mercante, A. S. *The Facts on File Encyclopedia of World Mythology and Legend.* New York and Oxford: Facts on File, 1988.

Miles, J. *God: A Biography.* New York: Alfred A. Knopf, 1995.

Milligan, J. L. *Judas Iscariot: A Poetical Play.* Toronto: Ryerson Press, 1929.

Milward, P. *Shakespeare's Religious Background.* Bloomington & London: Indiana University Press, 1973.

Monro, H. *Judas.* Cranleigh, U.K.: Samurai Press, 1907; London: S. Low, Marston, & Co., 1911.

Monstadt, B. *Judas beim Abendmahl: Figurenkonstellation und Bedeutung in Darstellungen von Giotto bis Andrea del Sarto.* Munich: 1995.

Montaigne, M. de. "On Repentance." In *Essays and Selected Writings,* 313–53. Trans. and ed. D. M. Frame. New York: St. Martin's Press, 1963.

Moo, D. J. "Tradition and Old Testament in Matt 27:3–10." In *Gospel Perspectives, Vol. 3: Studies in Midrash and Historiography,* 157–75. Eds. R. France and D. Wenham. Sheffield: JSOT Press, 1983.

Moodey, S. *Judas the Traitor Hung up in Chains: To Give Warning to Professors, that They Beware of Worldlymindedness, and Hypocrisy.* New Haven, Conn.: 1761.

Moore, J. F. "A New Christian Midrash: On the Frontier of Theology after the Shoah." In *What Have We Learned? Telling the Story and Teaching the Lessons of the Holocaust,* 269–313. Ed. F. Littell, et al. Lewiston, N.Y.: Edwin Mellen, 1993.

Moore, T. S. *Judas.* London: G. Richards, 1923.

Morel, R. *L'Évangile de Judas.* Paris: R. Julliard, 1946.

Morey, J. H. "The Death of King John in Shakespeare and Bale." *Shakespeare Quarterly* 45 (1994): 327–31.

Morin, J. A. "Les deux derniers des douze: Simon le Zélote et Judas Iskarîôth." *Revue Biblique* 80 (1973): 332–58.

Morley, S. *Judas, A Poem in 1932 Lines, One for Each Year of Our Lord.* Oxford: Basil Blackwell Publisher, 1932.

Mossenson, Y. *Judas, A Novel.* Trans. J. Harlow. New York: St. Martin's Press, 1963.

Mota, Atico Vilas-Boas da. *Quemicão de Judas: Catarismo, Inquisição e o Judeus no Folclore Brasileiro.* Rio de Janeiro: Ministerio da Educação e Cultura, Secretaria de Assuntos Culturais, Instituto Nacional do Folclore, 1981.

Munes, D. *Judas, traidor ou traído?* Rio de Janeiro: Gráf, 1968.

Münkler, H. "Judas Ischariot." In *Odysseus und Kassandra. Politik und Mythos*, 63–77. Frankfurt: Fischer Taschenbuch, 1990.

Munro, J. I. "The Death of Judas (Matt xxvii.3–8; Acts i.18–19)." *Expository Times* 24 (1912–13): 235–36.

Nagle, U. *Barter: A Drama in Four Acts.* London and New York: Longmans, Green, & Co., 1929.

Naselli, C. "Note sui 'Giudei' di San Fratello." In *Demologia e folklore*, 293–305. Ed. G. Bonomo, et al. 1974.

Nash, N. R. *Behold the Man.* Garden City, N.Y.: Doubleday, 1986.

Nestle, E. "Another Peculiarity of Codex Bezae." *Expository Times* 9 (1897–98): 140.

———. "The Name of Judas Iscariot in the Fourth Gospel." *Expository Times* 9 (1897–98): 240.

Nichols, W. B. *The Saga of Judas.* London: N. Wolsey, 1949.

Nicole, A. *Judas the Betrayer.* Grand Rapids: Baker Book House, 1957.

Niemann, R. *Judas, wer bist du?* Gütersloh: G. Mohn, 1991.

Nigg, W. "Judas Ischarioth." In *Grosse Unheilige*, 58–83. Olten: Walter-Verlag, 1981.

Niles, J. J. *The Ballad Book of John Jacob Niles.* New York: Dover Publications, 1960.

Nortjé, L. "Matthew's Motive for the Composition of the Story of Judas's Suicide in Matthew 27:3–10." *Neotestamentica* 28 (1994): 41–51.

Norwood, R. W. *The Man of Kerioth.* New York: George H. Doran Co., 1919.

O'Connor, F. *The Complete Stories.* New York: Farrar, Straus & Giroux, 1971.

Ong, W. J. *Orality and Literacy: The Technologizing of the Word.* London and New York: Methuen, 1982.

Origen. *Against Celsus.* Trans. F. Crombie. New York: Charles Scribner's Sons, 1899.

———. *Commentary on the Gospel of Matthew.* Trans. J. Patrick. Edinburgh: T. & T. Clark; Grand Rapids: Wm. B. Eerdmans Publishing Co., 1951. Available on-line at http://www.ccel.org/fathers2/ANF-10/TOC.htm

———. *Contra Celsum.* Trans. Henry Chadwick. Cambridge, U.K.: Cambridge University Press, 1965.

Paffenroth, K. "The Character of Judas in Bach's *St. Matthew Passion.*" *Midwest Quarterly* 36 (1995): 125–35.

———. "Review of *Judas: Friend or Betrayer of Jesus?*" *Journal of Religion* 78 (1998): 104–5.

———. "The Stories of the Fate of Judas and Differing Attitudes towards Sources." *Proceedings: Eastern Great Lakes and Midwest Biblical Societies* 12 (1992): 67–81.

Page, G. A. *The Diary of Judas Iscariot or the Gospel according to Judas.* London: Charles H. Kelly, 1912.

Pagels, E. *The Origin of Satan.* New York: Random House, 1995.

Pagnol, M. *Judas.* Monte-Carlo: Éditions Pastorelly, 1975.

Panas, H. *Wedlug Judasza.* Olsztyn: Pojezierze, 1973.

Pepler, H. D. C. *Judas, or, The Betrayal: A Play in One Act with Prologue and Epilogue.* Ditchling, U.K.: St. Dominic's Press, 1956.

Petruccelli della Gattina, F. *Memorie di Giuda.* Torino: Fògola, 1976.

Pflaum, H. "Les Scènes de Juifs dans la littérature dramatique du Moyen-âge." *Revue des études Juives* 89 (1930): 111–34.

Phillips, D. R. "We Don't Want to Own the Likeness: Contemporary Literature and Films Have Recast Judas as a Tragic and Therefore Noble Figure." *Christianity Today* 24 (April 4, 1980): 30–31.

Pinkham, D. *The Passion of Judas.* Boston: E. C. Schirmer Music Co., 1978.

Plath, M. "Warum hat die urchristliche Gemeinde auf die Überlieferung der Judaserzählung Wert gelegt?" *Zeitschrift für die neutestamentliche Wissenschaft* 17 (1916): 178–88.

Plummer, A. "Judas Iscariot." *Hastings Dictionary of the Bible* 2 (1905): 796–99.

Pope, L. "The Price of the Potter's Field." *Christianity and Crisis* 14 (1954): 33–34.

Pottecher, M. *Le mystère de Judas Iscariote en IV acts et un prologue.* Paris: P. V. Stock, 1911.

Powell, M. *God Off-Broadway: The Blackfriars Theatre of New York.* Lanham, Md., and London: Scarecrow Press, 1998.

Preisker, H. "Der Verrat des Judas und das Abendmahl." *Zeitschrift für die neutestamentliche Wissenschaft* 41 (1942): 151–55.

Puchner, W. *Studien zum Kulturkontext der liturgischen Szene: Lazarus und Judas als religiöse Volksfiguren in Bild und Brauch, Lied und Legende Südosteuropas. Österreichische Akademie der Wissenschaften.* Vienna: Verlag der Österreichischen Akademie der Wissenschaften, 1991.

Puget, C. A. *Un nommé Judas, pièce en trois actes.* Paris: La Table ronde, 1956.

Rand, E. K. "Medieval Lives of Judas Iscariot." In *Anniversary Papers by Colleagues and Pupils of George Lyman Kittredge,* 305–16. Boston: Ginn & Co., 1913.

Rayner, W. *The Knifeman.* New York: William Morrow & Co., 1969.

Reed, C. E. B. *The Companions of the Lord: Chapters in the Lives of the Apostles,* 2d ed. London: Religious Tract Society, 1883.

Rehkopf, F. "Mt 26:50: Ἑταῖρε, ἐφ' ὃ πάρει." *Zeitschrift für die neutestamentliche Wissenschaft* 52 (1961): 109–15.

Reid, D. "Elders' Ears in Appleton House." *Notes and Queries* 42 (1995): 447–48.

Reider, J. "Jews in Medieval Art." In *Essays in Antisemitism,* rev. ed., 93–102. Ed. K. S. Pinson. New York: Conference on Jewish Relations, 1946.

Reider, N. "Medieval Oedipal Legends about Judas." *Psychoanalytic Quarterly* 29 (1960): 515–27.

Reik, T. "Das Evangelium des Judas Iskariot" and "Die psychoanalytische Deutung des Judasproblems." In *Der eigene und der fremde Gott: Zur Psychoanalyse der religiösen Entwicklung,* 75–97, 98–129. Frankfurt am Main: A. Mitscherlich, 1972.

Renan, E. *Vie de Jésus.* Paris: Michel Lévy, 1863.

Rhoads, D., and D. Michie. *Mark as Story: An Introduction to the Narrative of a Gospel.* Philadelphia: Fortress Press, 1982.

Richard, A. *Judas, une drame en quatre actes.* Paris: B. Grasset, 1914.

Riedel, O. *Verrat aus Liebe: eine biblische Studie.* Berlin: Evangelische Verlagsanstalt, 1965.

Robbins, V. K. "Last Meal: Preparation, Betrayal, and Absence (Mark 14:12–25)." In *The Passion in Mark: Studies on Mark 14–16,* 21–40. Ed. W. H. Kelber. Philadelphia: Fortress Press, 1976.

Robertson, A. T. "The Primacy of Judas Iscariot." *Expositor* 8, no. 13 (1917): 278–86.

Robertson, J. M. *Jesus and Judas: A Textual and Historical Investigation.* London: Watts, 1927.

Roquefrot, D. "Judas: une figure de la perversion." *Études Théologiques et Religieuses* 58 (1983): 501–13.

Rose, M., ed. *The Wakefield Mystery Plays.* New York and London: W. W. Norton, 1969.

Rosenberg, E. *From Shylock to Svengali: Jewish Stereotypes in English Fiction.* London: Peter Owen, 1961.

Roth, C. *Iscariot.* London: Mandrake Press, 1929.

Russell, J. B. *The Devil: Perceptions of Evil from Antiquity to Primitive Christianity.* Ithaca, N.Y.: Cornell University Press, 1977.

Sahlin, H. "Der Tod des Judas Iskariot nach Ag 1,15ff." *Annual of the Swedish Theological Institute* 12 (1983): 148–52.

Sayers, D. L. *The Man Born to Be King: A Play-Cycle on our Lord and Saviour Jesus Christ.* New York: Harper & Brothers, 1943.

Scharlemann, R. P. "Why Christianity Needs Other Religions." In *Christianity and the Wider Ecumenism*, 35–46. Ed. P. Phan. New York: Paragon House, 1990.

Schendler, D. "Judas, Oedipus, and Various Saints." *Psychoanalysis* 2–3 (1954): 41–46.

Schiller, G. *Iconography of Christian Art. Vol. 2: The Passion of Jesus Christ.* Trans. J. Seligman. London: Lund Humphries, 1972.

Schläger, G. "Die Ungeschichtlichkeit des Verräters Judas." *Zeitschrift für die neutestamentliche Wissenschaft* 15 (1914): 50–59.

Schmidt, K. "Judas Ischarioth." *Realencyklopädie für protestantische Theologie und Kirche*, 3d ed., vol. 9, 586–89. Ed. A. Hauck. Leipzig: J. C. Hinrichs, 1896–1913.

Schonfield, H. J. *According to the Hebrews.* London: Duckworth, 1937.

Schueler, D. G. "The Middle English *Judas*: An Interpretation." *Publication of the Modern Language Association of America* 91 (1976): 840–45.

Schultess, F. "Zur Sprache der Evangelien. D. Judas 'Iskariot.'" *Zeitschrift für die neutestamentliche Wissenschaft* 21 (1922): 250–58.

Schwarz, G. *Jesus und Judas: aramaistische Untersuchungen zur Jesus-Judas-Überlieferung der Evangelien und Apostelgeschichte.* Stuttgart: Kohlhammer, 1988.

Schwarz, W. "Die Doppelbedeutung des Judastodes." *Bibel und Liturgie* 57 (1984): 227–33.

Schweitzer, A. *The Quest of the Historical Jesus: A Critical Study of Its Progress from Reimarus to Wrede*, 2d ed. Trans. W. Montgomery. London: A. & C. Black, 1936.

Schweizer, E. *The Good News according to Matthew.* Trans. D. E. Green. Atlanta: John Knox Press, 1975.

———. "Zu Apg 1:16–22." *Theologische Zeitschrift* 14 (1958): 46.

Sedgwick, S. N. *Judas, Which Also—A Tragedy.* London: Society for Promoting Christian Knowledge, 1936.

Senior, D. "A Case Study in Matthean Creativity (Matthew 27:3–10)." *Biblical Review* 19 (1974): 23–36.

———. "The Fate of the Betrayer: A Redactional Study of Matthew 27:3–10." *Ephemerides Theologicae Lovanienses* 48 (1972): 372–426.

———. *The Passion according to Matthew: A Redactional Study.* Leuven: Leuven University Press, 1982.

———. "The Passion Narrative in the Gospel of Matthew." In *L'Évangile selon Matthieu*, 343–57. Ed. M. Didier. Gembloux: Duculot, 1972.

———. *The Passion of Jesus in the Gospel of Matthew.* Wilmington, Del.: Michael Glazier, 1985.

Shachar, I. *The Judensau: A Medieval Anti-Jewish Motif and Its History.* Warburg Institute Surveys 5. London: Warburg Institute, 1974.

———. "Studies in the Emergence and Dissemination of the Modern Jewish Stereotype in Western Europe." Ph.D. diss., University of London, 1967.

Shapiro, J. *Oberammergau: The Troubling Story of the World's Most Famous Passion Play.* New York: Pantheon Books, 2000.

———. *Shakespeare and the Jews.* New York: Columbia University Press, 1996.

Sheen, F. J. "The Kiss." *Epiphany* 4, no. 3 (spring 1984): 47–49.

Smith, W. B. "Judas Iscariot." *Hibbert Journal* 9 (1911): 529–44.

Soocher, S. *They Fought the Law: Rock Music Goes to Court.* New York: Schirmer Books, 1999.

Spiteri, A. *Die Frage der Judaskommunion neu untersucht.* Theologische Studien der Österreichischen Leo-Gesellschaft 23. Vienna: 1918.

Spong, J. S. "Did Christians Invent Judas?" *The Fourth R* (March-April 1994): 3–11, 16.

Sproston, W. E. "Satan in the Fourth Gospel." In *Studia Biblica (1978).* 3 vols., vol. 2, 307–11.
Ed. E. A. Livingstone. Sheffield: Sheffield University Press, 1979.

———. "The Scripture in John 17:12." In *Scripture: Meaning and Method. Essays Presented to
Anthony Tyrrell Hanson on His Seventieth Birthday,* 24–36. Ed. B. Thompson. Hull: Hull
University Press, 1987.

Stade, R. "Der Verrat des Judas vom kriminalistischen Gesichtspunkt aus." *Zeitschrift für Religionspsychologie* 3 (1909): 273–82, 311–23.

Stalter-Fouilloy, D. "Les maudits." *Revue d'Histoire et de Philosophie Religieuses* 66 (1986):
451–58.

Stead, W. T. *The Passion Play at Ober Ammergau 1910.* London: Stead's Publishing, 1910.

Steinmetzer, F. "Judas, der Verräter." *Zeitenwächter* 22 (1928): 17–31.

Stein-Schneider, H. L. "'A la recherche du Judas historique: Une enquête exégétique à la
lumière des textes de l'ancien testament et des LOGIA." *Études Théologiques et
Religieuses* 60 (1985): 403–23.

Stendahl, K. *The School of St. Matthew and Its Use of the Old Testament.* Philadelphia: Fortress
Press, 1968.

Stern, R. C., C. N. Jefford, and G. Debona. *Savior on the Silver Screen.* New York: Paulist
Press, 1999.

Story, W. W. *A Roman Lawyer in Jerusalem.* Boston: Loring, 1870. Repr. as *In Defense of Judas.*
Wausau, Wisc.: Philosopher Press, 1902.

Stouck, M. "A Reading of the Middle English *Judas.*" *Journal of English and Germanic Philology* 80 (1981): 188–98.

Strauss, D. F. *The Life of Jesus Critically Examined.* Trans. G. Eliot. Philadelphia: Fortress Press,
1972.

Strecker, G. *Der Weg der Gerechtigkeit: Untersuchung zur Theologie des Matthäus.* Göttingen:
Vandenhoeck & Ruprecht, 1966.

Suarès, C. *The Passion of Judas: A Mystery Play.* Trans. M. and V. Stuart. Berkeley, Calif.: Sham-
bala, 1973.

Suggit, J. N. "Poetry's Next-Door Neighbour." *Journal of Theology for Southern Africa* 25
(1978): 3–17.

Symington, A. MacL. *The Apostles of Our Lord: Practical Studies.* London: Hodder &
Stoughton, 1880.

Tabachovitz, D. "Der Tod des Judas Iskariot." *Eranos* 67 (1969): 43–47.

Tannehill, R. C. "The Disciples in Mark: the Function of a Narrative Role." In *The Interpretation of Mark,* 134–57. Ed. W. Telford. Philadelphia: Fortress Press/London: SPCK,
1985.

Tarachow, S. "Judas the Beloved Executioner." *Psychoanalytical Quarterly* 29 (1960): 528–54.

Tasker, J. G. "Judas Iscariot." In *A Dictionary of Christ and the Gospels,* 907–13. Ed. J. Hastings.
Edinburgh: T. & T. Clark, 1911.

Taylor, A. "The Burning of Judas." *Washington University Studies* 11 (1923): 159–86.

———. "The Gallows of Judas Iscariot." *Washington University Studies* 9 (1922): 135–56.

———. "Judas Iscariot in Charms and Incantations." *Washington University Studies* 8 (1920):
3–17.

Teichert, W. *Jeder ist Judas. Der unvermeidliche Verrat.* Stuttgart: Kreuz, 1990.

Temple, S. "The Two Traditions of the Last Supper, Betrayal and Arrest." *New Testament Studies* 7 (1960–61): 77–85.

Thomas, W. *Outline Studies in the Gospel of Matthew.* Grand Rapids: Wm. B. Eerdmans Publishing Co., 1961.

Thompson, J. *The Lost and Undone Son of Perdition: or, The Birth, Life, and Character of Judas Iscariot.* Leominster, Mass.: Chapman Whitcomb/Adams & Wilder, 1800.

Thümmel, H. G. "Judas Ischariot im Urteil der altkirchlichen Schriftsteller des Westens und in der frühchristlichen Kunst." Diss., Greifswald, 1959.

Thurston, E. T. *Judas Iscariot: A Play in Four Acts.* London and New York: G. P. Putnam's Sons, 1923.

Tilborg, S. van. *The Jewish Leaders in Matthew.* Leiden: E. J. Brill, 1972.

———. "Matthew 27.3–10: An Intertextual Reading." In *Intertextuality in Biblical Writings: Essays in Honor of Bas van Iersel,* 159–74. Ed. S. Draisma. Kampen: J. H. Kok, 1989.

Timayenis, T. T. *Judas Iscariot: An Old Type in a New Form.* New York: Minerva, 1889.

Topping, C. W. *Jewish Flower Child: An Historical Novel.* Toronto: McClelland & Stewart, 1970.

Torrey, C. C. "The Foundry of the Second Temple at Jerusalem." *Journal of Biblical Literature* 60 (1936): 247–60.

———. "The Name 'Iscariot.'" *Harvard Theological Review* 36 (1943): 51–62.

Trocmé, E. *Le livre des Actes et l'histoire.* Paris: Presses Universitaires, 1957.

Trüdinger, L. P. "Davidic Links with the Betrayal of Jesus: Some Further Observations." *Expository Times* 86 (1975): 278–79.

Turner, F. "A Curious Custom. The Judas Penny." *Folk-Lore* 65 (1954): 47.

Unnik, W. C. van. "The Death of Judas in Saint Matthew's Gospel." *Anglican Theological Review Supplementary Series* 3 (1974): 44–57.

Upton, J. A. "The Potter's Field and the Death of Judas." *Concordia Journal* 8 (1982): 213–19.

Vanhoye, A. "Les récits de la Passion chez les Synoptiques." *Nouvelle Revue Théologique* 89 (1967): 135–63.

Vinson, J., ed. *Great Writers of the English Language: Poets.* London: Macmillan Press, 1979.

Vogler, W. *Judas Iskarioth: Untersuchungen zu Tradition und Redaktion von Texten des Neuen Testaments und ausserkanonischer Schriften.* Berlin: Evangelische Verlagsanstalt, 1983.

Wagner, H. "Judas: Das Geheimnis der Sünde, menschliche Freiheit und Gottes Heilsplan." In *Judas Iskariot: Menschliches oder heilsgeschichtliches Drama?* 11–38. Ed. H. Wagner. Frankfurt: Knecht, 1985.

———, ed. *Judas Iskariot: Menschliches oder heilsgeschichtliches Drama?* Frankfurt: Knecht, 1985.

Walker, A., trans. *Apocryphal Gospels, Acts, and Revelations.* Ante-Nicene Christian Library, vol. 16. Edinburgh: T. & T. Clark, 1873.

Wannamaker, O. D. "Iscariot." *Methodist Quarterly Review* 66 (1917): 537–38.

Weatherhead, L. D. "Judas." In *Personalities in the Passion: A Devotional Study of Some of the Characters Who Played a Part in the Drama of Christ's Passion and Resurrection,* 26–39. Nashville: Abingdon-Cokesbury Press, 1943.

Wehr, G. "Judas Iskariot, unser schattenhaftes Ich. Analytische Psychologie im Dienste der Bibelauslegung." *Deutsches Pfarrerblatt* 74 (1974): 146–47.

Weiger, J. *Judas Iskarioth: eine Betrachtung.* Munich: Kösel-Verlag, 1951.

Whelan, C. F. "Suicide in the Ancient World: A Re-examination of Matt 27:3–10." *Laval Théologique et Philosophique* 49 (1993): 505–22.

Wicker, J. "A Copy of Three Letters, Written by the Rev. James Wicker to His Daughter Eliza." Middlebury, Vt.: T. C. Strong, 1811.

Wiesel, E. *Night.* New York: Bantam Books, 1960.

———. *Trial of God.* New York: Random House, 1979.

Wilcox, M. "The Judas Tradition in Acts 1:15–26." *New Testament Studies* 19 (1973): 438–52.

Williams, D. J. "Judas Iscariot." In *Dictionary of Jesus and the Gospels*, 46–48. Eds. J. B. Green and S. McKnight. Downers Grove, Ill.: Intervarsity Press, 1992.

Williams, D. S. "Rub Poor Lil' Judas's Head." *Christian Century* 107 (October 24, 1990): 963.

Wrede, A. "Judas." *Handwörterbuch des deutschen Aberglaubens*, vol. 4, 800–8. Ed. H. Bächtold-Stäubli. Berlin: De Gruyter, 1927–42.

Wrede, W. "Judas Iscariot in der urchristlichen Überlieferung." In *Vortäge und Studien*, 127–46. Tübingen: J. C. B. Mohr, 1907.

Wright, A. "Was Judas Iscariot 'the First of the Twelve'?" *Journal of Theological Studies* 18 (1916): 32–34.

———. "Was Judas Iscariot the First of the Twelve?" *Interpreter* 13 (1917): 18–25.

Yanikian, G. *The Triumph of Judas Iscariot.* Los Angeles: Research Publishing Co., 1950.

Yoder, J. H. *The Politics of Jesus.* 2d ed. Grand Rapids: Wm. B. Eerdmans Publishing Co., 1994.

Zehrer, F. "Das Judasproblem." *Theologische-Praktische Quartalschrift* 121 (1973): 259–64.

Index of Scriptural References

Index of Authors

Index of Subjects and Names